PRAISE FOR *THE ESSENTIAL MARIO SAVIO*

"Robert Cohen has performed an invaluable service by collecting, annotating, and contextualizing the letters and speeches of Mario Savio, leader of the now iconic Free Speech Movement at Berkeley in 1964."

Nicholas B. Dirks, Chancellor of the University of California

"This is an extremely important collection of primary materials from the youthful pondering of Mario Savio, a vitally important but little-understood figure of the 1960s. The connections between activism in the South and activism on the Berkeley campus have never been more vividly expressed than in Savio's own words."

Paul Buhle, Brown University

"This powerful work deserves a wide reading. Mario Savio spoke with passion, clarity, and courage when he confronted injustice in Mississippi and again when he defied the suppression of free speech at the University of California. This well-edited introduction to the 'essential' Savio is a boon to both scholarship and citizenship."

Lewis Perry, author of *Civil Disobedience: An American Tradition*

"Lucid and persuasive, Robert Cohen is a leading authority on the history of student activism in the United States, most particularly in the 1960s and even more particularly at UC Berkeley in the fall of 1964."

Maurice Isserman, Publius Virgilius Rogers Professor of History at Hamilton College

The Essential Mario Savio

FSM march on campus, the day of the regents meeting, November 20, 1964. Savio, clad in jacket and tie, is second to the right of the banner. Photograph courtesy of Don Kechely, Bancroft Library collection.

The Essential Mario Savio

SPEECHES AND WRITINGS THAT
CHANGED AMERICA

Edited by Robert Cohen

Foreword by Tom Hayden
Afterword by Robert Reich
Epilogue by Lynne Hollander Savio

UNIVERSITY OF CALIFORNIA PRESS

University of California Press, one of the most distinguished university presses in the United States, enriches lives around the world by advancing scholarship in the humanities, social sciences, and natural sciences. Its activities are supported by the UC Press Foundation and by philanthropic contributions from individuals and institutions. For more information, visit www.ucpress.edu.

University of California Press
Oakland, California

Library of Congress Cataloging-in-Publication Data

The essential Mario Savio : speeches and writings that changed America / edited by Robert Cohen.
    p.   cm.
  Includes bibliographical references and index.
  ISBN 978-0-520-28337-4 (cloth, alk. paper) —
  ISBN 978-0-520-28338-1 (pbk., alk. paper) —
  ISBN 978-0-520-95926-2 (electronic)
  1. Savio, Mario.   2. Free Speech Movement (Berkeley, Calif.)—History.   3. Political activists—United States—Biography.   4. Civil rights workers—United States—Biography.   5. Student movements—California—Berkeley—History.   I. Cohen, Robert, editor.
JC599.U6E87   2014
378.1′981092—dc23   2014016260

Manufactured in the United States of America

23 22 21 20 19 18 17 16 15 14
10 9 8 7 6 5 4 3 2 1

In keeping with a commitment to support environmentally responsible and sustainable printing practices, UC Press has printed this book on Natures Natural, a fiber that contains 30% post-consumer waste and meets the minimum requirements of ANSI/NISO Z39.48-1992 (R 1997) (Permanence of Paper).

To the student activists of the 1980s, whose protests helped lead the University of California to divest its multibillion-dollar investments in companies that did business in apartheid South Africa.

It's wonderful, and I know you feel it too, to be part of such a change for good that's sweeping across our country. I really believe that the history of the world is pivoting on the internal changes that are going on today in America—and we are in part the agents of that change. A breath of freedom. But what about Vietnam?

Mario Savio to Cheryl Stevenson
Holmes County, Mississippi, 3 July 1964

By our courage, . . . by dignity in the face of unprovoked violence, by the insatiable adherence to principle of the students on this campus, . . . we've shown ourselves guilty of one thing—of passionately entering into a conspiracy to uphold the First and Fourteenth Amendments.

Mario Savio, Free Speech Movement rally, 16 October 1964
steps of Sproul Hall, Berkeley, California

Contents

Illustrations

Acknowledgments

This collection of Savio's writings and speeches would not have been possible without diligent archival work. Lynne Hollander Savio's archive of Mario Savio documents was indispensable, and I am grateful to her for support of this project. Kathryn M. Neal, university archivist in UC Berkeley's Bancroft Library, offered invaluable advice on locating Savio documents, tracking down contextualizing data, and enabling me to use the recently accessioned files on the post-1960s history of the University of California's struggle over whether and how to honor Savio and the FSM. There could not have been a chapter in this book on Savio's work in Mississippi had Cheryl Stevenson not saved and made available the letters Savio sent her from the front lines of the Southern civil rights movement during Freedom Summer. I am also grateful to Cheryl for sharing her memories of Savio and that summer. Barbara Stack, of the Free Speech Movement Archives, has been more than generous in sharing the documents on both Savio and the FSM, and I owe her a special debt for helping to bring to light a formerly lost letter Savio wrote from Santa Rita jail. My thanks to Will Morgan, of the Mississippi Department of Archives and History, for helping locate the court records of the case against Savio's KKK assailants. My thanks to Savio's childhood friend Art Gatti, who recorded Mario's speech at Queens College and made the tape available to me; it is the only surviving speech of the East Coast tour that Savio and other FSMers made right after their victory in December 1964. For crucial assistance with the photo research for the book my thanks to Gregg Parrish and Lynne Hollander Savio.

As a former *Daily Californian* editorial page editor, it is with a special sense of pride that I acknowledge the Berkeley student newspaper's work—via the Freedom of Information Act (FOIA)—in uncovering the FBI's covert and unconstitutional efforts to slander and spy on Savio and the Berkeley student movement. This important probing of the FBI's role in Berkeley has been carried on for decades by journalist Seth Rosenfeld, also a *Daily Californian* alumnus, whose FOIA requests and reportage have brought to light valuable and revealing FBI documents on Savio and the FSM.

My work setting Savio's speeches and writings into historical context has been facilitated by the excellent oral histories of Savio and his fellow FSMers by Max Heirich, Bret Eynon, Marston Schultz, Ronald Shatz, Lisa Rubens, David Pickell, David Lance Goines, and filmmaker Mark Kitchell—whose classic documentary, *Berkeley in the Sixties,* has endured as a source of valuable insights into the FSM. My thanks to Suzanne Goldberg for sharing her memories of Mario in their Berkeley student years and for her generosity in supporting my research on him. My NYU students and their oral histories with FSM veterans last semester also proved illuminating, and it is a pleasure to thank Maryanne Greenaway and Allyson McGinty and their interviewees, Kate Coleman and Jean Golson Moule, for their insights.

The suggestions and criticism offered by the historians who served as readers of the manuscript—Wesley Hogan, Paul Buhle, Maurice Isserman, and Jennifer Snow—were of great value, and I am grateful to each of them. Bettina Aptheker, as always, was generous in taking time to discuss Savio with me, and she offered invaluable insights that enabled me to better understand the dynamics of the Bay Area civil rights movement of the early 1960s.

For deepening my understanding of the New Left and the 1960s, I am grateful to Tom Hayden—as I am for his friendship and support. Jack Weinberg, the FSM's master strategist, taught me an immense about the dynamics and meaning of the Berkeley revolt in a memorable, marathon oral-history session. The late Reginald E. Zelnik was very close to Mario Savio for years, and I can't imagine having completed two books on Mario without the inspiration that came from working with Reggie on our FSM anthology more than a decade ago. My teachers Leon Litwack, Jesse Lemisch, and the late Lawrence W. Levine all, in their own special ways, led me to this work. My interest in the 1960s has been sustained by the friendship and the privilege of co-teaching an undergraduate course on that era here at NYU with Marilyn Young. Bob Moses, Martha Noonan, Marshall Ganz, and Robert Osman generously shared their knowledge of the Mississippi freedom movement, in which they participated.

My understanding of the legacy of Savio and the FSM at Berkeley has been enhanced by my correspondence with two Cal faculty members, Colleen Lye of the English department and David Hollinger of the history department, as well as with Lynne Hollander Savio.

The historical profession has done surprisingly little research on Savio or the FSM, which makes all the more valuable the work FSM veterans have done to archive FSM documents and to foster discussion of the movement's history. For this work, I thank the late Michael Rossman, Jack Radey, Jackie Goldberg, Lee Felsenstein, Gar Smith, Barbara Garson, Margot Adler, Susan Druding, and the other board members of the Free Speech Movement Archive. The work that my generation of Berkeley graduate students did with these FSM veterans and with Savio himself in 1984, at the commemoration of FSM's twentieth anniversary, played a pivotal role in leading me to this book and my other work on Savio and the FSM. My thanks to Pedro Noguera and Nancy Skinner for helping to make that commemoration possible, through their leadership of Berkeley's Graduate Assembly.

I join with the publisher in gratefully acknowledging the generous contribution to this book by Stephen M. Silberstein, which made it possible for this selection of Savio documents from 1964 to be so comprehensive.

This book came about thanks to the initiative of my editor at UC Press, Naomi Schneider, and I thank her for all her help on the book. Christopher Lura at UC Press provided additional editorial assistance that is much appreciated. My thanks to Jennifer Eastman for her fine work copy editing this book.

My family's support has been crucial in making this book possible and my life joyful. I'm not quite sure how my wife, Becky, and my son, Daniel, put up with me through all the sleep-deprived months that I worked on this book, and just thanking them seems ungrateful. Let's just say that I owe them both big time.

This book is devoted to Berkeley's most famous student activist, who battled racism and cared deeply about making freedom and justice more than mere words; it is dedicated to my generation of Berkeley student protesters, whose names and speeches are less well known than Mario's but who carried this same torch.

Editor's Note

Since this is a collection of Mario Savio's speeches and writings, it cannot be—nor is it intended to offer—a complete transcription of the Free Speech Movement's rallies and press conferences. The focus in the two FSM chapters is more on Savio's ideas and expression than on crowd response to them. In fact, to avoid having such crowd response distract readers from Savio's words, I have, where possible, deleted the crowd reactions to his speeches (applause, laughter, and other responses). Exceptions were made in three kinds of cases: (1) where Savio asked for crowd approval; (2) where crowd response was essential to understanding Savio's words and thought: (3) police transcripts of two of Savio's speeches, which are offered verbatim, including their account of crowd reactions. Readers will note that these police transcripts are low quality and garbled at points. I have repaired most of the rough spots in those transcripts with bracketed inserts, but left a few ungrammatical sentences that provide readers with the best available accounts of what Savio said.

To keep the speeches as concise and cogent as possible, I have edited out redundancies, which occurred fairly frequently, since Savio tended to repeat subjects and adjectives (the last vestige of Savio's youthful speech defect). Toward this same end, I have usually deleted interjections (most notably, such phrases as "you know"). So when readers encounter ellipses in the speeches, they should understand that these denote not large excisions but small deletions made for the sake of tightening up Savio's discourse in such a way as is appropriate in converting the spoken word to print. All these edits have been made in such a way as to preserve Savio's ideas, phrasing, and tone.

Foreword

Tom Hayden

It is a worthy time to study and treasure the eloquent speeches of Mario Savio, "freedom's orator," as the historian Robert Cohen rightly calls him.

I didn't know Mario well, mainly because of our separate geographic orbits, but our paths were intertwined. As a student editor from Ann Arbor, I hitchhiked to Berkeley in summer 1960, where I stayed in an apartment belonging to activists from SLATE, the campus political party that was demanding a voice for students stifled by university paternalism. SLATE activists were among those hosed down the steps of San Francisco's City Hall after protesting the House Committee on Un-American Activities (HUAC) that spring. The FBI opened a file on me for simply writing an editorial in the *Michigan Daily* supporting the student critics. I remember interviewing the aptly named Alex Sherriffs, the aggressive UC vice chancellor who wanted to shut down the tiny Bancroft strip where I was first leafleted by the friendly student who found me a place to stay. In a memo at the time, Sherriffs called the SLATE activists "office seekers and publicity hounds . . . misfits, malcontents and other politically-oriented individuals who do not conform to the normal political activity in the university community."[1] My kind of people.

This was the dawn of the sixties. A counter-community was forming, and the simple idea of student rights was infectious. The SLATE leaders pushed me to create a similar campus political party in Ann Arbor, which I helped to do that fall; known as VOICE, it became the first chapter of the national SDS (Students for a Democratic Society).

Our strategy in SDS was to excite students nationally by the model of students putting their lives on the line down South. It worked. In late 1961 I was a Freedom Rider in Georgia and had been beaten and expelled from McComb, Mississippi, while writing a pamphlet about a voting rights campaign. By spring semester 1964, Berkeley activists, Mario among them, were copying the Southern sit-ins against Jim Crow lunch counters in their own sit-in against racist hiring at San Francisco's Sheraton Palace Hotel. That experience propelled Mario to volunteer in the 1964 Mississippi Freedom Summer project in McComb, where he was subjected to the same kind of radicalizing violence I had experienced in 1961.

The links kept being forged. In June 1962, the first SDS convention in Port Huron, Michigan, adopted a lengthy statement calling for students to forge a participatory democracy based on the direct-action model of SNCC (the black-led Student Nonviolent Coordinating Committee) and the radical notions that students could be "agents of social change" and universities the laboratories of reform. That Port Huron vision was realized when the Free Speech Movement burst into history in 1964. Mario himself spoke favorably of participatory democracy, and activists like Jackie Goldberg carried the Port Huron Statement in their backpacks.

I lived later in Berkeley (1968–1970) during the post-FSM years, when the rhetoric was more revolutionary, the campus often was choked by tear gas, student strikes were frequent, armed Black Panthers sold Red Books on the Sproul steps, the early utopian moment was clouded by internal strife, and the community was anything but blessed. During the People's Park march of 1969, I witnessed sheriffs coldly kill one bystander and blind another with buckshot while they sat on a rooftop overlooking Telegraph Avenue. This lethal moment came just four and a half years after the FSM's rise and one year before the murders at Kent State and Jackson State. The Berkeley free speech area looked like a war zone. The idealistic movement that first gave Mario his magical voice, after he had grown up with a stuttering shyness, now left him stranded and alone amidst its fragmentation and demise.

Looking back, were we only pawns in a larger game? That's the troubling conclusion of a book by the former *Daily Californian* reporter Seth Rosenfeld, based on FBI documents finally divulged by federal court order four decades later and published in the *San Francisco Chronicle* in 1992. Altogether the files came to over two hundred thousand pages, including 4,600 pages from the secret FBI counterintelligence program (COINTELPRO).[2]

Thanks to Rosenfeld's dogged Freedom of Information Act requests, we know that the FSM was targeted by FBI and CIA operations intended to improve the political fortunes of Ronald Reagan and Richard Nixon, both of whom rose to political power on promises to crush Berkeley radicalism. Mario was demonized as a virtual Fidel Castro, and the Berkeley hills were his Sierra Madre. Here is J. Edgar Hoover from a 1966 memo: "Agitators on other campuses take that lead from activities that occur at Berkeley. If agitational activity at Berkeley can be effectively curtailed, this could set up a chain reaction that will result in the curtailment of such activities on other campuses throughout the United States."[3]

This was a full decade before the U.S. Congress held its explosive inquiry, the Church Committee hearings (for its chairman Senator Frank Church), which uncovered widespread and illegal spying and disruption against domestic protest in America. Nothing revealed in those hearing could fully match what happened in Berkeley in the sixties. Hoover's FBI, along with UC Regent Edwin Pauley and former CIA director John McCone, plotted to uncover alleged "reds" among the Berkeley faculty; remove the university president Clark Kerr; conspire with Ronald Reagan, a onetime informant; and alter the course of American political history.[4] All these deeds were, of course, far beyond the agency's legal mandate. The FBI could get away with its crimes because of the climate of opinion in those Cold War times.

Led by Hoover, the political elite looked at "campus unrest" through a Cold War lens, completely missing the rise of millions of idealistic young people representing demands for relevance, justice, equal treatment, peace, and a voice in the decisions affecting their lives. If this was only a Cold War misunderstanding, perhaps the dreadful mistake could be forgiven. But there was another agenda that began at Berkeley as well: after being elected to "clean up" Berkeley, Reagan quickly imposed tuition for the first time in the history of the university. The conservative attack on "permissive" UC officials and "communist" professors shielding the "spoiled brats" was also an assault on the liberal tradition of public-sector institutions. The current era of privatization and neoliberalism was born in Berkeley as a countermovement to the sixties.

We have not recovered, but America's progressives have survived to fight back. It took three decades, but UC chancellor Chang-Lin Tien wrote in 1997 that Mario was "a gifted leader whose passionate conviction and eloquence inspired a generation of students across America. His name is forever linked with one of our nation's most cherished freedoms—the right to freedom of expression. We are proud that he was part of the community at the University of California."[5] The Sproul steps were renamed for Mario too. This year, in memory of the fiftieth anniversary of the FSM, the university is distributing eight thousand copies of former Berkeley graduate student Robby Cohen's comprehensive Savio biography, *Freedom's Orator*, as required reading for its first-year class. The FSM is being acknowledged as a leading example of America's own democracy movement.

It is difficult not to be slightly cynical about this latter-day praise. Many of Mario's worst fears have come to pass—for example, in the skyrocketing tuition and room and board levels, which now reach $35,000 per year for in-state students and more than $56,000 for nonresidents. In November 2011, UC police pepper-sprayed nonviolent student tuition protestors at Davis and wielded batons in Berkeley to evict a tent encampment for Occupy Wall Street–allied protests. (It was deemed that the tents were not protected under freedom of expression rulings, unlike private campaign dollars.) Nonetheless, in recent years, the University of California has incorporated the FSM and student activism in its brand promotion. Some from the FSM generation have become wealthy donors (one, Stephen Silberstein, gave $3.5 million to UC Berkeley's libraries, complete with an FSM archive and café). A new generation of administrators wants to make amends for a past in which their predecessors overreacted to political pressure. And in Machiavellian terms, the image of a Free Speech America is helpful when chastising other countries for suppressing student protest.

History provides this lesson, and a cynical one: again and again, the persecuted radicals of one era are venerated as prophets and saints in another. Only consider Tom Paine, whose rhetoric ignited the American Revolution, but was castigated as a scoundrel by the Revolution's elite and buried without honor by a small handful of friends. John Adams denounced Paine as "a mongrel between a pig and a puppy, begotten by a wild boar on a bitch wolf."[6] Mario Savio was a Paine of the sixties.

I sometimes saw Mario after his media stardom had declined, after he spent a period in a psychiatric hospital coping with posttraumatic stress disorder (which afflicted civil rights movement veterans as well as GIs), and after the university rejected his application to resume his studies. When I saw him last, it seemed to me he was in a fitting phase of a noble life. Mario was teaching at Sonoma State University, focused mainly on remedial work with students of color, in a program called the Intensive Learning Experience (ILE). Immigrants were being scapegoated for the state's woes. It was the early 1990s, and California was cutting its higher education budgets while building one of the world's largest prison systems. Mario joined the fights against rising tuition rates, for what was free speech if universities were unaffordable and inaccessible to working people?

Many are unaware that Mario was returning to his roots when he worked among those young students at Sonoma. During 1963, the year before the San Francisco hotel sit-ins, before his time in McComb and the rise of the FSM, Mario spent a summer immersed in a Catholic antipoverty project in central Mexico. There he instinctively applied the basic techniques of community organizing, long before he would be trained for the Mississippi summer project. Listening to villagers recount their needs, Mario and his student band began the construction of a community laundry, where the poor could wash their clothes during Mexico's dry season.

That summer experience planted in Mario a lifelong connection to the poor, from Mexican and Central American peasants to Mississippi sharecroppers to his resistance to the U.S. military interventions in Central America. The circle was closed in his organizing against California's anti-immigrant initiative, Proposition 187. When the burden of confronting anti-immigrant hysteria was falling mainly on Latinos in California and border states like Arizona, Mario was one of those few on the white radical left standing with them. He wanted to rearrange America's vision from a nation caught up in an East-West Cold War framework to one centered in the Americas from South to North. Mario realized early on what only a few—Cuba's Jose Marti, the *Nation's* Carey McWilliams, and today's Juan Gonzales of Pacifica—have realized: that our ultimate destiny lies here in "Our America." Mario was a prophet of our permanent destiny in the Americas.

What does it mean to declare that Mario was "freedom's orator"? His philosophical and mathematical training prepared him to communicate in plain but lucid language, rich with references to past great thinkers. His podium, however, was on the top of a police car or the Sproul steps. Mario did not deliver The Word from a mountaintop or dictate official dogma for devotees to memorize and go forth. He was given the gift of speech—that is, he stopped stuttering—from the movement community. In return, he gave them the gift of being heard, thinking aloud, for the first time. Amid the pandemonium of the movement awakening all around him, Mario could sift the good arguments from the bad, engage the crowd in dialogue, and crystallize whatever consensus that was needed at the moment. It's almost unfortunate that his most famous speech—calling on the students to place their bodies on the gears and stop the machine—was more like a call to battle than the usual Socratic speeches he gave almost daily at mass meetings. Oratory implies a solo performance, but a speech by Mario was an exercise in reasoning out loud, essentially unrehearsed, yet perfectly clear in the end. It was a *participatory oratory* that left the listeners better informed and empowered. In later times, with the movement gone, many of his speeches and articles are sharply reasoned and on the cutting edge, but lack the exciting vitality that comes when many minds are in motion at once.

Mario, of course, was an original thinker, not just a stylist. He attacked the premises of the Cold War before others did. He went on to challenge the neoconservative assumption of the "end of history" after the Cold War had ended. Perhaps his most interesting and still-relevant speculations were about Marxism and liberation theology, leading him to identify with what he called "secular liberation theology."[7] How did he arrive there? First, Mario and the New Left could not abide the traditional liberalism of many in the Democratic Party. Liberalism had reached a compromise with corporate capitalism that delivered a welfare state, but within the context of a Cold War corporate state dominated by distant elites. Liberals, at least as we knew them in the sixties, were late to join the civil rights movement, had rejected the Mississippi Freedom Democratic Party in 1964, opposed the Cuban Revolution, and supported the Vietnam War. That seemed to leave only varieties of Marxism, an important tradition without deep roots in the American past. Mario acknowledged that understanding Marxism was essential to being politically literate, yet he hesitated to embrace it philosophically. His reasoning was this: "Marxism, even at its most poetic, is a kind of economism."[8] The thesis of Marxism, he believed, was that the very workings of the capitalist system led to mass immiseration, which in turn led to an oppositional consciousness. But capitalism, spurred by the New Deal and the threat of socialism, developed a white-collar middle class represented by the likes of Mario and me. As the opening sentence of the Port Huron Statement declared: "We are people of *this generation,* bred in at least *modest comfort,* housed now in universities, looking *uncomfortably* at the world we inherit." This was hardly the Communist Manifesto. Shortly after, the FSM began issuing its grievances against the "multiversity," in which students were treated like IBM punch cards. These were not narrow, privileged, middle-class sentiments alone, since the movements were aligned with struggles for voting rights, farm worker rights, and the "other America" brought to light by Michael Harrington. But we wanted something more than the New Deal. We also realized that any immiseration of workers under capitalism could drive them far to the right.

While the Marxist model produced an inherent sense that history was on our side, Mario instead argued that "we have to be prepared on the basis of our *moral insight* to struggle even if we do not know that we are going to win."[9] He believed the antidote lay in having spiritual values and was therefore inspired by the rise of liberation theology in Latin America. His skeptical nature, however, required for him a "secularized liberation theology." It is only my conjecture that the strains of Catholic and Greek philosophy in his intellectual upbringing perhaps led him to an alternative to the dialectic, a deep belief that we all might dwell in a spiritual realm of truth and beauty.

For whatever mix of reasons, during the immigrant rights struggles in the nineties, Mario pointed out that the Catholic Church was in the forefront and noted that there "is probably no other institution in the United States in which there is a heavier representation of righteously working class people than in . . . that church. We ought to be talking to them as well as to one another."[10]

One can only imagine what Mario would have thought of the rise of Pope Francis who, in 2014, seems to be the left wing of the world. Pope Francis's moral denunciations of capitalism are important, but even more interesting is the pontiff's answer to a question about homosexuality: "Who am I to judge if they are seeking the Lord in good faith?" In those few simple words, the pope was subverting the whole doctrine of an Infallible Center. Marxism in recent decades has experienced the same loss of doctrinally infallibility, opening a chapter of history that Mario would have delighted in.

Equally, he would have delighted in the emergence of the Dreamers' movement on UC campuses and in communities across the country, young undocumented immigrants who were brought to America as children, acting in the spirit of the militant civil rights movement, demanding their constitutional rights and willing to face deportation.

He would have delighted in the Occupy movement as a harbinger of the next wave of economic populism. He would salute those who fight against soaring tuition and debt. He would have reveled in dialogue with these new young American rebels. He would have exchanged reading lists with them. He would have happily joined their ranks.

Mario Savio has been missed. Thanks to the FSM's coming fiftieth anniversary, however, his challenging words can be felt among us once again, sermons and parables for an unpredictable dawn.

Introduction

REVOLT ON THE CAMPUS: MARIO SAVIO AND
BERKELEY'S FREE SPEECH BATTLES, 1964

The Free Speech Movement's fiftieth anniversary is an opportune time to publish this first comprehensive collection of Mario Savio's speeches and writings from 1964, since he was that movement's great orator and most prominent leader. Savio's fame began on October 1, 1964, when, in the middle of the University of California at Berkeley's Sproul Plaza, the twenty-one-year-old philosophy major climbed atop a police car and used its roof as a podium to explain and defend the blockade of that car by his fellow free speech activists. According to the police report, this nonviolent human blockade began just before noon, "when approximately fifty persons laid [sic] down in front of the car" and immobilized it. The police inadvertently sparked the blockade when they arrested and dragged into their squad car Jack Weinberg, a civil rights activist and former math graduate student charged with trespassing, whose only "crime" had been defying the UC administration's ban on campus political advocacy. The crowd surrounding the car quickly swelled to include hundreds and then thousands of students sitting in on behalf of free speech, which at the moment meant stopping the police from taking Weinberg off to jail in their squad car. The police car blockade would last thirty-two hours—

1

Figure 1. Savio atop the police car, in front of Sproul Hall, October 1, 1964.
Photograph courtesy of Lon Wilson, Bancroft Library collection.

constituting to that point the longest, most disruptive act of civil disobedience ever seen on a university campus in the United States.[1]

Savio's speech not only explained and justified the blockade but also launched an almost surreal car-top rally, in which a parade of mostly student speakers—who, like Savio, took their shoes off so as not to damage the car—spoke from the roof of the police car and championed an end to both the campus ban on political advocacy and the UC administration's attempts to quell opposition to that ban through suspensions and arrests. The speeches went on, hour after hour, engaging the masses of protesters around the car. It was an unprecedented oratorical marathon, a kind of free speech festival, and it continued into the night. The speeches, together with the communal act of sitting in around the police car—a risky form of civil disobedience—inspired a deep sense of solidarity and community that the protesters would never forget. The blockade remained nonviolent despite the provocations of rowdy fraternity members who, ironically, in the name of law and order, turned up late in the night to hurl rotten eggs and lighted cigarettes at Savio and his fellow activists.[2]

The next night, the car-top rally ended—as it had begun—with a Savio speech from atop the police car. Faced with an imminent police invasion of the campus, Savio and other leaders of the protest negotiated with UC's administration and signed the Pact of October 2. When Savio read and explained that agreement to the protesters—which amounted to a truce while negotiations on the free speech issue and disciplinary proceedings began—they approved it by acclamation and heeded Savio's plea to disperse the blockade "quietly and with dignity," avoiding a potentially bloody confrontation with the police.[3]

By early November, however, these negotiations would break down, and so would the truce, as Savio and other Free Speech Movement leaders, realizing that UC's administration would not voluntarily surrender its power to regulate the content of political speech on campus, resumed mass protest. These protests included a march of more than three thousand students on UC's Board of Regents meeting on November 20 and the mass occupation of Sproul Hall, the Berkeley administration building, on December 2, at which Savio gave his most famous speech. Echoing Thoreau, Savio, from the steps of Sproul, urged students to put their "bodies upon the gears" to stop "the machine" of injustice—offering one of the most powerful calls to civil disobedience ever heard in America.[4] The Sproul Hall sit-in began with that Savio speech and a procession of more than a thousand students into the building, serenaded by folk singer Joan Baez singing "We Shall Overcome," the anthem of the civil rights movement.

California governor Edmund "Pat" Brown responded to the sit-in by ordering in an army of police officers to clear the protesters out of Sproul Hall, culminating in the largest mass arrest in California's history. The scale of the Sproul arrests was so unprecedented that both the police and UC administration had difficulty even counting the total number of arrestees. The police initially claimed that they made 801 arrests at Sproul, then revised their figures downward to 761, and then up again to 773, while UC officials came up with numbers as high as 814. All agreed, however, that most of those who sat in and were jailed were students.[5] The arrests, which started in the middle of the night, took hours. In broad daylight the next morning, protesters were still being physically removed from Sproul Hall and carted off to jail in police buses, a shocking sight for faculty and students arriving for classes. This immediately ignited an effective strike of teaching assistants and a student boycott of classes, supported by many professors.[6]

Four days later, Savio was at the center of yet another act of political theater, which took place literally on stage—that of the Greek Theatre, Berkeley's huge outdoor amphitheater. UC president Clark Kerr had cancelled classes so that he and his allies among Cal's department chairs could impose a badly flawed peace settlement, which did not address the FSM's call for an end to university regulation of the content of speech on campus. The Greek Theatre convocation was supposed to be a carefully scripted event addressed only by Kerr and his faculty supporters, with no student speakers allowed. Just as the meeting ended, however, Savio, determined to speak, walked onto the stage and up to the podium. Before Savio could utter a syllable, he was jumped and dragged away by the police, an electrifying moment of political theater, a symbolic act of censorship, acted out before an outraged crowd of thousands of students and faculty.[7] The next day, Berkeley's faculty responded to "the tragedy at the Greek" and the larger leadership vacuum it represented by finally opting to side with Savio and the FSM, voting overwhelmingly (824–115) in its Academic Senate to adopt the historic December 8 resolutions, one of which backed the FSM's central demand "that the content of speech or advocacy should not be restricted by the University."[8]

The December 8 resolutions, which Savio praised as the university's new "Constitution and Magna Carta," represented a stunning victory for civil liberty and the Free Speech Movement.[9] This triumph heralded the rise of a new student politics in the 1960s, teaching students across the country and the globe that if they emulated the Berkeley rebels by uniting and strategically deploying nonviolent civil disobedience on campus, they could be an effective voice for change. It was a lesson students would apply first in building a mass movement against the Vietnam War in the mid-1960s and then on a host of campus issues ranging from supporting racial and gender equity, free speech, and black studies to toppling the old *in loco parentis* restrictions on student social life.[10]

This same lesson filled many college and university administrators with fear and foreboding. They sought above all to avoid "another Berkeley," to stop FSM-style disruptive student protests from spreading to their campuses.[11] Such fear was shared and fanned by the FBI and its antiradical director, J. Edgar Hoover, whose agents spied on Savio and the FSM. Hoover publicly depicted the organizers of Berkeley's movement for free speech as un-American and dangerously subversive—a view reinforced by red-baiting press stories, some of which the FBI planted.[12]

Although Clark Kerr, as a liberal, had little in common with the FBI's reactionary director (who detested him), it must be recalled that Kerr was a Cold War liberal whose antiradicalism was different not in kind but only in degree from Hoover's. That antiradicalism led Kerr to red-bait the Berkeley student movement at crucial early points in the conflict. On the second day of the police car blockade, Kerr publicly stated that leaders of the student revolt were "impressed with the tactics of Fidel Castro and Mao Tse-tung," a charge that, in the Cold War climate of the time, equated Berkeley's rebels with America's Communist enemies. Similarly, less than a week later, Kerr told the press that the FSM's "hard core group of demonstrators" contained "persons identified as being sympathetic with the Communist Party and Communist causes."[13] Kerr and other top UC administrators spoke in a similar vein in private, as when UC chancellor Edward Strong, in a call to Kerr, characterized Savio as "an intractable fanatic," and Kerr concurred, adding that Savio "could not be restrained or controlled."[14]

Neither Savio nor the FSM was un-American, of course. In fact, Savio was in love with the Constitution's First and Fourteenth Amendments—a love so evident in his oratory that it helped draw mainstream students into the FSM.[15] Both he and his fellow FSMers—including the few Communists among them—risked their academic careers, suspension from school, and arrest struggling to ensure that the free speech and due process rights embodied in those amendments did not become dead letters on the Berkeley campus.

Savio and the FSM were subversive, but not in the way Hoover or Kerr meant. The Berkeley rebels proved very adept in subverting undemocratic decision making and unjust authority. Just think of the police car blockade. There you had a police car, the symbol of state power and authority, paralyzed by a crowd of student protesters who insisted that such power not be used to suppress resistance to UC's illiberal ban on political advocacy. The symbolism was striking: Savio spoke from atop the car—dissent trumping authority, liberty over order—in an iconic act that embodied the antiauthoritarianism of the 1960s. The power and authority being subverted were not merely that of the police but also of university administrators whose restriction of free speech had provoked the protest and arrests. Savio and his fellow protesters on Sproul Plaza challenged that administration's authority to govern unilaterally and by fiat. They demanded a voice in the decisions impacting their lives and education—enacting the principle of participatory democracy articulated in the New Left's founding document, SDS's Port Huron Statement, two years earlier.[16]

In seeking to give voice and power in university governance to students, a group that historically had lacked both, Savio and the FSM challenged hierarchy and bureaucracy, prodding students and faculty to assert their right to govern themselves rather than being dictated to by administrators. Savio and the FSM went beyond merely questioning authority; they pushed for it to be reconstituted democratically and did so through a movement that was itself hyper-democratic (much too democratic to have a president, the FSM was governed by its Steering and Executive Committees and by consensus decision making) and battling for freedom of speech.[17] The victory the FSM won for civil liberty helped usher in an era when even high school and middle school students asserted free speech rights. Before the decade was out, the Supreme Court affirmed in *Tinker v. Des Moines* (1969) that neither students nor teachers lose their First Amendment rights at the schoolhouse door.[18] In winning this epic battle for free speech and student rights, Savio and his fellow FSMers also made possible a rare moment of democratic campus governance in which the Berkeley professoriate effectively overruled a powerful university administration.

In all these ways, Savio's story and the FSM's amounted to an important chapter in the history of the university, the New Left, and American democracy. Savio himself has thus been depicted—in some of the best histories of the 1960s—as an icon of democratic rebellion, whose eloquent oratory and political daring embodied a classic American struggle for freedom. Rick Perlstein, for example, portrayed Savio in heroic terms, writing of Savio's ascent to the police car: "Boston Harbor, Harpers Ferry, Omaha Beach: this time the stand for freedom would be made atop a dented squad car roof."[19]

THE FREE SPEECH MOVEMENT AS AN EXTENSION OF THE CIVIL RIGHTS MOVEMENT

Savio and the rebellion that he helped to lead at Berkeley in 1964 cannot be fully understood, however, simply as a part of American history, for their story is also a part of *African American* history. At first glance, this might seem a strange statement, since Savio and most participants in the FSM were white. Yet while there were few African American students at Berkeley or in the FSM, the black presence in the FSM was strong politically, intellectually, and personally.[20] Savio and most of the FSM's key organizers were living far less in the era of Lyndon Baines Johnson than in what Martin Luther King Jr. biographer Taylor Branch has termed the King era, in which Dr. King and the black freedom movement set the moral and political agenda for America. In fact, Savio's frame of reference in speaking and writing about the FSM was, at crucial moments, that of the civil rights movement. He saw the Berkeley rebellion as an extension of the black freedom movement and drew comparisons between the two movements. As early as November 1964, he was likening the tense confrontation around the police car on Sproul to Birmingham and the FSM's decorous mid-semester march on the regents meeting to the March on Washington. Even in his humor, Savio at times used this frame of reference, as when he opened his letter home from Santa Rita prison, after the mass arrest at Sproul, by joking that he guessed his family "might like to receive a letter from the 'Birmingham Jail.'"[21]

Since Savio and his most dynamic fellow FSM leaders came of age as part of the student wing of the civil rights movement, we might broaden Branch's "King era" to include not only Martin Luther King Jr. but also other leaders and heroes who inspired the Berkeley activists, including Bob Moses, Ella Baker, Diane Nash, John Lewis, Fannie Lou Hamer of SNCC, King aide Bayard Rustin, and James Farmer of CORE. Savio and the FSM's leadership, we might then say, were living in the King-SNCC-CORE era, and so they saw sit-ins as a legitimate and empowering expression of their dissident politics.[22] Indeed, a key reason why the Berkeley rebellion succeeded was that it brought *on campus* the democratic ethos and civil disobedience tactics that SNCC and the black freedom movement had pioneered *off campus*.[23] That movement inspired and mentored these Berkeley students in community organizing in the battle against racism in the San Francisco Bay Area and the Deep South.

To see how direct and important the connections were between the Free Speech Movement and the civil rights movement, all you need to do is look closely at the police car blockade. Savio, the first student protester to speak from atop the car, was the head of UC Berkeley's Friends of SNCC chapter. He had first engaged in civil disobedience and been arrested a half-year earlier at a sit-in against racial discrimination in San Francisco's Sheraton Palace Hotel. While in a holding cell for that arrest, he learned from his cellmate of the Mississippi Freedom Summer project being spearheaded by young African American organizers who led SNCC. Savio volunteered for the project. He would spend the summer registering voters among Mississippi's black population and teaching African American students in a Freedom School.[24]

Savio saw UC Berkeley's ban on political advocacy as a crude attempt to prevent the civil rights movement from continuing to recruit students—as he himself had been recruited into Bob Moses's nonviolent army of freedom workers in Mississippi—to assist in its historic struggle for racial equality. So Savio was deeply committed to battling the ban.[25] Having done grassroots organizing in Mississippi and having stood up to racist police there—as well as the Klan—Savio had the political skills and daring to confront Berkeley authorities even from the top of a police car. But Savio was not the only veteran of the civil rights movement. Inside that police car sat Jack Weinberg, a leader of Campus CORE, who had dropped out of UC to become a full-time civil rights organizer and who had been arrested in nonviolent Bay Area protests against racially discriminatory hiring at the Cadillac agency, Mel's Drive-In, and the Sheraton Palace.[26]

As a veteran of these and other civil rights protests, Weinberg knew to go limp when the police arrested him on Sproul Plaza, which slowed the cops as they sought to move him into their car. This gave the crowd time to react. Other movement veterans on the scene had the presence of mind to shout "sit down," which the crowd did, beginning the nonviolent blockade. One of the first protesters near the car to call for the blockade, a graduate student in sociology, later explained that in making that call, he had in mind civil rights movement strategist Bayard Rustin's ideas about collectively confronting police when they used their authority unjustly.[27] Civil rights work in the Bay Area also provided CORE veterans with negotiating experience, since that movement centered on winning fair-hiring agreements, which spotlighted the negotiating process. So it should come as no surprise that two-thirds of the students who negotiated the Pact of October 2 ending the police car blockade, were, like Savio, civil rights movement veterans who had been arrested in Bay Area protests against discriminatory employers the previous semester.[28]

But this only begins to get at the connection between the police car blockade at Berkeley and the King era. The struggle that Martin Luther King and Rev. Fred Shuttlesworth led against Jim Crow in Birmingham was broadcast on television. The images of the brutality that Birmingham's racist public safety commissioner, Bull Connor, unleashed on the civil rights protesters—attacking them with vicious police dogs and high-powered fire hoses—in May 1963 moved millions of Americans, especially such idealistic students as Savio. Recalling how the civil rights movement "just burst on the United States right on the tube," Savio felt both shamed that such injustice could exist in "the land of the free" and inspired by how the black "people on the tube overcame their fear by holding one another, against the snarling and snapping dogs we saw, against the torrents of water from the hoses—and they held one another! And that got to the children of white America." The result was the stirring of an activist impulse, because, as Savio put it, "we threw ourselves ardently into their movement. We wanted to be part of them."[29]

Nationally, during the seven months following Birmingham, some one hundred thousand Americans participated in civil rights demonstrations, in which at least fifteen thousand protesters were arrested.[30] Such activism was fostered all the more in the wake of the tragedy of the Medgar

Evers assassination in June 1963, the exhilaration of the March on Washington in August 1963, and the horror of the bombing of a black church in Birmingham a few weeks later, killing four young black girls. These events intensified student concern with civil rights and added momentum to local protests against racism, even on the West Coast. Berkeley students aligned with local African American activists in mounting effective protests against racially discriminatory employers on both sides of San Francisco Bay during the 1963–1964 school year, targeting downtown Berkeley's stores, picketing at San Francisco's Auto Row, the *Oakland Tribune*, and Mel's Drive-In, organizing shop-ins at the Lucky supermarket chain, and sitting in at the Sheraton Palace Hotel.[31] To Savio—and many of his classmates—it seemed as if in the Bay Area, there "were civil rights demonstrations, massive ones, every week. . . . The country had changed very, very quickly; I . . . found myself at the place which was the cutting edge, absolutely the most advanced of any place in the north or west" in the struggle against racism.[32]

This intensifying civil rights activism paved the way for the Free Speech Movement in two important ways. First, it provided a political baptism and training ground for Savio and hundreds of other students, so that when the administration banned political advocacy on campus, it faced not deferential kids or political novices, but dedicated, even courageous, civil rights movement veterans accustomed to risking arrest in the freedom struggle. Second, the surging student involvement in the Bay Area civil rights movement—and especially the arrest of more than one hundred students who sat in at San Francisco's Sheraton Palace Hotel in March 1964—led to a backlash against Berkeley student radicalism and to pressure on the UC administration from conservatives, especially in the California state legislature, to punish students who broke the law in such protests.[33]

President Kerr responded timidly to these pressures. In a speech at UC Davis in May 1964, Kerr asserted that the campus grounds could not be used to organize such unlawful civil rights protests. The Davis speech proved a fateful one, since it led UC Berkeley administrators to believe they were adhering to university policy when, in September 1964, they banned political advocacy in what had been the traditional free speech area—the sidewalk strip on Bancroft Way and Telegraph Avenue, outside the campus' south entrance—when they discovered that this area, formerly thought to belong to the city, actually rested on land owned by the university.[34] The ban ignited the Berkeley student rebellion.

The timing of the ban was also connected to civil rights movement. The involvement of UC students in the anti-Goldwater civil rights protests at the Republican convention in San Francisco during the summer had led a reporter from the pro-Goldwater *Oakland Tribune* to inquire if those protests had originated on the Berkeley campus—and this, in turn, led to the discovery that the Bancroft strip was on campus property. Dean of Students Katherine A. Towle, who signed the historic memo banning political advocacy on campus, later confirmed that two student civil rights pickets—the anti-Goldwater protests at the Cow Palace and demonstrations against hiring discrimination at the *Oakland Tribune*—had yielded the complaints that precipitated the ban.[35] Even more than a month after the police car blockade, Kerr privately made clear that his ongoing worries about off-campus civil rights sit-ins being organized from campus prevented him from acceding to the Free Speech Movement's demands that the university cease regulating the content of speech. Kerr took issue with the university's own attorney, Thomas Cunningham, who behind closed doors told Kerr that UC's ban on advocacy was likely unconstitutional. "Kerr argued that we have a responsibility to put people on notice [that advocating on campus] ... what becomes subsequently unlawful—we can't ignore it, said Kerr. For example—Palace Hotel incident."[36]

BERKELEY TRADITIONS IN CONFLICT: ADMINISTRATION RESTRICTIONS ON SPEECH VS. STUDENT ACTIVISM

Kerr's Davis speech was part of a hoary tradition of University of California administrators seeking to steer the university away from political controversy—by disassociating it from the activist inclinations of its students—to avoid antagonizing conservatives in the legislature who might jeopardize UC's state funding. Restrictions on outside speakers, prohibitions on using campus ground for political advocacy, and other attempts to curtail left-wing student activism at UC dated back to the 1930s, the era of America's first mass student movement, which at Berkeley took the form of surging student protest led by communists, socialists, Popular Front liberals, and pacifists against war and fascism and in solidarity with the labor movement.[37] The West Coast red scare, sparked by the San Francisco general strike in 1934 led Kerr's predecessor, UC President Robert Gordon Sproul, to codify the ban on campus political advocacy that Kerr still clung to in 1964. Under Sproul and then Kerr, students were forced to do their political agitating off campus—which they did, just outside the university's south campus entrance.[38] This meant students had more freedom off campus than on, a testament to the fact that the University of California, in spite of its increasing academic stature, had a long-standing free speech problem. Kerr had made a few liberalizations, notably lifting the campus ban on Communist speakers, but these were offset by rules he issued to discourage student protest, such as the provision in his so-called Kerr Directives of 1959 "that student governments and their subsidiary agencies" on UC campuses "may not take positions on any . . . off campus issues without the consent of their Chief Campus Officer" (which at Berkeley meant the chancellor). He also required that outside speakers appear only after a seventy-two-hour wait for administration approval, that tenured faculty moderate when controversial speakers appeared, and that student groups pay for police at such events.[39]

Despite these and other attempts to curtail dissent, Berkeley had a lively tradition of student activism, which endured even into the darkest days of UC Loyalty's Oath and the McCarthy era. By the late 1950s, Berkeley student activists had created a Left-liberal political party, Towards an Active Student Community (TASC), which ran candidates for student government united on a single-plank platform calling for an end to racially discriminatory admissions policies in fraternities, sororities, and other campus organizations. This practice of running a slate of such candidates on the basis of political principle rather than personal popularity was so novel on campus that the progressive ticket (and the party that selected it) began to be referred to simply as SLATE, and the name stuck. The UC administration harassed SLATE in ways that anticipated the free speech battle of 1964, as when, in 1959, it forbade SLATE from holding a rally on campus in support of Proposition C—which would have outlawed racial discrimination in the Berkeley housing market—on the grounds that such a rally violated the university's nonpartisan status. SLATE

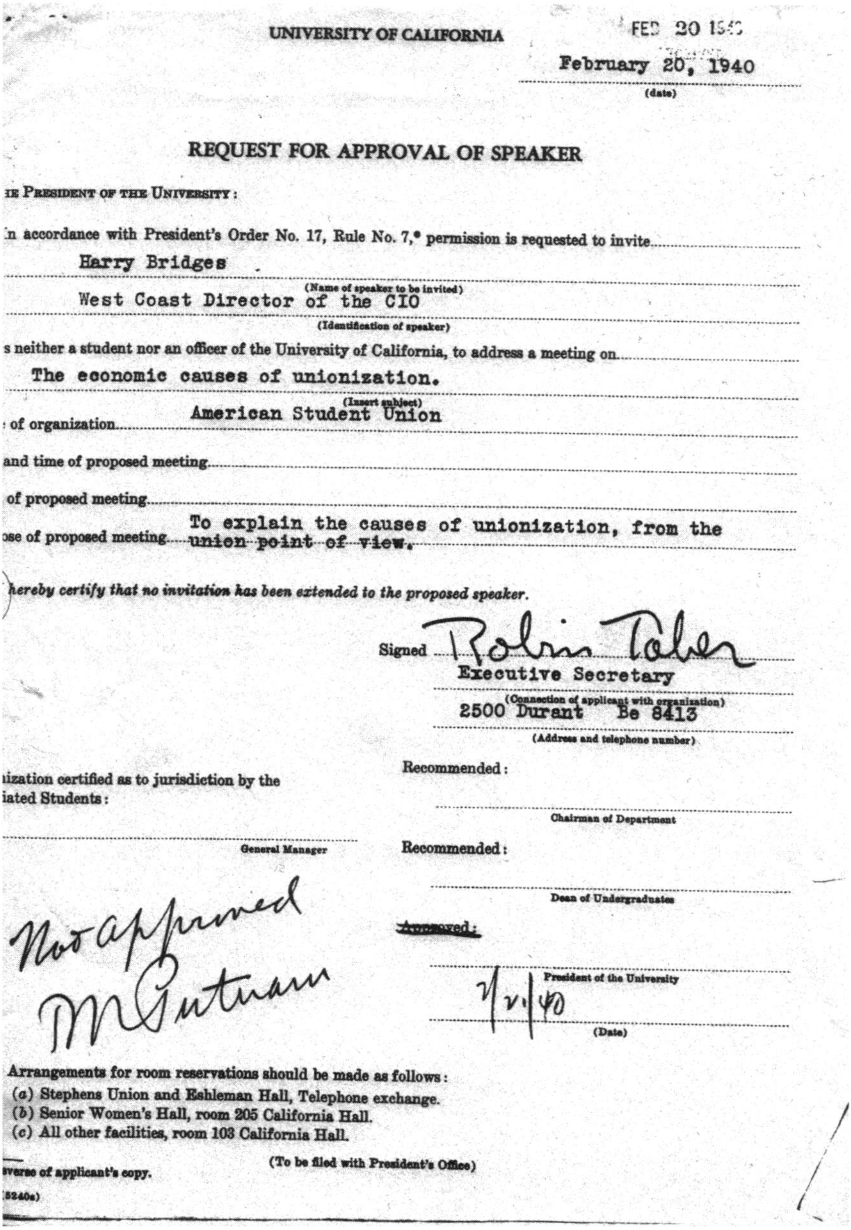

UNIVERSITY OF CALIFORNIA

FEB 20 1940

February 20, 1940
(date)

REQUEST FOR APPROVAL OF SPEAKER

IE PRESIDENT OF THE UNIVERSITY:

:n accordance with President's Order No. 17, Rule No. 7,* permission is requested to invite

Harry Bridges
(Name of speaker to be invited)

West Coast Director of the CIO
(Identification of speaker)

s neither a student nor an officer of the University of California, to address a meeting on

The economic causes of unionization.
(Insert subject)

: of organization **American Student Union**

and time of proposed meeting

of proposed meeting

ose of proposed meeting **To explain the causes of unionization, from the union point of view.**

hereby certify that no invitation has been extended to the proposed speaker.

Signed *Robin Taber*

Executive Secretary
(Connection of applicant with organization)

2500 Durant Be 8413
(Address and telephone number)

Recommended:

ization certified as to jurisdiction by the
iated Students:

General Manager

Recommended:
Chairman of Department

Not approved
Mc Putnam

Recommended:
Dean of Undergraduates

~~Approved:~~
President of the University

1/v/40
(Date)

Arrangements for room reservations should be made as follows:
(a) Stephens Union and Eshleman Hall, Telephone exchange.
(b) Senior Women's Hall, room 205 California Hall.
(c) All other facilities, room 103 California Hall.

(To be filed with President's Office)
verse of applicant's copy.
:5240s)

Figure 2. Restricting free speech: Dean T. M. Putnam, in an act typifying the UC administration's tradition of political intolerance, indicates on this speaker request form that radical labor leader Harry Bridges is barred from speaking on campus, February 1940. Sproul Hall files, courtesy of Hal Reynolds.

proved an effective umbrella organization for the embryonic New Left of the late 1950s and early 1960s, pushing for an end to compulsory ROTC, protesting the nuclear arms race, opposing capital punishment, expressing solidarity with the civil rights movement, and seeking to banish the legacy of McCarthyism.[40]

It was on this last issue that SLATE members made their biggest mark (and national headlines) when they—borrowing the tactics of the lunch counter protests of black students—sat in at San Francisco's City Hall in May 1960 to demonstrate against the local hearings of the red-hunting House Committee on Un-American Activities (HUAC). Police used high-powered water hoses to evict the protesters, washing them down the steps of City Hall. HUAC inadvertently added to Berkeley's national reputation for student activism by producing a film, "Operation Abolition," which so crudely attacked these protesters as reds and Communist dupes that it evoked admiration for Berkeley student activists.[41] Berkeley became a magnet for students weary of Cold War orthodoxies and eager to defy the political and cultural repressiveness of those antiradical times.

MARIO SAVIO'S POLITICAL EDUCATION AND CIVIL RIGHTS LETTERS

This history of Berkeley student activism in the early 1960s intersected directly with Mario Savio's political trajectory. Savio had begun his higher education in his native New York City, first as a scholarship student at Manhattan College and then as a transfer student at Queens College. When his parents moved to Southern California, in 1963, Savio decided that he too would head west to continue his education. Savio was drawn to Berkeley in part because of its activist reputation. He had learned about that reputation "while browsing at the paperback stand in the local corner candy store" and "skimming David Horowitz's book *Student*."[42] Horowitz, a Berkeley teaching assistant when he published this book, in 1962, portrayed SLATE and the campus's student activists glowingly, as champions of civil rights, peace, academic freedom, civil liberties, and serious-minded social reform who broke with the conformity and political apathy of the "silent generation" of college students of the 1950s. Savio read with interest

Horowitz's dramatic account of the Berkeley student role in the demonstrations against the House Committee on Un-American Activities in San Francisco. "This was," as Savio put it, "my first encounter with the Berkeley students. . . . I just had a feeling that this was an exciting place to be. . . . Once my *father* decided to move the family to California I was on my way to the Berkeley campus."[43]

The fact that Savio found Berkeley's activist reputation attractive attests that he was already politically conscious and inclined toward social action before he ever set foot on the Berkeley campus. This social consciousness and activist disposition evolved out of his religious background. Raised in a working-class Italian immigrant home as a devout Catholic, Savio had been an altar boy, and he had aunts who were nuns and a mother who hoped he would become a priest. As a teen, Savio, broke with the church but retained from his Catholic background a deep sympathy with the poor and oppressed, reading Dorothy Day's *Catholic Worker* for a time, feeling a desire to promote social justice and "resist evil"—a mindset he later referred to as a kind of "secularized liberation theology."[44] Consistent with all this was his volunteer work in the summer of 1963 on antipoverty projects in Mexico, an effort organized by a Catholic student group at Queens College. Remnants of Savio's religious sensibility stirred his sympathy with the civil rights movement, which he saw as struggling for a cause that was righteous, even holy—a beloved community struggling against hatred and evil, against the sin of racism.[45] Given this moral sensibility, it would have been surprising if Savio had not been drawn to Berkeley and to the black freedom movement. He saw that movement as the most important, moral, and inspiring form of social activism in America, and he saw anything that interfered with it—as the UC administration seemed be doing with its free speech ban in fall of 1964—as an evil to be resisted.[46] This was a mindset that, given Savio's intellectual and political skills, would not bode well for Clark Kerr and the UC administration.

The interconnectedness, the overlap, and the synergy between protest movements are central to understanding the history of dissent in the 1960s. And this is one of the key reasons that the writings and speeches of Mario Savio from 1964, the year he emerged as the most famous student protest leader in the United States, are so valuable. In this single year, we see Savio involved in three distinct yet interconnected protest movements and in different roles in each. During spring semester of 1964 he became increasingly involved in civil rights work, tutoring inner-city students in a program founded by Campus CORE and University Friends of SNCC, doing political canvassing in San Francisco's black community, and participating in local protests against discriminatory employers. This activism culminated in his participation in the sit-in at the Sheraton Palace Hotel, where he was arrested for the first time in his life. Savio's engagement with the local civil rights movement was serious and deepened with his arrest. But it was still only part-time work, which he was at least trying to balance with his studies at Berkeley as a philosophy student deeply interested in science.[47]

Savio's commitment to the civil rights movement increased exponentially after he signed up to spend the summer of 1964 in Mississippi, where he joined some eight hundred other volunteers (mostly students) and their hosts from SNCC registering voters and teaching black children in a Freedom School. This was *full-time* civil rights organizing, conducted at—to put it mildly—considerable personal risk. The black voter registration drive that SNCC's Bob Moses began in 1961 had enraged white supremacists in Mississippi, resulting in bombings, beatings, and shootings. This murderous violence claimed the life of Herbert Lee, a local African American supporting Moses's work. Lee was killed in broad daylight, and the black witness to that crime, Louis Allen, was also murdered. Savio understood before he ever set foot in Mississippi that to do this freedom work, he might be giving up not merely his summer but his life. In fact, in late June, while Savio and his cohort of Freedom Summer volunteers were in Ohio undergoing their orientation and training, word came that three civil rights workers on the project—James Chaney, Andrew Goodman, and Michael Schwerner—were missing and assumed dead (their bodies would be found later that summer), a chilling reminder of the dangers of freedom work in the Deep South. Once in Mississippi, as his letters from Holmes County and McComb attest, the threats from night riders and racist police were real and immediate, as was the fear this engendered among both the volunteers and the local African American community. Before his first month in Mississippi ended, Savio came face-to-face with racist violence when he, a fellow civil rights worker, and a local African American youth were assaulted by club-wielding Klansmen in Jackson.[48]

Savio's correspondence reveals deepening thought about civil rights as he shifted from part-time civil rights activism in the Bay Area to full-time voter registration work and Freedom School teaching in Mississippi. The Mississippi letters evoke the heady democratic idealism that brought Savio to the South and show how it intensified as he witnessed black Mississippians risking their lives to assert their voting rights. For Savio the most memorable moment of that whole summer was witnessing the quiet courage of an elderly black farmer he had recruited in his voter registration work and brought down to the courthouse in Lexington. The farmer persisted in his attempt to register despite a racist white official's efforts to silence, insult, and humiliate him. Later that summer, Savio was again moved profoundly—and wrote a euphoric letter home that embodies a feeling known in the movement as a "freedom high"— as he witnessed local blacks, who had been barred from even voting before, working with SNCC and the summer project to organize their own interracial party, the Mississippi Freedom Democratic Party. Bringing democracy to life right before his eyes, these black Mississippians held party meetings in which they caucused, wrote platforms, and nominated candidates to challenge the state's lily-white segregationist Democratic Party.[49]

We also see in his Mississippi correspondence a deepening of what might be termed Savio's sociological sensibility. From his antipoverty work in Mexico and Bay Area civil rights organizing, Savio was already aware of how power worked to reinforce class and racial inequities. Mississippi heightened Savio's concern about the way political and legal authorities resisted democratic change. In Mississippi Savio saw how the police and the courts locally enabled the Jim Crow system to persist in all its violence, and how black poverty and white economic power left African Americans aware that they were risking their livelihoods, if not their very lives, if they joined the movement for their voting rights. Savio also saw that local black farmers were armed to the teeth to defend their families from the Klan, and he quickly realized that the issue of how nonviolence played out was far more complex at the grassroots than one might have gathered from Dr. King's speeches. His survival and that of other nonviolent civil rights workers in their Freedom Houses was made possible by their location in this well-armed black community.[50]

Whatever impact their civil rights activism had on the struggle for black rights in Mississippi and the San Francisco Bay Area, there is no question that it provided Savio and his fellow Berkeley students—and their counterparts across the nation—with a memorable political education. There were many levels at which this worked and was disseminated. There was a reciprocal relationship between the freedom movement in the South and on the West Coast. The high drama involved in the life and death struggle in the South helped draw Berkeley students into the movement locally, who then raised money and recruits for the Southern struggle. Even though Berkeley's activist community was relatively small—a few hundred students became directly engaged with the Bay Area civil rights movement, and a few dozen went South, as Savio did—they were part of very dynamic movements that made headlines and elicited broad support on campus. That support arose and spread because it was obvious that activists were fighting a historic struggle for democratic change against racist forces and courageously using militant but nonviolent means for demands that were self-evidently just and moderate—that blacks be accorded their Fifteenth Amendment right to vote in the South and be considered for jobs beyond menial labor in the Bay Area. So even if relatively few Berkeley students went to the South, many more did so vicariously. Thus when, at the height of the Birmingham struggle, James Baldwin came to speak at Berkeley, an astonishing crowd of nine thousand assembled to hear him.[51] So *even the perception* that the UC administration's restrictions on free speech in 1964 were designed to disable the student wing of the civil rights movement would prove explosive—all the more so because the most visible and eloquent leader of the Free Speech Movement was Freedom Summer and Bay Area civil rights veteran Mario Savio.

MARIO SAVIO'S FREE SPEECH MOVEMENT ORATORY AND LEADERSHIP

With the battle over free speech in the fall of 1964, sparked by the ban on political advocacy at Berkeley's Bancroft strip, Savio entered the third and final stage of his year of activism. For the first time, he would be thrust into the *leadership* of a mass movement. Although his work in the civil rights movement helped prepare him for his leadership role in the FSM, he had been a rank-and-file activist and organizer, not a movement leader. This change in role brought with it a new involvement with public speaking. Even when Savio took on full-time activist work in Freedom Summer, it had not been as an orator speaking to large crowds but as a local organizer going door-to-door, speaking mostly one-on-one in voter registration work, and as a Freedom School teacher mentoring small groups of students. Not until the Berkeley revolt that fall would Savio emerge and become famed for his eloquent dissident oratory. For this reason, readers will notice a shift in the Savio documents from the letters that dominate the Freedom Summer chapter to the speeches that predominate in the Free Speech Movement chapters.

In this role as the Free Speech Movement's key orator and spokesperson, Savio made his biggest mark on history. This leaves readers of Savio's speeches with the task of understanding what made them so distinctive and historic. How could someone so young—a twenty-one-year-old undergraduate—and so new to public speaking create and deliver a speech so memorable as his "Bodies upon the Gears" oration, which has come to be seen as a classic in the history of dissident oratory? This was not a question contemporary press accounts probed, since most reporters on the scene failed to recognize that Savio's speeches would come to be seen as historic. The media in 1964 was so antiradical that few reporters or editors were inclined to rise above their hostility to the student movement and seriously delve into the meaning and appeal of Savio's oratory.[52]

Time magazine was typical in this regard, offering little more than Fidel Castro analogies that were designed to be insulting but that in retrospect sound silly: Savio had "an almost Latin American eloquence . . . a sense of demagoguery and a flair for martyrdom."[53] The demagogue image was common, and so was the idea that this rabble-rouser behind the Berkeley "riots" (another common term in the media, and one that ignored the movement's nonviolence) appealed to the emotions rather than reason. So Savio was characterized not as speaking persuasively but as ranting angrily, as in this typical Bay Area report: "He harangues in rapid staccato, shrill at times, emotionally charged always. He's a slender 6 foot 1, sloping at the shoulders, clad usually in baggy slacks and a heavy jacket, bushy hair . . . unkempt. His blue eyes sparkling and intense."[54]

Neither Savio nor his fellow Free Speech Movement organizers bothered to challenge the media's caricature of him as demagogue, because their egalitarian, New Left approach to political organizing meant that they saw the movement's leadership as collective, and they were not terribly concerned about how the media explained the appeal of any one their leaders. So it would not be until decades after the FSM—in fact, not until after Savio died in 1996—that his friends and fellow movement veterans began to comment in public about the nature and appeal of his oratory and to debate how crucial a role it played in the Berkeley rebellion.[55] Nor have historians done much to delve into these questions, as should be obvious from the fact that here we are a half-century after the Berkeley rebellion, and you hold in your hands the first reasonably complete collection of Savio's FSM speeches, press statements, and writings.

In thinking about Savio's oratory, one has to keep in mind that it is both what Savio said and how he said it that matters, that his ideas (and the movement's) were refracted through his unique persona and style of speaking, which almost needs to be seen and heard—not just read on the printed page. His speeches convey more than the sum of their parts, and they reflect a kind of charisma, even though Savio and the movement he represented were much too democratic to be comfortable with the very idea of charismatic leadership. It would be going too far to say that with Savio, as with Bob Dylan, what is on the page is just the lyric without the music. Still, it would be useful before you start reading his speeches to put down this book, go to your computer and watch Savio delivering his "Bodies upon the Gears" speech (on YouTube) and then watch his speech at the FSM victory rally (at https://diva.sfsu.edu/collections/sfbatv/bundles/209401) to get a sense of how he sounded and looked. There you will see what the late Reginald Zelnik, a Berkeley history professor, FSM ally, and Savio friend, meant when he recalled how the young Savio,

> tall and somewhat gangly . . . [as] he hovered above the mike on the steps overlooking Sproul Plaza, . . . cut an extraordinary figure. . . . His face was exceptionally mobile, at times telegraphing the thought that was still being formulated or whose utterance was delayed by an occasional stutter. When he spoke, Mario made full use of his arms, perhaps revealing his Italian

origins. . . . He sounded like the New Yorker he was. . . . [Savio] was the most original public speaker I would ever hear.[56]

What was it, then, that made Savio's oratory so distinctive? FSM veterans have answered that question quite differently than the hostile press did in 1964. Even those acknowledging the presence of the anger or intensity displayed in the "Bodies upon the Gears" speech insist that reasoned argument and logic were central to his oratory. FSM veteran and rock critic Greil Marcus argued in this vein as he observed that "there was often a scary rush in his speeches, sometimes a tense brittle calm, but always a vehemence, an insistence that choices were being made, as you listened, which meant that you too had to choose."[57] Journalist Robert Scheer, a Berkeley antiwar activist and peace candidate for Congress in the Vietnam era, saw Savio's thoughtful oratory as a standing rebuke to those "who denigrate the student activists of the 1960s as anti-intellectual." The New Left's detractors "inevitably stumble over the lanky figure of Savio in his sheepskin coat . . . cerebral to a fault . . . and in all ways an American original."[58]

Moving yet further from the firebrand image, Zelnik wrote that "the piercing words" and angry tone of the "Bodies upon the Gears" speech were not typical of Savio's oratory. It was because Savio had earned the student body's trust all semester with "many . . . other slower . . . more stammering, more considerate, more complex speeches" that students found his angry call for civil disobedience in "Bodies upon the Gears" so compelling. Jack Weinberg agrees that Savio's most famous speech was not typical of his FSM oratory, since the bulk of his speeches focused on explaining the state of the free speech struggle and the strategic and tactical situation facing the movement, linking FSM leaders to their classmates, and building community, rather than urging some immediate act of defiance or civil disobedience.[59]

Readers can judge for themselves how "Bodies upon the Gears" relates to his other FSM oratory. This collection, as the most complete yet assembled of Savio's FSM speeches, makes it possible to view that speech in context and not to have it stand as the be-all and end-all of his oratory—as it has for too long, since that speech alone (and actually only a brief excerpt from it) is the one that most often gets anthologized, screened on YouTube, dubbed into films, and quoted in history books.[60] If one fixates on that speech, Savio and his oratory come off as one-dimensional and perpetually angry. It is quite true that no student radical on an American campus had ever before given such a memorable, poetically incendiary, and angry speech summoning student resistance to oppression. But Savio's FSM speeches on other occasions were, as Zelnik and Weinberg suggest, quite different in focus and tone from "Bodies upon the Gears." In those speeches, Savio comes off as more hopeful in his idealism, humorous, calming, lawyerly, and explanatory in a way that could be so intricately detailed and analytical as to be almost Talmudic. How illusory it is to think that one speech and one emotion—anger—defined Savio's FSM discourse can be gleaned from the memories of FSM veterans, such as David Stein, who recalls being "entranced" by Savio's "brilliant description of his ideas about democracy." Stein writes, "I have never been so affected by a vision of a better world, even to this day." Even an FBI agent reporting on a Savio speech characterized it not as angry but as "rambling and philosophical."[61]

This is not to deny that Savio was effective in articulating and fanning student anger against the campus administration and other forces he saw arrayed against free speech. But since there was more than anger to Savio's oratory, we need to go beyond that one emotion and the firebrand /demagogue image to comprehend his oratory's effectiveness with his fellow students. Zelnik thought the key was the dialogical quality of Savio's oratory, his willingness to question himself and to engage back and forth with those to whom he was speaking, making them feel as if they were part of a dialogue, as opposed to being merely talked at. Savio had, as Zelnik put it, "an ability to engage his listener at the visceral level, speaking to their own doubts and apprehensions. And . . . students had lots of apprehensions and doubts that fall. And by feeling that the person addressing them shared them, his speeches became that much more powerful and persuasive."[62] This was certainly a form of speech that Savio was aiming for, since he admired and emulated the plain-spoken and candid narrative style that he encountered in SNCC's oratory, where the goal was honest communication—free of cant—instead of harangues.[63]

Perceptive as Zelnik's observations may be, there are no easy or certain answers as to what made Savio and his oratory so memorable, and no single way to explain how form and substance, politics and personality, lyricism and polemic, intellect and emotion came together so powerfully in his speeches. This is not something that has been tested empirically, and it is not clear it ever can be. At some level it is akin to an aesthetic question, as in determining what makes great poetry or literature and why certain works prove popular at different times. Thus literary critic Wendy Lesser may be onto something when she invites us to think of Savio's speeches in aesthetic terms, arguing that Savio was "the only person I have ever seen or met who gave political speech the weight and subtlety of literature." Terming Savio the Berkeley rebellion's Demosthenes, journalist and FSM veteran Kate Coleman also stressed the aesthetic dimension of Savio's oratory, "which took all of our inchoate desires and yearnings and articulated them with metaphors. . . . The man was a poet . . . incredibly moving. He was the glue that held the FSM together." Lesser links this power and the literary quality of Savio's oratory to his honesty and earnestness, even going so far as to say, "[Savio was] the only political figure of my era for whom language truly mattered. He was the last American perhaps who believed that civil, expressive, precisely worded emotionally truthful exhortation could bring about significant change." In other words, there was a direct connection between Savio's character and his discourse; his speech was not artifice, not something contrived, but reflected who he was—expression rich in authenticity, so that if his thinking was complex, so was his language. As Lesser explains, "The sentences he spoke were complicated and detailed, with clauses and metaphors and little byways of digression that together added up to a coherent grammatical whole. When he spoke, he seemed inspired—literally so, as if he were breathing thought through language."[64]

Whether or not we accept all of Lesser's and Zelnik's arguments about the structure and appeal of Savio's oratory, there is one point they both share—and Weinberg agrees with them—regarding trust and community building. Whatever gifts Savio had as an orator reinforced the trust students had in him and genuinely reflected who he was. Savio's fellow Steering Committee member Bettina Aptheker underscored this point as she recalled that from the start of the FSM, Savio rejected the normal prerogative of leadership to keep secrets and monopolize information. This too was in the democratic tradition of the early SNCC. Savio insisted on sharing, in a very detailed, narrative style, all that had transpired in the movement's leadership meetings and even in the negotiating sessions with the administration. It was an open, transparent leadership style that reinforced the perception of Savio as an honest leader whose oratory was completely candid.[65] All of this makes comprehensible the morally freighted way Berkeley students in Sara Davidson's group portrait, *Loose Change: Three Women of the Sixties*, venerated Savio as

> the spiritual leader of the Free Speech Movement. He stuttered badly but when he faced a crowd, words came in a silken flow. Jeff thought he was one fucking genius of a speaker. Susie thought he was a great man, a prophet. She heard kids compare him to Moses, who had also stuttered. "Mario could never lie. . . . He had this morality thing, right and wrong, no compromise on your principles." He inspired universal respect.[66]

Davidson draws attention to one reason why Savio's emergence as an orator could not have been more surprising. During his school years, including the start of his college years, Savio had had a severe stammer. This is why not only Savio's childhood friends but even his fellow Freedom Summer volunteer Marshall Ganz, who had roomed with him in the Holmes County Freedom House, were amazed when they first learned that Savio—whose stammer had at times been so bad, even during Freedom Summer, as to be, as Ganz put it, "defining"—had become famous as the Free Speech Movement's most eloquent orator. Reflecting back on this startling change in his ability to speak, Savio noted that for him the Berkeley rebellion's very name, the Free Speech Movement, was a pun, since the revolt led to the free movement of his own speech.[67]

Savio's history of blocked speech made the issue of free speech especially powerful. It resonated viscerally and personally—all the more so because he had found it so upsetting in the South to see the free speech rights of African Americans trampled. The idea that Berkeley students should have their free speech rights narrowed so that they could not aid blacks in the South—who suffered far worse denials of their rights—would outrage any student concerned about civil liberty. But for Savio, who knew what it meant to be literally unable to speak fluidly, this free speech issue registered in a personal way that is almost impossible to overstate.[68] Here too one needs to consider Savio's religious sensibility, which, even long after he had broken with the church, still led him to express himself in almost theological terms. Free speech was not a mundane thing, but almost a divine gift, and our ability to speak was a defining element of our humanity. Just how deeply Savio felt all this and how unique he was in the way he expressed this reverence for freedom of speech can be seen in an interview he gave on the Free Speech Movement's thirtieth anniversary, where he *spontaneously* grew lyrical in describing his commitment to free of speech, quoting Diogenes.

> He said, "The most beautiful thing in the world is the freedom of speech." And those words are in me, they're . . . burned into my soul, because for me free speech was not a tactic, not something to win for political [advantage]. . . . To me, freedom of speech is something that represents the very dignity of what a human being is. . . . That's what marks us off from the stones and the stars. You can speak freely. It is almost impossible for me to describe. It is the thing that marks us as just below the angels. I don't want to push this beyond where it should be pushed, but I feel it.[69]

This passionate, personal commitment to freedom of speech was so evident in Savio that it made him an ideal spokesperson for the Free Speech Movement. It enabled him to connect with mainstream students, political novices who were far less radical than he was, and far more numerous than the campus's core of civil rights activists. Savio had a gift for explaining the principles of free speech and due process at stake in the battle over the ban on political advocacy. By the end of the semester, it was very clear to the majority of students and faculty—whose support was essential if the FSM was to prevail—that this was no mere technical quibble over university rules. All the best oratory of the FSM, not just Savio's, made it evident that the First Amendment, the Fourteenth Amendment, the civil rights movement, and the very raison d'être of the university—to promote intellectual freedom—were all endangered by the ban. Savio's admirers point to a special quality of "sincerity and thoughtfulness" in his oratory that, as Berkeley immunology professor Leon Wofsy noted, "just lifted him above the others. He wasn't doing it for show. . . . He was speaking from his heart and from his head." Savio spoke so effectively that his would be the only speeches from the FSM that continue to be listened to, reprinted, and quoted in history textbooks and studies of the 1960s.[70]

Savio's speaking style was also distinctive because it was shaped by his disability as well as his ability, his experience as well as his aspirations, his intellect as well as his emotions. During his adolescent years and beyond, as he struggled with his speech blockage, he studied poetry and elocution, developing a poetic sensibility, a love of words and wordplay, a sensitivity to the cadences and tone of effective speech that left him sounding like no one else when his stammer finally lifted. In terms of ability, it was not merely that Savio was intellectually gifted—a high school valedictorian and a national Westinghouse Talent Search finalist—since that was true as well of other Berkeley students. It was that he tapped into his knowledge and reading in ways that were illuminating and accessible and could make the writings of Herodotus, Plato, Karl Popper, Thomas Aquinas, Herman Melville, Clark Kerr, Martin Luther King Jr., Karl Marx, and Henry David Thoreau seem equally relevant to the Berkeley rebellion. Savio never talked down to his fellow students; he respected their intelligence and challenged them to use it to join the FSM's dialogue about free speech, democracy, and the university. He had an ability to impart intellectuality with clarity and without pretense. As his philosophy professor John Searle noted, "A typical Mario speech . . . has a kind of freshness which combines an awareness of the problem that he can state in an ordinary common sense, non-intellectual level with a certain deep intellectual vision."[71] The anger in Savio's speeches rested on a reasoned critique of the university administration—informed by his training in logic as a philosophy major—not on impulsive venting or personal pique. His speeches drew on his experiences in the civil rights movement, tapping into recent history that was accessible and a moral cause that many students found admirable. From that movement, Savio had inherited a hyper-democratic ethos that he applied to university affairs, pressing a hierarchical and bureaucratic administration to cut the red tape and move toward the simple and elegant ideal of campus governance resting in the consent of the governed.

It would be a mistake, however, to see Savio's oratory as a solo act. Savio's speeches were shaped by the larger political and intellectual milieu of the Berkeley rebellion and were as much an outgrowth of that milieu as they were of Savio's own intellect. If his speeches were idealistic at times and bitterly disillusioned and angry at others, it was in part because the movement itself changed its tone as it experienced ups and downs. If

Savio dug below the surface to probe how the university served the power elite while slighting the powerless, it is because the student movement at Berkeley was trying to determine why a university supposedly committed to the free exchange of ideas was limiting free speech on campus.

Most of Savio's oratory, especially his speeches in the opening phases of the Berkeley rebellion, must be read differently from those of scripted politicians. Savio was not working from a script. At the start of the movement, the protests were spontaneous; there was no time for Savio to prepare a speech. The speeches from atop the police car were as improvised as the blockade itself. When Savio cited Thoreau in seeking to justify the ideal of civil disobedience to the hecklers around the blockade, he was thinking on his feet. The same is true of his speech rebutting Dean Barnes the day before, when Savio cited the eruption of racist violence in Mississippi and the Tonkin Gulf incidents as examples of crises where UC's rule requiring a seventy-two hour delay for nonstudent speakers on campus derailed an urgent need for timely discourse and free speech. Those early speeches were made even before the Berkeley rebels had named their cause the Free Speech Movement. Later, when the FSM had the time and organization to plan rallies and press conferences and decide on speaking topics, Savio could develop outlines for his speeches and gather quotes of FSM detractors that he would rebut and mock in his oratory.[72] But never did he work from a fully prepared text. Even his most famous speech, "Bodies upon the Gears," which Savio did think about in advance and delivered at a rally the FSM had planned, was not made from a written text, and in fact, the speech opened with a spontaneous rebuttal to the preceding remarks at the rally made by Berkeley's anti-FSM student body president.[73] This spontaneity gives much of his FSM oratory a special improvised quality, much like a jazz riff, and it enables us to see Savio thinking out loud. But it also means that the speeches tend to be unpolished and that their deepest and most memorable phrases often have to be tracked down.

Among the most important problems readers confront in assessing Savio's oratory is determining the extent and the nature of its radicalism. Savio, in the early SNCC-New Left tradition, avoided the leaden and jargon-filled oratorical style of the Old Left. As an ex-Catholic, he was allergic to doctrinaire expression and totalistic approaches to social thought. His one reference to Karl Marx in his FSM discourse was humorous and done to mock the red-baiting press. He mentioned Mao, Fidel Castro, and Soviet "democratic centralism" in a similar vein. Savio's document of choice during the FSM was the First Amendment, not the Communist Manifesto. Yet he did not shy away from class analysis, and he echoed radical sociologist C. Wright Mills when he asked critical questions about the class interests of UC's Board of Regents and those who pressured the university to bar civil rights organizing on campus.[74]

Savio was an emerging New Left student organizer based at a university, not an Old Left union organizer of blue-collar workers at an industrial plant. This means that much of the radical thought in his FSM speeches would be directed toward the educational process, the socializing role of the university, and the psychological oppression and alienation of college students rather than the material issues raised by bread-and-butter unionists. Savio's nemesis in the realm of ideas about higher education was the same university leader that he opposed in the free speech fight: UC president Clark Kerr. In his influential book *The Uses of the University* (1963), Kerr proudly placed the modern research university—which he called the "multiversity"—at the center of postindustrial America as the harbinger and training ground of the knowledge industry, which he correctly predicted would be the dominant sector of the U.S. economy in the information age. But what Kerr saw as the academic fulfillment of the American dream, Savio saw as a nightmare. Kerr's vision, Savio charged, would reduce the university to a service station for big business and the Pentagon. Higher education would lose its independence, both economically and politically, becoming so much a part of the military-industrial complex that it would dare not criticize the inequities of American capitalism or the conversion of Cold War America into a garrison state. A university bent on serving the power elite would have little time or inclination to help the powerless.[75]

In the rush for research contracts, the university would, Savio maintained, devote less and less attention to teaching undergraduates. The vocational ethos of the university would infect undergraduate education as colleges were virtually reduced to trade schools devoted to readying students for their elevated places in the corporate order rather than fostering critical thought about that order. This grooming of students as conformists was, from Savio's perspective, seeding an existential crisis. Students were denied a chance to question corporate America and their role in it, never afforded an opportunity to define what meaningful work was or to ponder what a better, freer society would look like. Savio bemoaned the fact that at these huge and growing universities, under-graduates were treated impersonally, like IBM cards used for data process-ing. This charge resonated with students tired of standing in long lines and sitting in the back of almost stadium-sized lecture halls. Appealing to the democratic values of his classmates, Savio suggested that democracy would be a casualty if Kerr's multiversity aped large corporations, which functioned autocratically and were managed by a new class of bureau-crats. Savio called on students and faculty to reject Kerr's corporate vision and refuse to be cogs in the "knowledge factory" he had built. Savio argued that students and faculty *were* the university and should demand the return of its government to their hands, reducing administrators to their rightful, subordinate role as the servants of the university—that is, serv-ants of the faculty and students—rather than allowing these bureaucrats to continue their usurpations as campus managers or dictators.[76]

At first glance, Savio's vision of the university as a self-governing, dem-ocratic community seems radical, even socialistic, since he was advocating that academics take control of their workplace. And to the extent that the FSM won a momentary toppling of administration authority on December 8, 1964, when the faculty, prodded or inspired by the FSM, overruled President Kerr, it did something revolutionary. Nonetheless, Savio called the movement academically conservative and liked to say that his was a very traditional Christian ideal of the university as being *in but not of soci-ety*.[77] He claimed that when it came to a vision of higher education, Kerr was the revolutionary, the innovator, who wanted to more closely inte-grate the modern research university with the capitalist economy, while he (Savio) clung to the old vision of a campus whose gates marked a dividing line that preserved the university's independence from the socioeconomic, political, and military elites devoted to sustaining the status quo.[78] This critique was a natural outgrowth of the Free Speech Movement, since, in Savio's eyes, it explained why Kerr lacked the independence to preserve free speech on campus. The university so closely identified with the busi-ness and political elites that it barred its students from using the campus as a base for organizing demonstrations against local business interests even when those businesses provoked and deserved protests on account of their racist hiring practices.

While popularized in the 1960s, Savio's critique of the corporatization of the university has a twenty-first-century ring to it. The line separating higher educational institutions from corporate America has all but disappeared in our century of massive partnerships between the campuses and multinationals, with Berkeley and British Petroleum being a prime example.[79] The trend toward such partnering has accelerated not only because of the needs of an increasingly high-tech corporate economy but also because of the decline of public funding for higher education. It has reached the point where today's most prominent critics of corporatization, those who see Savio's warnings as prophetic, are not student radicals, but middle-aged professors. There is a whole field of higher-education studies devoted to monitoring and fretting over the commercialization of the university. David Kirp, one of the leading scholars in this field, notes that in twenty-first-century UC Berkeley, the business school is headed by the "Bank of America Dean," and so asks "Was Savio simply ahead of his time?"—a question that readers of Savio's writings (especially on the cupidity of American higher educational institutions) would do well to consider.[80]

As a historical figure, a student leader in 1964, however, what matters most about Savio is not his prescience about the future (and our depressing academic scene today) but his appeal in his own time on his own campus. Were he a singer, we would say that he had crossover appeal. Savio could attract the campus Left with his biting critique of the elite class interests represented on the Board of Regents and the autocratic managerialism of the administration. But by avoiding stilted Old Left rhetoric, he could and did prove equally adept at connecting with the much larger number of non-radical students. He spoke passionately in defense of the very civil liberties they had been taught to cherish in their high school civics classes and by their parents, and he invoked the idea of a university that would treat them as adults rather than as children. Savio's intellectuality, ability to think independently, and his engagement with history and philosophy made him at times sound like a graduate student, enhancing his appeal to graduate students and faculty. Having an orator with such

crossover appeal gave the FSM an advantage over many subsequent student movements and is certainly a key reason why few could quite dupli-
cate the victory Savio and the FSM won in December 1964.

REFLECTIONS ON YOUTH REVOLT AND MAKING
HISTORY AT TWENTY-ONE

The most startling fact about Savio's letters and speeches from 1964 may
be that the person who did this writing and speaking was all of twenty-one
years old. Youth and studenthood do have their limits, and these can be
gleaned from Savio's FSM speeches and writings. Attending college in an
era of liberal hegemony, when such establishment liberals as Clark Kerr
and Pat Brown were in power and the university richly funded, young
Savio could not have even dreamed that California's illiberal, intolerant,
antiradical, tax-averse right wing would come to power and decimate
state funding for the university and the state's entire public school system.
Savio was brilliantly critical of Kerr's timidity in defending free speech on
campus but did little to explore the historical sources of that timidity, particularly Kerr's wariness of stirring the sleeping dogs of the California
right—a wariness born of Kerr's experience dating back at least to UC's
Loyalty Oath debacle and the McCarthy era.

    In 1964 Savio could have had no way of knowing how much those on the
right loathed Kerr, most notably FBI director J. Edgar Hoover, who covertly slandered Kerr and sabotaged his career, and Ronald Reagan, who in
1967, just three weeks after his ascension to California's governorship,
abruptly fired Kerr.[81] Euphoric that the use of civil disobedience had finally
won free speech on campus—and exhausted from that consuming struggle—Savio did not consider that the California electorate's resentment of
the movement's militant tactics would become so widespread, and he could
not have anticipated how Reagan would tap into that resentment—making
his pledge to "clean up the mess in Berkeley" a key theme in the campaign
that won him the governorship.[82] But then again, it may have been impossible for Savio and the FSM to have won over a California electorate that,
even in early November 1964, well before the FSM ended, already displayed strongly illiberal tendencies—voting, for example, by an overwhelm-

ing 55 percent to 29 percent margin to repeal the state's fair housing law, giving a huge boost to racially discriminatory realtors and homeowners.[83] It seems unrealistic, moreover, to expect Savio to have viewed Kerr more sympathetically or to have seen that, in his own way, UC's president was trying protect the university from dangers Savio lacked the age and experience to recognize. After all, the young student rebel and his middle-aged university president viewed one another in a similarly harsh light—as one might expect of political combatants. In fact, as we have seen, Kerr even stooped to red-baiting the FSM's leaders in the heat of political battle.[84] Still, there is something sad about the way this Left-liberal feud played out, that Savio and Kerr, the FSM and the UC administration, inadvertently empowered California's right, which has left UC with campuses where today speech is free but tuition is not.[85]

Such critical reflections, however, are grounded in knowledge that Savio could not have had at the time and in a twenty-first-century view of UC's depressing decline in state funding. We would be guilty of what is for historians the cardinal sin, presentism, if we expected him to be able to see his world as we can now—from a post-Reagan, post–Proposition 13 perspective.[86] But if we change to a more appropriate lens and view Mario Savio in 1964 from the perspective of all that he said, wrote, and achieved in that year, it seems almost astonishing that a twenty-one-year-old undergraduate could have accomplished so much. It is difficult to think of another student whose words would be so worthy of being collected and published. A biographer might argue that the tremendous outburst of ideas and activism charted in these pages reflects Savio's brilliance and his passionate commitment to social justice, fueled by an ex-Catholic's secularized commitment to a Christ-like mission to help the oppressed.[87] And a biographer might say that Savio's political activism also reflected a yearning to chart his own course personally, breaking free of his parents by straying from the academic stardom he'd previously maintained as part of their immigrants' assimilationist version of the American dream, and rebelling against academic administrators as surrogates for his overbearing father—in the process finally shedding his oppressive speech defect.[88] A historian, on the other hand, would likely lay more emphasis on the times, setting Savio in the context of the activist subset of the baby-boom generation that collectively said no to Jim Crow and the legacy of Joseph

McCarthy and that managed to crack the Cold War consensus, paving the way for an America where racial disenfranchisement was a crime, where it became possible to elect an African American president, and where free speech reigned on campuses that were increasingly engaged with dissident politics.

Since 1964 was by far Savio's most politically active period, his writings in that year were much more centered on politics than on his personal life. His expanding activist role, from part-time to full-time civil rights organizer and then to FSM leadership, left him relatively little time to reflect on his relationships and the psychological dynamics of his young life.[89] Nor did it leave him time to write about the plusses and minuses of being in the media's spotlight because of his oratory and leadership in the Berkeley revolt—a spotlight that Savio would flee in the months and years after the Free Speech Movement. A fuller account of the personal side of Savio's life is available in my biography of him.[90] These civil rights letters and speeches, however, are not devoid of the personal. We see in Savio's Mississippi letters his hopes for a loving relationship with his fellow activist Cheryl Stevenson, his determination to confront and overcome his psychological problems, and his youthful agonizing about the focus of his studies. Moreover, if we think dialectically about the 1960s feminist notion that the personal is political and realize that the political is also personal, these writings can be seen as both personal and political. Savio's personality, ideas, ethics, language, and education shaped the unique way he wrote about and spoke for the democratic mass movements whose fellow activists and egalitarianism he loved and whose ideas and ethos he articulated so eloquently.

Though he did not have time to write about it in fall 1964, Savio's personal life was obviously impacted by the FSM. Becoming a political celebrity almost overnight proved difficult, and the intensity of being at the center of a mass movement disrupted his relationship with Cheryl Stevenson.[91] Savio grew closer to his fellow FSM leaders on the Steering Committee who spent endless hours together in their political meetings. Steering Committee member Suzanne Goldberg, a philosophy graduate student, collaborated with Savio on a number of key movement writings. She later recalled, "we worked very well together," writing "a lot of [FSM] pamphlets together. We respected each other." She was impressed by the way his character shaped his politics, that Savio's honesty and integrity led him to express himself in a way that was devoid of inflated rhetoric, resulting in a straightforwardness in communicating. Soon after the FSM semester drew to a close, Goldberg and Savio spent a good deal of time speaking privately too, talking "a lot about ourselves and our pasts," and she came to appreciate his "ironic sense of humor."[92] Mario and Suzanne's friendship evolved into a romantic relationship, and they would later marry. For Savio personally, then, the FSM semester, which had disrupted his academic work—with his suspension from the student body—had led to this important new relationship, as well as to new friendships with other movement leaders that would prove enduring. The FSM kept Savio so engaged politically and personally that he showed no signs of the depression that would afflict him in later life.[93]

Perhaps what may be most striking are the educational implications of the story of Berkeley's most famous student radical (who, come to think of it, may be the most famous *student* in the history of the University of California). Had Savio and his friends been obsessed with grades, coursework, and careers, they might well have rushed past the Bancroft strip without taking the leaflets that led them to participate in the Sheraton Palace demonstration for fair hiring. Savio would have missed the sit-in, arrest, and the jail-house conversation that led him to volunteer for Mississippi, and likely would not have led the Free Speech Movement. Berkeley has had dozens of Nobel Laureates, but none of their oratory has been elevated to the pantheon of great American speeches. No Berkeley professor or administrator, but only Savio, a student, had his words selected for inclusion in the Library of America's collection of historic American speeches since Lincoln. This is not to say that Savio's speeches and writings were flawless—they do have their problems, exaggerations, and omissions. But the richness of the ideas and the significance of the civil rights and free speech activism documented in these pages attest that some of Savio's most important learning experiences went on outside the classroom, as a participant in movements for social change.

What Savio learned in his classes, whether about Thoreau, Thucydides, Diogenes, Marx, or any of the other thinkers he mentioned in his FSM oratory, was tremendously important in enabling him to think critically about the inequities of power and the limits on freedom both on campus and off. But Savio recognized that thought connected to action, and learning "by doing," as he put it, made knowledge all the more meaningful and powerful.[94] He also recognized that for all its educational riches, the university, if divorced from the struggle for a more democratic world, risked becoming an enclave of class and racial privilege, promoting a selfish materialism and mind-numbing conformity. By going beyond Berkeley's classrooms, Savio was able to learn from and work with Bob Moses and other African American organizers, obtaining the kind of interracial education that was not available in Berkeley's mostly white classes in 1964. By looking beyond the campus, Savio was able to test the limits of freedom and become part of movements that expanded freedom in 1960s America, exercising his First Amendment rights in the way he found most meaningful—by engaging in what he liked to call "consequential speech," speech that led to action. This meant pushing America to become more truly democratic by taking steps to end the restriction on freedom of speech on campus and to eliminate the country's ugly racist restrictions on black voting and employment rights.[95] Viewed in this way, the collected works of the twenty-one-year-old Mario Savio constitute a standing invitation for the young in our own century to consider how their education too might be extended beyond the classroom.

SAVIO'S WRITINGS AND SPEECHES AS A GUIDE TO A HISTORIC YEAR OF STUDENT ACTIVISM

The structure of *The Essential Mario Savio: Speeches and Writings that Changed America* is chronological, and each chapter uses Savio's own words to carry us through his intensifying activism in 1964. Chapter 1, "The Making of a Berkeley Civil Rights Activist," traces Savio's emergence as a part-time civil rights worker, whose local activism in the spring semester of 1964 culminates with his arrest in the mass sit-in at San Francisco's Sheraton Palace Hotel. Chapter 2, "Going South," uses Savio's Mississippi letters to tell the story of his work as a full-time civil rights worker during Freedom Summer, on the front lines of the struggle for racial equality in the Deep South's most violently racist state. The last two chapters—"Leading the Free Speech Movement" and "No Restrictions on the Content of Speech"—center on Savio's oratory in the Free Speech Movement, in the fall semester, showing how the Berkeley revolt emerged, evolved, and triumphed, and how quickly and effectively Savio transitioned from a rank-and-file civil rights worker to a leader of the Berkeley student movement—a transition eased by the lessons he learned and skills he developed in the black freedom struggle.

While each of these chapters centers on Savio's words from 1964, my introductions to the chapters and the documents they contain also draw on Mario's later reflections on his civil rights activism and Free Speech Movement leadership. In this way, the insights Savio had as he looked back on his student activism—preserved in interviews and the outlines he drafted for an uncompleted memoir—are used to help readers contextualize the letters and speeches from that period of youthful activism.

BEYOND THE 1960S: SAVIO AND THE FSM IN HISTORY AND MEMORY

The documents are followed by a coda that briefly discusses what became of Savio after the FSM and then focuses on the struggle over the history, memory, and commemoration of Savio and the Free Speech Movement at UC Berkeley. Here the story is told of a protracted process in which Savio and the FSM went from being feared to being embraced by the UC administration, thanks to the efforts of Berkeley students, faculty, FSM veterans, and one 1960s-era Cal alumnus and software pioneer turned philanthropist. Savio's leadership in the struggle for free speech on campus led to his suspension from the student body and to his arrest in 1964, the denial of readmission to UC in 1966, and to a three-month jail sentence in 1967, yet three decades later he would be honored by the same university that once shunned him. The steps in front of the administration building, from which he gave many of his rebellious speeches, were renamed the Mario Savio Steps. By 2000 UC had named a major endowment and a café next to its undergraduate library in honor of Savio and the FSM. These acts of recognition represented change that was dramatic, almost poetic—as a great university paid tribute to one who led and sacrificed on behalf of a movement to make the university more free.

I say *almost* poetic because the recognition was so belated that Savio did not live to see it. Of course, Berkeley was not alone in taking years to honor a key figure its history who represented democratic change in 1960s America. Universities in the Deep South took decades to honor those African American students who desegregated them in the early 1960s.[96] It took the U.S. government fifteen years following Martin Luther King's death to honor the slain civil rights leader with a national holiday. No campus, no nation responds to change or sorts out its history as quickly as one might hope or expect. My hope is that this volume will contribute to this process of both rethinking the history that Savio and the FSM helped to make in the 1960s and reflecting on their vision of a more democratic society and university.

1 The Making of a Berkeley Civil Rights Activist

For Mario Savio, college never represented a mere career track; it was part of a moral and intellectual quest, a path toward meaning and identity, a crucial part of what he called a "period of personal transition [that] revolved about [his] breaking away from the Catholic Church." At the behest of his parents, he had, as a star science student, accepted a scholarship in 1960 at a local Catholic institution, Manhattan College. Majoring in physics, his first act of intellectual rebellion grew out of his study of the classics, taking "a full year course in ancient history, literature, and philosophy," and using ancient Greek culture as a kind of counterculture that helped him move further away from the church. "I fell in love with the Greeks," Savio recalled, "because they represented a pre- and really a non-Christian culture. . . . For me Greek philosophy and literature provided a first vantage point from which to examine the Church critically."[1]

After a year at Manhattan College, as another step away from the church, Savio transferred to Queens College, in the New York City College system, which he found attractive because its "secular, predominantly Jewish," liberal student body reminded him of the friends he had grown up with in Floral Park. Even though he left the church, he still was connected to its social action wing or, as he termed it, "Social Catholicism, which would culminate in the Second Vatican Council [that] was [then] approaching flood tide." And under its auspices, Savio took up his first venture in social activism, volunteering for antipoverty work in Taxco, Mexico, in the summer of 1963. This was part of what he called a "private peace corps project" initiated by the Newman House at Queens College—building a laundry facility and starting work on a school for the poor.[2]

During this pre-Berkeley period, Savio was already drawn to the civil rights movement, which he saw as a meaningful alternative to the materialism, repressiveness, and boredom of the America he had grown up in during the 1950s. The movement's moral seriousness, its struggle for justice, left Savio "deeply impressed" when he first encountered its activists "on the nightly news."[3] The black freedom movement would soon fill the void left by Savio's break with the church.

> For me it [the freedom struggle] was in some ways a religious movement I could believe in. . . . I was not a careerist. I was someone who took good and evil exceptionally seriously. . . . I could have been a priest. And, suddenly there's the Civil Rights Movement. And since I'm breaking with the Church I see the Civil Rights Movement in religious terms. . . . [In the] Civil Rights Movement there were all those ministers; . . . it was just absolutely rife with ministers. And so to me, this was an example of God working in the world. . . . The spirit of "do good" and "resist evil" was an important part of my religious upbringing. I saw that present in the Civil Rights Movement— and I wanted to ally myself with that.[4]

Savio's first in-person encounter with the civil rights movement occurred when he observed the picketing of a Woolworth's store in his Queens neighborhood. Even though the protest was nonviolent and "absolutely respectful, decorous," the protesters picketing the store were, in Savio's words, "behaving differently" than the conformist norms of the world in which he was raised.

> You see, people in those days obeyed the rules. All the rules . . . that were written down . . . [and] a whole bunch of rules that weren't written down. . . . How you're supposed to dress. Everything was so rigid. . . . There was an internally imposed regimentation. . . . So just the idea of people walking around in a little oval in front of Woolworth's was massively non-conformist for the time. Something's going on here. That has to be seen against the

background of absolutely day after day nothing going on. So it was attractive, because it was real. . . . I'd never seen anything like it before.[5]

Savio later saw the civil rights movement as working with other strands in his intellectual and political development to ready him for an activist role at Berkeley: "The liberal Jewish culture of my high school friends, a deep encounter with the Greeks, and the opening acts in the civil rights drama were the three forces leading me away from home and toward Berkeley, already a center of activism in 1960."[6]

When Savio transferred to UC Berkeley in the fall of 1963, drawn by its reputation for student activism, John F. Kennedy was president. But Savio was not impressed with JFK and looked not to the White House but to the streets and the civil rights movement for inspiration. Kennedy, in Savio's eyes, "failed . . . at crucial places . . . to connect with reality somehow. He wasn't leading. . . . He was the official leader, but he wasn't leading," and seemed more flash than substance. By contrast, "the Civil Rights Movement," as Savio put it, "wasn't flash. It wasn't a fake. It wasn't fantasy land. . . . The Civil Rights Movement was leading America," morally and politically, to an expanded and more inclusive vision of freedom.[7]

Savio's first academic year at Berkeley (fall 1963–spring 1964) coincided with a surge in the Bay Area civil rights movement that he found "amazing."[8] Hundreds of students would be arrested that year in protests against racially discriminatory employers, protests that, for the West Coast, seemed unprecedented in their size, frequency, and militancy.[9] The dynamism of the Bay Area movement was obvious, and so was the role of Berkeley students in it. Berkeley had not one but two activist student groupings, which, despite their differences, cooperated with each other in leading major civil rights actions. Campus CORE was especially active and militant and had connections to the local black communities' CORE chapters. Leadership in Campus CORE tended to come from students in or close to UC Berkeley's Independent Socialist Club. Its main competitor was Berkeley's Communist-led W. E. B. Du Bois Club. The Communist Party had connections in the Bay Area's black communities, and Du Bois Club organizers used those to link Berkeley's predominantly white student activists with such black organizations as Youth for Jobs in Oakland and dynamic young African American civil rights activists such as Tracy Sims.

Out of this collaboration came the Ad Hoc Committee to End Discrimination, the organization that coordinated student and black community protests against the Sheraton Palace Hotel and other racially discriminatory employers.[10]

Berkeley's stores and San Francisco's auto dealers, restaurants, and hotels proved attractive targets for these protests, because all of these employers—facing little state and no federal governmental pressure to hire on a nondiscriminatory basis, since this was before the Civil Rights Act of 1964—had terrible records of employment discrimination. The U.S. Civil Rights Commission, for example, found that in 1960 less than 2 percent of the employees of downtown Berkeley's stores were African American.[11] The few blacks hired tended to be relegated to the most menial, low-paying jobs. The Bay Area civil rights protests usually proved quite effective. When confronted with their hiring record by sustained protest, most of these businesses were forced to capitulate.

As a transfer student at Berkeley, it took a little time for Savio to get sufficiently settled. Living in a noisy student apartment building and attending large and impersonal lecture courses, Savio went through a rough transition to his new academic home that first month. In October, however, he made connections with the local activist community. Savio began "tentatively to walk the picket line" in protest against racially discriminatory hiring at Mel's Drive-In, even though he did not yet have friends in the movement.[12] Nor did he know much about the protest other than the worthiness of its fair-hiring goals.

But by the middle of the fall semester, Savio had become more active with University Friends of SNCC, helping with its inner-city tutoring program. Savio later recalled that, for him, SNCC embodied the Southern black freedom movement at its best and was America's most "unsullied" and moral form of social activism. He compared his attraction to SNCC to "a moth to a light."[13]

But while committed to the goal of banishing the scourge of racism from America, Savio, in his first six months at Berkeley, was not yet a radical when it came to protest tactics. He thought CORE's use of sound trucks in its protests was foolish and a poor way of communicating with the community.[14] Savio also disliked the "shop-in" tactic used in February 1964 to pressure Lucky supermarkets to end its discriminatory hiring practices, because he found that tactic—which involved disruption of the store by protesters carrying groceries to the check-out stands and then just leaving them there—"messy" and lacking in "self-restraint and dignity."[15]

Given Savio's later political trajectory, it may sound strange to characterize him as a moderate, but tactically that was what he was in his early Berkeley days. The bulk of his activist energies were devoted not to risky protest activity but to tutoring young black students. Savio soon became aware, however, that the tutoring project was a "finger in the . . . [dike] operation," and that whatever good it was doing was undermined by the poor schools that seemed to beat down whatever enthusiasm the tutors managed to inspire in their students.[16]

Savio's leap from tactical moderation to radicalism came suddenly, in the spring semester, and it was linked to his deepening connection to the student activist community. He began to make friends with students who, like him, were attracted to civil rights activism, including Cheryl Stevenson, the first woman he would date at Berkeley. In March, while socializing with this circle of activist friends at a party, Savio and some of the others decided to drive across the Bay Bridge to join the protests for fair hiring at San Francisco's Sheraton Palace Hotel—protests he had first read about from leaflets he had been given at Berkeley's free speech area on Bancroft Way and Telegraph Avenue.[17] In light of Savio's later fame as a critic of university education for breeding conformity, it is ironic that he would later credit his education with paving the way for his decision, and that of fellow activists, to join their first sit-ins in these civil rights protests. As Savio explained, "Civil disobedience was studied in class in discussions of Socrates and Thoreau, and acted out at Bay Area businesses in demonstrations that were frequent, massive, and often successful."[18]

In this chapter, the details of Savio's decision to engage in civil disobedience at the Sheraton Palace Hotel will be told in his own words, through the documents he wrote soon after his arrest for participating in this mass sit-in. Savio's subsequent reflections on this event are worth considering as you read those documents. Unlike today, when symbolic arrests for nonviolent civil disobedience are quite common, in March 1964 this was not the case. Risking arrest and prison by sitting in was far from a casual act, especially if it was your first arrest—as it would be for Savio. Thus he saw the arrest as an important symbol of a deepening commitment to the

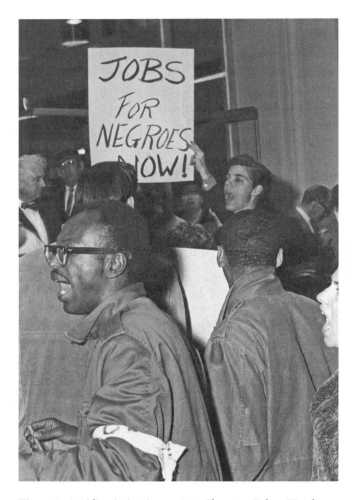

Figure 3. Antidiscrimination protest, Sheraton Palace Hotel, San Francisco, March 1964. Photograph courtesy of Ronald L. Enfield.

civil rights movement, a rite of passage, which he likened to a Native American brave killing and bringing home his first bear. Since the struggle to eliminate racism in the hotel's hiring "had the stamp of morality on it," for Savio, "the issue wasn't whether this was the right thing to do, but whether you had the courage to do it."[19]

Equally significant, this sit-in was the first protest at which Savio experienced the deep sense of solidarity and community of mass protest. It had "a righteous, even sanctified power," which had a profound impact upon him.[20] Under its influence, Savio, who had previously been so moderate on tactics, not only opted to sit in and face arrest, but even favored more militant tactics, such as going to the upper floors of the hotel and waking up hotel guests. While aware that this would have disturbed these guests, Savio thought they ought to be disturbed by the hotel's racism.[21] Savio was also growing more sensitive to political process and the need for protest movements to make decisions democratically, even in the heat of battle, and so was willing to reflect critically on the movement's deliberative style even as he supported its ends. Finally, Savio was aware that his deepening civil rights activism and that of his friends served not only the community, in battling racism, but the activists' humanity and character. "The civil rights movement" enabled the committed activist "to be an agent in . . . [his or her] own life." Those so committed, "more than anyone else, are causing things to occur rather than having things occur to them." Savio concluded, "It's very different from watching television or being a spectator at spectator sports. There seemed to be a real wedding of thought and action; that's a very abstract way to think about it, but I think that's a lot of what was attractive" about civil rights activism.[22]

DEFENDANT STATEMENT, SHERATON
PALACE HOTEL SIT-IN

MARCH 1964

Written for the attorneys representing Savio and his fellow protesters arrested in the civil rights sit-in/sleep-in at the Sheraton Palace Hotel in San Francisco on March 7, 1964, Savio's defendant statement is the first document generated by his civil rights activism. The demonstration at which Savio was arrested was the largest civil rights protest in the Bay Area, involving several thousand demonstrators. Savio was one of 167 protesters arrested, the majority of whom were students. Fair hiring at San Francisco's hotels had been an issue for years in the black community, because African Americans encountered persistent discrimination when seeking jobs in the hotels. The sit-in was the culmination of a surge of militant fair-hiring agitation at the hotel that had begun in February, which the Sheraton Palace initially resisted with an injunction and lawsuit. The pickets and sit-in spurred San Francisco mayor John Shelley to intercede. He presided over negotiations that resulted in the Sheraton Palace and more than thirty other hotels agreeing to adopt a non-discriminatory hiring policy—a major victory for the movement. Savio's defendant statement is his only contemporary account of the events leading to his first arrest, and it reflects his solidarity with the goals of the protests, his criticism of its tactics, and his disdain for police misconduct at the sit-in.

A. Why I took part in the Demonstration
   1. To protest the racially unfair hiring practices of the hotel.
   2. To protest the previous arrests at the hotel.
   3. To support those negotiating to obtain—
     a) from the hotel, assurances that its hiring practices would be liberalized.
     b) From the hotel owners' association, assurances that city-wide hotel hiring practices would be liberalized.
   4. To focus community attention on the racial injustice in San Francisco, and, in particular, in the hotel industry.
B. What I Was Doing Prior To the Arrests

    With a large group of those demonstrators who had entered the hotel I was sitting on the floor blocking the main entrance. We were waiting there for a decision from the demonstration leaders on whether we should be arrested. Conflicting reports reached us regarding this decision, but finally Tracy Simms announced to us that those who themselves chose to undergo arrest should continue to sit in the entrance (behavior which, she said, the police had said they would reward with arrest), whereas those not desiring arrest should "sleep-in" in the hotel lobby, the hotel having assured that none sleeping-in would be arrested.[23]

    I felt that this proposed splitting of the demonstration members would weaken the overall effectiveness of our protest. Although I could not decide whether all sleeping in or all being arrested was the better (i.e. more effective) procedure, nevertheless I did believe that making it a purely individual decision was a tactical error.

Undecided as to what I should do, and even deciding for a while to sleep-in, I finally went to the side entrance where arrests had begun. After watching the arrests for some time, I concluded that although unanimity would have been best, nevertheless, lacking unanimity, a large number of arrests would still be quite effective in focusing public and government attention on our demonstration and its aims. However, it seemed that in comparison with the great size of the demonstration, the number of those arrested was quite small. Deciding, therefore, that increasing this number was the best course of action, I lay down with those blocking the side entrance.

C. Concerning the Arrests

At first I considered the police to be "just doing their jobs," and while I held those jobs in contempt, and although I would have greatly admired one of the officers refusing to continue his assignment, nevertheless I recognized no clear moral imperative for such action. However, my good opinion of these men suffered due to the following:

A policeman dressed in plain clothes (whom I originally mistook for a hotel official), on the occasion of one of the demonstrators being taken with a fit of seizure, exhorted the group lying in the entrance to go home before someone else got hurt, saying that we'd made our point. Though there was an unmistakably patronizing quality (a "be good little boys and girls" quality) about his speech, still I believed that he too was "just doing his job" and was speaking, for the most part, with sincerity. I was rudely awakened to the cinicism [sic] and callousness of this man when not five minutes after giving his pretty little speech, he bent his fingers upward under the chin of one of the demonstrators, gouging the latter's throat violently in an effort to pull him away from his fellow demonstrators. This took place while two other policemen attempted, with fair success, to block the view of this brutality from the press photographers who were present.

When my turn came to be arrested, I offered moderate resistance to the officers, but was carried to the waiting wagon without notable incident.

Mario R. Savio
2283 Hearst, Apt. 2
Berkeley, California

Mario Savio archive, copy in editor's possession, published by permission of Lynne Hollander Savio.

TO THE DEAN OF THE COLLEGE OF LETTERS AND SCIENCE, UNIVERSITY OF CALIFORNIA, BERKELEY

20 MAY 1964

In the initial stages of Savio's civil rights activism, he tried to balance this political role with his academic work. This proved increasingly difficult, especially after his arrest at the Sheraton Palace sit-in, when the court required him to attend the trial resulting from his arrest, which caused him to miss many classes. So he wrote the dean at Berkeley requesting permission to withdraw from his chemistry course. The letter offers the earliest expression of Savio's views on the university's responsibility to support movements for democratic change. It also articulates an idealistic view of the university as a "great and free" democratic institution, which may come as a surprise to those who associate Savio only with his criticism of the university during the FSM. But actually, that criticism can be seen as an extension of the idealism displayed here, in that it grew out of his disappointment over UC's failure to live up to his lofty ideals about the democratic role a university should play in society. The letter also offers Savio's view of his acquittal in the case resulting from his arrest at the Sheraton Palace.

Gentlemen:

I am writing this letter in support of a petition for permission to withdraw from Chemistry IA. I was arrested in the second Sheraton Palace Hotel demonstration for equal opportunities in employment for minority peoples. As a result of my arrest I was required to be present in court for two and one half weeks; accordingly, I shall be unable to complete my courses satisfactorily unless I am permitted to withdraw from my chemistry course. I single out this course because it is by far the most difficult to "catch up" in, since it has time-consuming laboratories, several of which I have now missed.

In my opinion, consideration of my petition should be based upon the following three principles:

(a) Any person acting in his role as citizen should be prepared to suffer the *probable consequences* of his acts.

(b) The University of California should not *ordinarily* interfere with its students when the latter are acting in their roles as citizens.

(c) As a great and free institution of higher learning with a vital interest in the extension of democratic process, the University of California should *defend* the right to use any legal means to secure civil rights and civil liberties whenever these have been denied or abridged.

Concerning (a), most difficulties of application will arise out of disagreement as to the force of the words *"probable consequences."* For though a given consequence may well have been probable, the citizen whose action is in question might easily have been ignorant of the fact, in which case the university must judge whether the consequence in question is such that the student-citizen can reasonably have been expected to know of it. Of course, when the consequence of a citizen's act is contingent not merely upon that act but also upon some subsequent judgment of a second party (e.g., the court), then the probability of that consequence is put seriously in doubt.

Concerning (b), difficulties occur in the interpretation" of *"ordinarily."* For there are some crimes (e.g., rape) such that if a student be convicted of one of them, sufficient grounds may exist for denial of readmission to that student. However, there are other grounds for qualification of (b). Thus, due to the very nature of a university, it is expected that there are certain matters upon which it cannot remain neutral. An example is offered in (c). Hence there will be instances in which (b) and (c) may appear to be in conflict. These instances will demand a prudential judgment on the part of the appropriate university officials. A prudential judgment is never simply the drawing of consequences from premises by a strict application of the laws of inference. Rather, it is the application of a working principle which is adopted in view both of the particular case and of antecedently accepted general principles. I suggest that in the case in question, an appropriate working principle is:

If a student is subject merely to the probable consequences of some action undertaken in his role as citizen, then the university is under no obligation to aid him in shouldering those consequences. If, however, the student is subject to consequences of his action which cannot honestly be considered probable, and if the action was a legal one, and if furthermore, (1) the university has it within its power to lessen the effect of those consequences, and (2) the student's interest in the matter is one with which the university must be presumed to be deeply concerned (see (c) above), then the university is under a clear obligation to assist the student to a reasonable degree.

I submit that in the case of my petition, all the elements are present for an application of this working principle in a manner favorable to my request, since:

(1) The matter in question clearly falls under principle (c); for although I performed that act which I believed would result in my arrest, nevertheless, being arrested is not a crime, and furthermore, I was subsequently acquitted proving that my action was perfectly legal.

(2) I had no reason to believe that I would be required to appear in court at all; but if required to do so, I was advised that I would only have to appear for the first court session, and that presence at subsequent sessions would be required of counsel only. Furthermore, even if appearance at all court sessions be supposed a probable consequence of being arrested and demanding a jury trial, nevertheless, I can scarcely be supposed to have expected this to take more than two or three days since breach of the peace is a relatively simple matter to decide. It was the court's decision to try fifteen defendants at once that caused the trials to take so long; but the subsequent decision of the court can hardly be counted a probable consequence of my action (see above, final sentence of paragraph beginning "Concerning (a) . . . ").

To conclude, let me remark that I have framed principle (c) in such a way as to avoid asserting that the university is obliged to defend the tactic and philosophy of civil disobedience. This is not to imply that I do not hold there are circumstances under which the university is so obligated; but merely that for simplicity I have adopted the more restricted statement, since civil disobedience is not an issue in this case. Also, although not all the defendants were acquitted, this is not a clear indication that they committed any crime. For in some cases the court judge admitted in evidence facts establishing the constitutionality of our demonstration. In these cases acquittals were brought in. Indeed, I believe that Judge Welsh's instruction concerning the constitutional questions involved was a major factor in my acquittal. On the other hand, at some of the trials no discussion of the constitutional guarantees of freedom of speech and of lawful assembly was permitted. In some of the latter instances convictions or hung juries resulted. Naturally the convictions will be appealed, and in accord with the spirit of our system of justice, the university and the public should presume the defendants innocent until it is clear that all appeals have failed, an eventuality which, in view of the facts, is highly unlikely.

In short, then, the defendants in these cases have missed as much school as they have because of an unforeseen decision of the court. That this decision was unforeseeable as well as unforeseen follows directly from the nature of the prejudgments that certain of the judges involved made with respect to the guilt of the defendants. That these prejudgments were made is clear from what has already been indicated; namely, that the instructions that a given judge gave the jury and whether that judge would admit in evidence facts pertaining to the constitutional issues involved were important factors in the decisions of the juries. The question resolves itself in this, therefore: Should the student demonstrators be assisted by the university in shouldering the hopefully highly improbable consequences of their actions, that certain judges foreseeing the ultimate acquittals took it upon themselves to impose the penalties of fines (i.e., daily carfare) and of missed classes for periods of upwards of two weeks? I believe it has been amply demonstrated that it is the responsibility of the university to assist these demonstrators.[24]

Respectfully submitted,
Mario R. Savio
Junior, Letters and
Science

Mario Savio archive, copy in editor's possession, published by permission of Lynne Hollander Savio.

APPLICATION FORM FOR THE MISSISSIPPI SUMMER PROJECT, 7 JUNE 1964–25 AUGUST 1964

CIRCA APRIL–MAY 1964

Savio learned of the Mississippi Freedom Summer project from John King, his cellmate following his arrest at the Sheraton Palace. Savio was immediately attracted to the idea of the project—especially its quest to secure voting rights for black Mississippians, who had been disenfranchised for generations by a Jim Crow system that had made a mockery of the Fifteenth Amendment. For Savio, this crusade for democratic rights was so important—his "kind of religious" feeling that this was the most morally compelling battle against evil in America at that time was so strong—that he felt an urgency about both applying and being accepted for the project. Savio knew that those running the project would be selective, since Mississippi was "a dangerous place," where civil rights workers had to "rely on one another," and so they needed to be sure that the applicants chosen for the project were "clearly committed, but . . . also had some maturity about the thing."[25] *So Savio did not apply in a casual way, and his application reflects this, offering a thoughtful summary of his past activism and how the experiences and skills growing out of that activism could be useful to the Mississippi freedom movement—all of which reflects his growing confidence in his political abilities.*

Name: Mario R. Savio . . . . Age 21 . . . .
Schools Attended . . . . Graduation year

> Martin Van Buren H.S.: Queens Village, NY, June 1960
>
> Manhattan College; Bronx, N.Y., transferred out June 1961
>
> Queens College; Flushing, N.Y. transferred out (to move to California, June 1963)
>
> University of California at Berkeley; presently attending

. . . High School and College activities

> High School: National Honor Society (Valedictorian of class of 1,200) . . .
>
> President of Student Association
>
> National Finalist, Westinghouse Science Talent Search

Queens College: Charter member of Philosophy Club (unfortunately short-lived)

Member of Queens College Mexico Volunteers (with which I did

Community development work in Mexico last summer)

University of California: University Friends of SNCC (last semester)

One of the organizers (and presently a member-tutor) of

S(tudent) E(ducational) A(ssistance) L(eague), tutorial

And study hall for Negro elementary and high school students in the Berkeley area whose education is substandard due to de-facto segregation.

Member of SLATE, off-campus, left-wing political party: This is an "umbrella" organization whose members are of various political views which are left of center. . . .

Arrests . . . .

The Sheraton-Palace Hotel in San Francisco (a demonstration organized by the Ad hoc Committee to End Discrimination). At about 4 A.M. on the morning of March 7, 1964; the police began making arrests after the demonstrators, lying down with arms linked, began blocking the exits of the hotel. We were charged with disturbing the peace. We have been booked and arraigned, and are presently out on bail awaiting trial. Our attorneys will probably enter a plea of not guilty.

Skills and experience . . . for work on the [Freedom Summer] programs . . .

Last summer I went to Taxco in Mexico with the Queens College Mexico Volunteers to do community development work. I was the one of the group with the best knowledge of Spanish; accordingly, I was chosen to explain our work to the wealthy citizens and to the local government. Also, I had to request financial assistance of these citizens. Among the government officials, we encountered considerable hostility toward our efforts. Though not so extreme as the situation in Mississippi, what we encountered in Taxco was comparable: we had to explain to hostile and influential members of the community the nature of our work. . . .

I was one of the organizers and am presently a tutor in SEAL. This was a joint project of University Friends of SNCC and Berkeley CORE. . . . [I]

have done public speaking on political subjects. . . . I believe I could be successful in convincing Negro citizens of the importance of registering to vote, again on the basis of my work in Mexico last summer where I had to persuade the poor farmers of Taxco of the importance of helping us to help themselves; several of them expressed the belief that nothing could improve their situation, so deep had become their desperation.[26]

Mario Savio archive, copy in editor's possession, published by permission of Lynne Hollander Savio.

TO DORA E. SAVIO, BERKELEY, CALIFORNIA
26 MAY 1964

Savio was close to his mother, and in this letter he confided to her some of his second thoughts about going to Mississippi, after he was accepted as a Freedom Summer volunteer. His list of reservations centered on economic and logistical concerns, which serve as a useful reminder of his working-class background and how important it was to both him and his parents that he complete his education and become the first member of his immediate family to graduate from college. The list is also notable for what it did not include—any discussion of the violence and dangers faced by civil rights workers in Mississippi. This likely reflects a desire to avoid worrying his mother. The letter also reflects how deeply Savio had internalized the struggle for racial justice—that he was trying to convince his mother to join and promote a consumer boycott against a racially discriminatory bank—and it shows Savio's Left trajectory and disaffection from the two-party system.

Dear Mom,

I'm sorry to hear that Tom will not be giving the Valedictory.[27] On the other hand, we would—none of us—have wanted him to say pointless things. Also, although the speech which will be given may well be nonsense, let's not say so just because Tom isn't the Valedictorian—I'm sure that's not the case though.

Concerning this semester: I am definitely completing three of the four courses in which I enrolled. In addition, on the basis of a long letter which I wrote to the dean's office, the university had reconsidered its policy toward student demonstrators, and is permitting us to defer completion of our courses. Accordingly, I shall received credit for every course in which I enrolled this semester.

Concerning the summer: A number of things have moved me to reconsider my plans, even though I have been finally accepted by SNCC.[28]

a. I am not *perfectly sure* what my motives were in applying in the first place.

b. *My family* is very short on funds, and in the event of an arrest (which would be quite likely), you (i.e., Dad) would be called upon to post bail bond.

c. It will be difficult to obtain an adequate loan from the university in the fall if I have not worked through the summer.

d. There are several worthwhile projects here in the Bay Area from among which I can choose, so that the rationale for going South is considerably weakened.

e. I shall be far more useful to myself and to the community if I have completed an adequate education—as soon as possible.

f. I am determined to remain in the Bay Area: accordingly next semester I shall be 100% self-supporting; therefore it is desirable that I build up at least a small reserve of cash.

g. I believe I become a California resident (for university purposes) if, upon my 22nd birthday I have been in the state for one continuous year; this would require my remaining here through the summer (I am not absolutely sure about this last point, but will find out tomorrow, and will make my final decision on that basis).

Concerning this coming Saturday: by all means come and if you can, please bring *all* my belongings—books and otherwise (clothing, camping gear, etc.). Unfortunately we'll not be able to talk for long as I will have to be preparing a paper but at least we'll be able to spend several enjoyable hours together—and perhaps, if I can complete more of the paper by then than I have anticipated, we will be able to spend most of the day together.

One more thing: please immediately withdraw all your money from the Bank of America, asking to see the manager when you do so; tell him that you are severing your connection with the B. of A. in support of the state-wide C.O.R.E. campaign to bring about fair hiring practices at the

B. of A. (e.g., B. of A. officials admit that only 2.2% of their employees are Negro); also please tell the manager that you deplore the refusal of the bank to recognize C.O.R.E. as a legitimate bargaining agent. If you've made any friends who bank at B. of A. (e.g., the Bezalis, or your neighbors on the block—*ask* to be sure, it won't hurt!) ask them to do the same. Also get whomever you can to oppose the anti-Rumford initiative when it comes up for a vote—and *please don't sign* the anti-work rules (railroad petition—ask Tom, he'll explain all about it).[29]

> *My best to Dad, Noni,*
> *Tom—See you soon.*[30]
> *Love—your son*

P.S.—I am a paid up member ($1) of the American Socialist Party.[31] This is not—I repeat this is *not* a subversive organization. In fact, some SP members regularly work within the liberal wing of the Democratic Party (although some SP members are opposed to this practice). Many members of the San Francisco section are Cranston supporters, although I think he's a bit too conservative on several issues![32]

> *See you soon—love.*

P.P.S. I really like the Bay Area, and for the foreseeable future at any rate I shall make it my home. I have been doing a considerable amount of driving under various conditions (e.g., night, light rain at night, freeway, mountains, etc.) and I have become quite proficient, for a beginner anyway—I shall soon take my road test.

Tom should be encouraged to apply at the very best college he can possibly be accepted at. Perhaps, if necessary he could do this after one or two years at a less than ideal institution. Likewise, it would be exceedingly wise if *at least* the final two years of college be spent away from home—DISTANCE MAKES THE HEART GROW FONDER!!

Mario Savio archive, copy in editor's possession, published by permission of Lynne Hollander Savio.

2 Going South

FREEDOM SUMMER, 1964

To Mario Savio, "going South" to work in Mississippi's civil rights movement represented "entry into a different order of existence. It was danger and righteousness."[1] The racist terrorism that the KKK and other white supremacist groups in Mississippi directed against this nonviolent movement had been impossible to miss, which is why Savio later wrote that those going South "who weren't afraid weren't serious."[2] Much blood had been shed in the Mississippi movement before Savio set foot in that state, including the assassination of NAACP leader Medgar Evers, the beating of Bob Moses, the wounding of Jimmy Travis of SNCC, and the murder of Herbert Lee when he participated in the black voter registration drive Moses was leading— followed by the murder of Louis Allen, who had witnessed Lee's murder. There had been bombings of black churches where movement meetings had been held. It was, in fact, one such bombing in Neshoba County that Freedom Summer activists Mickey Schwerner, Andrew Goodman, and James Cheney were investigating when they disappeared in June 1964. The news broke that Cheney, Schwerner, and Goodman had gone missing and almost certainly had been killed while Savio's group of Freedom Summer volunteers was in the project's "staging gathering" in Oxford, Ohio. "This was," as Savio later wrote, "all becoming very real very quickly. We talked seriously about death."[3]

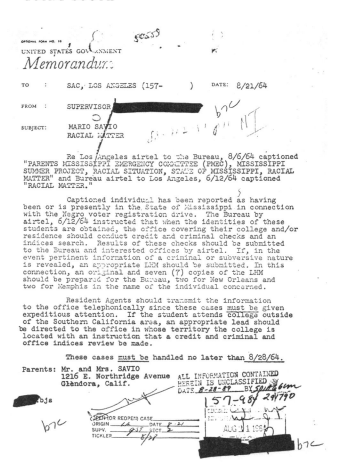

Figure 4. FBI document indicating that instead of protecting Savio and his fellow civil rights workers, who were seeking to promote the Fifteenth Amendment right to vote in Mississippi, the FBI was investigating them, August 21, 1964. Savio FBI file.

Not just the danger but the level of commitment to the movement required to stand up to it in Mississippi was so much greater than had been the case with his activism in the Bay Area civil rights movement that after Mississippi Savio came to reflect critically on his pre-Mississippi civil rights work. He thought that "despite the arrest" at the Sheraton Palace, "my own commitment was still callow and lacking in seriousness."[4]

Though the struggle against the Sheraton Palace Hotel's racist hiring polices was a just one, which he was proud to have supported, he thought that his motives at the time were mixed and his commitment level limited. Savio later conceded that part of the reason he had gone to that protest was because "there was this girl I wanted to impress."[5] "Going South in the summer of 1964 changed all that for me," wrote Savio decades later. "Whatever was still feckless or callow in my political commitment was seared out of me. . . . Mississippi changed my life."[6]

The intimately interracial way the danger in Mississippi was experienced made his work there all the more novel and memorable. Even his arrest at the Sheraton Palace had come after only a brief venture out from the mostly white, middle-class student enclave in Berkeley and into a demonstration against a white-owned downtown San Francisco business. By contrast, the civil rights work in Mississippi involved living in Freedom Houses in black communities and organizing full-time in those communities. This meant experiencing the threats that those communities and their activists faced from white supremacists almost continually, as well as seeing the results of racist violence and experiencing such violence personally. It also involved witnessing at close range the fear that the police, white employers, and the officialdom of Jim Crow Mississippi imparted as they sought to enforce black submission and prevent black Mississippians from asserting rights that were supposed to be guaranteed by the First, Fourteenth, and Fifteenth Amendments.

In this violent, racially charged atmosphere, the examples of courage displayed by ordinary black Mississippians beginning to assert their rights were for Savio so inspiring as to be personally transformative. Over the course of Freedom Summer, it was the courage of an elderly black farmer that moved Savio most deeply. Savio had recruited him to come to the courthouse in Lexington to register to vote. The courthouse was the center of Holmes County's white, segregationist establishment, so it took courage for this black farmer, who had never voted in his life, to even go there. As he sought to register, a belligerent white official mocked him and tried to put him off registering, calling him "boy" and acting as if what he wanted was a mystery, since he said he was there to "reddish," which was how rural blacks pronounced *register*.[7] But the man persisted until he got and completed the forms. This scene, which Savio witnessed, was, as he later put it, "burned in my memory." The quiet determination of "this courageous old man," who stood up to ridicule and intimidation, was so impressive that for Savio it "became emblematic" of his own "changed identity, a commitment" to the movement and its struggle for equality, "deep beyond equivocation or skepticism."[8]

SNCC's African American organizers, who had spearheaded the Freedom Summer project, made an equally deep impression on Savio, both for their courage and for their open and democratic leadership style. The embodiment of all this was SNCC leader Bob Moses, who had put his life on the line in Mississippi since 1961, when, in coalition with local black leaders, most notably Amzie Moore, he launched the state's historic black voter registration campaign. This drive to restore voting rights denied black Mississippians for generations so threatened white supremacy that it led to waves of racial violence, which the federal government did precious little about. In fact, a key reason Moses initiated Freedom Summer was the hope that the presence of students—mostly white—from top colleges and universities across the country would shine a national spotlight on Mississippi, forcing Washington to finally do something to curb the racial terror. But from the outset, Moses was candid about the risks, and when Schwerner, Chaney, and Goodman went missing, Moses told Savio's group of volunteers in Ohio, "People have been killed. You can decide to go back home, and no one will look down on you for doing it."[9]

For Savio, Moses's response to the murders typified the whole early SNCC approach to organizing. Unlike mainstream politics, in which "manipulativeness . . . seems to come with the territory," Moses and SNCC were to Savio "the least manipulative people you'll ever want to meet."[10] Savio admired the SNCC style of public speaking, with its straight talk, unadorned narrative, and conversational oratory designed to communicate and engage rather than harangue. The goal was to empower the community so it could lead itself rather than rely on celebrity leaders giving big speeches.[11] SNCC's hyper-democratic ideal of the effective organizer was one who organized himself or herself out of a job as the community produced its own movement and leaders.

Savio admired Bob Moses with an intensity that qualifies as either reverence or love—or perhaps both. "If I'm nominating people for sainthood," Savio would later say, "Bob Moses wins hands down."[12] This reflected Savio's admiration for Moses's unaffected leadership style as well as Savio's gratitude for being able to participate in the Mississippi freedom movement. These warm feelings were also connected to how Savio retrospectively viewed Moses's Freedom Summer initiative itself—as "the most creative political endeavor . . . that I've experienced or heard about. . . . It may be . . . the most creative political endeavor of the 20th century in the United States."[13] Savio meant this in two ways. First, Freedom Summer was a key step en route to the Voting Rights Act and black enfranchisement. He saw Moses, SNCC, and his fellow Freedom Summer volunteers as fitting the term historian Howard Zinn used when he titled his history of SNCC *The New Abolitionists*. Savio believed they were completing "the unfinished . . . business of the Civil War, not in a violent way, but rather to prevent violence, to overturn a violent order." In the Jim Crow South, "the 14th Amendment and the 15th . . . didn't mean anything." We saw ourselves," Savio recalled, as "going down to make" those Reconstruction Amendments "mean something."[14]

The other major impact of Freedom Summer, as Savio came to see it, extended far beyond Mississippi and the South. In working to change and democratize the South interracially, the Freedom Summer workers were themselves transformed—radicalized—as they came to grasp the nature of oppression in America and how to organize against it, even in the most violently racist state in the Union. Savio saw this as a wave of liberation that began with SNCC and the Mississippi movement and reached across America: "SNCC and the other black workers in the South liberated themselves. In the process, they helped liberate us."[15] When these volunteers came back to their own campuses as veteran organizers, they helped lead the FSM and the many other social movements that spread across 1960s America. In this sense, Freedom Summer was, as Savio put it, "the trigger for very deep change."[16] It was "the event which more than any other created the [New Left], the [predominantly] white student movement. It put an historic period to the mechanism of isolation by which white and black America had been kept apart since the end of Reconstruction," provoking the activist core of the 1960s generation to reject and battle racism.[17]

Savio thought Freedom Summer, by giving the 1960s generation this initial antiracist raison d'être, enabled white, middle-class students to puncture bourgeois America's bubble of self-centered materialism—the privatistic, avaricious consumer culture that had been so suffocating in the 1950s—a breakthrough that played a crucial role in what "turned the '60s loose as we know them." Bob Moses's Mississippi crusade had, in Savio's words, promoted "that interface between the poorest stratum of society that was on its own struggling for liberation and . . . [those in the] privileged stratum, who had all sorts of comforts but . . . a very hollow kind of existence. I mean the notion of a wasteland really applied." This "interface" enabled white students to connect with real purpose through a politics of liberation, in alliance with the black freedom movement, and it was this that "actually turned the '60s loose" and served as a seedbed for the decade's subsequent liberation movements.[18]

Savio's responses to the dangers, as well as the joys, of Freedom Summer and his democratic idealism and deepening criticism of an America that tolerated the racial inequality, disenfranchisement, and terror he confronted during Freedom Summer are documented thoroughly in his correspondence from Mississippi. Most of these letters were written to Cheryl Stevenson, a fellow Berkeley student who was active in the Bay Area civil rights movement. Stevenson and Savio had met in a Berkeley philosophy class at the start of the spring semester of 1964, developing a friendship that evolved into a romantic relationship toward the end of the semester. Stevenson admired Savio for volunteering for Freedom Summer—and had considered going too—but chose instead to continue her Bay Area civil rights work.[19] Savio's letters to her came from different places in Mississippi, reflecting his evolving role in the movement there. Courageously, Savio, even after the news of the disappearance of Schwerner, Chaney, and Goodman, volunteered to go to Klan-infested southwest Mississippi, the most violent part of the state. But the situation in Amite County and McComb was so unstable that he was first sent to Holmes County, where he did voting rights work in July. Thus, his first Mississippi letters came from the Freedom House in Mileston, Holmes County. Later in the summer, he moved to a Freedom House in McComb and shifted to the role of Freedom School teacher, so most of the late summer letters came from there, with a few from Jackson, where he stayed briefly to testify against the KKK members who assaulted him and fellow civil rights workers. The letters in this chapter enable us to learn from Mario Savio's own writings about the events, the people, and the spirit of the Mississippi movement, as well as its

Figure 5. Civil rights activist Cheryl Stevenson, whom Savio was
dating and to whom he wrote frequently from Mississippi,
spring semester 1964. Photograph courtesy of Cheryl Stevenson.

foes, and to see why these two months in the Deep South would be among
the most memorable and politically formative in Savio's life.

TO CHERYL STEVENSON

3 JULY 1964, HOLMES COUNTY, MISSISSIPPI

*Savio's first two letters from Mississippi were written to Stevenson the
same day, shortly after he arrived and began voter registration work in*

Holmes County. The first letter discusses his initial impressions of conditions in the Freedom House, located in the black community of Mileston. In the second letter, Savio articulates his idealism about the democratic change that the movement represents, mentions the dangers he and other freedom workers face in Mississippi, and reflects self-critically on why he has not been turned back by them. The second letter ends with Savio's sketchy map of the Freedom House environs, which included two sheds, an outdoor water pump, an outhouse, and a barn—all facing a dirt road (see figure 7).

Dear Cheri,

This is the first opportunity to write—I asked for today not to go canvassing so that I could take care of some "personal matters." I hope you're well—more important, I hope you're happy. I honestly believe there's every bit as much danger here from food poisoning as from night riders! Some of us are living with local (Negro) families. Today I took a bath in a bowl of water—we heat it after pumping it from the ground, yesterday the pump broke. Alas! The water is very peculiar. As you heat it, iron rust is precipitated. I volunteered to cook yesterday on a marvelous kerosene stove—spaghetti and tomato sauce. Well, more and more rust collected at the bottom of the pot, the water got redder and redder. After about 45 min. the water had not as yet boiled. I suppose the pot (a very large basin) was too large for the little stove. By about 10 o'clock we were filtering rusty water through one of my new handkerchiefs and we ended up having the spaghetti after all—we were done by about 11 o'clock. We play it by ear, each day is a comedy of errors. What they did not orient us in at Oxford could fill several volumes.[20]

The people here are very hospitable and quite responsive. Canvassing here for voter registration—which subjects the people to considerable personal risk—is easier (so far) than we had it in the Fillmore.[21]

I hope the money your [sic] sending will arrive, the address I gave you in a cocky moment should be amended to read: Mario Savio, 708 Avenue N; Greenwood, Mississippi. Others have been writing things like c/o COFO or c/o SNCC, but all (like c/o Freedom) are very unwise.

Figure 6. Savio bathing himself at the water pump outside the Freedom House, Mileston, Holmes County, Mississippi, July 1964. Photograph copyright Matt Herron. Take Stock/The Image Works.

I have tons of work to do, and people are working all around me—one pushed a pe[a]nut sandwich into my mouth a few minutes ago. Hoping you too are looking forward to our camping trip in the Fall.

> Yours,
> Mario

Mario Savio correspondence: Mississippi, to Cheri Stevenson, Bancroft Library, University of California, Berkeley, published by permission of Lynne Hollander Savio.

TO CHERYL STEVENSON

3 JULY 1964 (LATER), HOLMES COUNTY, MISSISSIPPI

Dear Cheri,

Your letter just came from Greenwood. I was so happy to receive it. No, I'm not just being "nice"! At the end of the letter I wrote earlier today ("Hoping you too . . .") I was really uncertain as to how you felt. Whether you were thinking about me too. You're right, it does get lonely, and it's wonderful to know that there's someone somewhere who's concerned— not just as a mother! Those three words came to my lips again—I don't really know just how I feel toward you. About your coming down to Greenwood, I really can't advise you—I'd love to see you! I do plan to return in August, though I might change my mind (very unlikely but possible). Our standing "date" is a strong attraction.

However do you find the time for school with all the things you're doing? It's wonderful, and I know you feel it too, to be part of such a change for good that's sweeping across our country. I really believe that the history of the world is pivoting on the internal changes that are going on today in America—and we are in part the agents of that change. A breath of freedom. But what about Vietnam? Please work hard for KPFA, especially on news from the South. We need the PR! Hold open that block partner(ship) opening.[22]

When I see you I'll talk for a month straight on the orientation in Oxford and our further "adventures." We were originally going to the Southwest, and if the decision is not changed (as Donna Moses—1st

Lady!—has hinted it will be) we shall still go.[23] I volunteered for Amite County, but the KKK is so active there that the project may well be called off. Since the beginning of the year five Negroes have been murdered down there. It was a damned sobering experience to hear the volunteers talking about the real, concrete possibility of being shot dead. All the Southwest volunteers (*all*, including yours truly) realize how ambiguous is the question "Why have I volunteered?" Nevertheless, none of us have backed out, even after the disappearance of those three volunteers in Neshoba County.[24] I don't want to die. I never want to die. But dam[n]it I can't bear to sit safe at home while others are risking their lives. But I don't know why I feel this way. And I think that may be the reason for the hesitation I felt—the fact that I don't really know why I have to take part, I know why *one* should take part and I can't stand to be safe while others are involved, but—and we might die—I might die! Have you ever really thought of what that means?

We're set up, in an old, abandoned farm house. I include this layout so you might have some idea of our surroundings. Even if this letter is opened it won't make any difference because almost every farm in Holmes Co. appears to be layed out in the same way. The house belongs to Mr. Howard, I don't know which one however, there are hundreds of them—one of the few families in Holmes Co. (eh, eh!). Seriously, we're surrounded on both sides by friendly houses (which are not as non-violent as we).[25] So this is a safe place for our office. Our yard is "full of (cow's) shit."

Mario Savio correspondence: Mississippi, to Cheri Stevenson, Bancroft Library, University of California, Berkeley, published by permission of Lynne Hollander Savio.

TO CHERYL STEVENSON

5 JULY 1964, HOLMES COUNTY, MISSISSIPPI

Security in the Freedom House was a serious, persistent concern, especially at night. As nonviolent civil rights activists, Savio and the other residents of the Freedom House were unarmed and had few options in the face of armed assailants other than fleeing or ducking. Windows were, as Savio stressed in

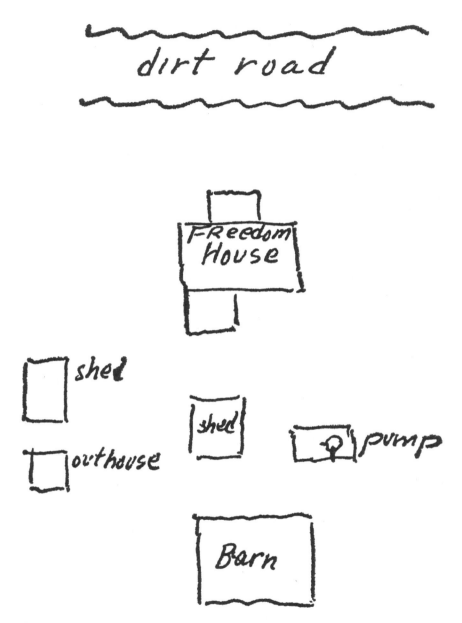

Figure 7. Savio's sketch of the Freedom House environs, Mileston, Holmes County, Mississippi, July 3, 1964. Savio letters to Cheryl Stevenson, Bancroft Library.

his later reflections, a special source of tension. One had to avoid peering out windows, since that made one vulnerable to getting caught in the sights of snipers. Yet patrolling at night to prevent a bomb from being planted outside the house made looking out the windows unavoidable. Such tensions were exacerbated, as this letter makes clear, when explicit bomb threats came in.

Dear Cheri,

I have nothing important to say—I just all of a sudden felt the need to communicate with you. It's so difficult to separate the "important" from the "unimportant" anyway. It's five of eleven Sunday morning. The bomb never materialized. And paranoia was a bit less intense than the first night spent here when we posted watches and crawled about on hands and knees to keep from standing or walking before a window. Now we cover the windows and turn the lights on, uncovering them only when in bed (sleeping bags on the wooden floors). Uncovering the windows lets in more air. I didn't stay up all night writing letters after all. My fatigue "overcame" my sense of the prudent, and I decided to wait to complete my letters. I have so many to write to so many people, so I thought I'd write you another.

I'm sitting outside the Freedom House under a tree. The intense heat of the late afternoon has given no prior hint—every now and again a gentle breeze blows. Looking back toward the back of the house I see Steve Bingham washing his loins at the pump by reaching down into his bathing suit, while Carol (Matthews?) pumps his water.[26] Carol is a Negro girl very sensitive of her bourgeois background; Steve is a white, Yale, pre-law student from a New England patrician family with segregationist relatives in Tennessee—my how integration proceeds apace! . . .

On Sundays we do no canvassing, as the negroes here are very religious. Yesterday we did no canvassing because the local citizens decided to hold a Fourth of July picnic—they celebrate the white man's freedom! I don't want to write any more. Wait for me.

Love,
Mario

Mario Savio correspondence: Mississippi, to Cheri Stevenson, Bancroft Library, University of California, Berkeley, published by permission of Lynne Hollander Savio.

TO CHERYL STEVENSON

7 JULY 1964, HOLMES COUNTY, MISSISSIPPI

This was Savio's last letter from Holmes County, though he would spend several more weeks living there and doing voter-registration work in the area before moving to McComb. Here for the first time, Savio mentions the way local white supremacist organizations and the police intimidated the African Americans he and his fellow civil rights workers targeted in their voter-registration work. And he begins to offer some class analysis, connecting with the Jeffersonian idea that economic self-sufficiency enabled yeoman farmers to be politically independent, which in 1964 Mississippi meant that they were best equipped to resist the intimidation of white supremacists.

Dear Cheri,

You must consider me a fanatic or some other kind of nut—from writing no letters, I've begun writing one most every day. But don't fear for my health, it's only in your case that I've violated principle.

With each person with whom I talk, my desire to remain here past August increases. I'm ever more feeling this as a personal fight. By the time I'm ready to go to the Southwest, I'll feel the full personal commitment that I've ~~decided~~ desired to feel from the start (notice the significant slip: "decided" for "desired"!).

Two nights ago we had to suddenly flee to our barn. Cars were coming from two sides, and it seemed they were out to get us. Fortunately the cars left w/out incident. Next time we'll take to the woods and fields instead, in the hope to be able to run to friendly farm-houses.

Twice a private plane has buzzed us, probably spying. Also the police—who've promised at least minimal protection—have supplied only harassment. While we were canvassing Negro homes in Tchula (a nearby town), the Deputy Sheriff and Citizen's Council radio trucks rode up and down the "streets" past where we were working.[27] The people at once clammed up for fear of being identified as "uppity" Negroes. These people are deathly afraid of losing their jobs. The only Negroes really active are the independent farmers who do not depend upon whites' good pleasure for their livelihood.[28]

Yesterday I spoke w/one man who said he had been "uplifted" by our visit. He gladly welcomed the coming freedom, and would work to hasten it. I too was "uplifted." Today I spoke w/a lady who has worked without any rest since the day her father died when she was very young. Now her husband is dead also. She's very old. Her poor body has finally given out—and the doctors who've taken what little money she could give, have done nothing for her.

Please number your letters so I can know if any have been stopped in case I don't answer every one of them. SNCC is trying to get information to bring suit for tampering with the mails. . . . I'm so glad your letter came today. I wish you were here right now so I could kiss you. . . .

> With love,
> Mario

P.S. There's a lot I would have said in this letter that I can't say for security reasons. There's been a bomb threat—I don't intend to sleep tonight. I hope we'll *be able* to go to sleep tomorrow night. (Love).

Mario Savio correspondence: Mississippi, to Cheri Stevenson, Bancroft Library, University of California, Berkeley, published by permission of Lynne Hollander Savio.

STATEMENT TO THE FBI, JACKSON, MISSISSIPPI
23 JULY 1964

In the process of moving southwest from the Mileston Freedom House in Holmes County to McComb, in Pike County, Savio stopped off in the city of Jackson. Walking together in downtown Jackson, Savio, fellow Freedom Summer volunteer Robbie Osman, and John, an African American high school student (whose surname the FBI deleted from its records), were assaulted in broad daylight by two club-wielding men who were later identified as Ku Klux Klan members. Below is Savio's statement to FBI agents describing the assault.

FEDERAL BUREAU OF INVESTIGATION
   Date 7/24/64
MARIO ROBERT SAVIO was interviewed at the office of the Resident Agency of the Federal Bureau of Investigation (FBI), United States Post Office, Jackson, Mississippi, on July 23, 1964. The information he furnished was incorporated in a statement signed by SAVIO which reads as follows:

"July 23, 1964
"I MARIO ROBERT SAVIO hereby make the following voluntary statement to JOSEPH B. MC ALEER AND HAROLD F. GOOD, both of whom have identified themselves as Special Agents of the Federal Bureau of Investigation.

   "I arrived in Jackson Mississippi about 12:00 noon on July 22, 1964, having worked on the Voter Registration Drive in Holmes County, Miss. I was on my way to another part of Mississippi to continue this work. I had lunch at a church on Farish Street with ROBERT OSMAN, also a worker on the Voter Registration Drive, and we met a local Negro outside the church who said he could walk with us toward the Council of Federated Organizations (COFO) office because we did not know where it was located.[29] We had just passed the intersection of Gallatin Street and Amite Street and were next to the McKesson building at about 3:40 P.M. when a grey Chevrolet automobile in the early 1950s pulled ahead of us and stopped at the curb. It had, what appeared to me, 1963 Mississippi license plates with the county designation covered. It had light blue letters on a white background with numbers which I believe were 501611. Two white males sprang from the vehicle and both had wooden billyclubs. They came at us and we ran and they chased us. The Negro fellow, whose name I don't know, and I ran back toward the intersection. At the intersection he went left and I ran to the middle of the street in front of the McKesson building and stopped and looked back. If the Negro fellow was struck I didn't see it. I was struck once and possibly twice by the billyclub as I was running. I was hit on the rear part of my left shoulder but it was a glancing blow and I feel as though there is no permanent injury. There are no marks showing on the rear of my left shoulder and no swelling. I didn't hear the one who chased me say one word.

When I turned into the intersection of the street I could see ROBERT OSMAN being beaten on the back with a billy club, He was doubled up with his hands clasped over his heard [head]. The one who chased me ran back in the direction of the car and very shortly thereafter both of them fled in the vehicle. We then went into the McKesson building and called the police. About ten to fifteen minutes after the call two uniformed police arrived and questioned us in a general way about the incident. They then took us to the Police Department and we were interviewed separately by two plainclothesmen and thereafter one of the latter drove us back to COFO headquarters. Since I didn't feel as if I was seriously injured I did not seek any medical assistance in any form. ROBERT OSMAN did ask to be brought to either a doctor or a hospital and police said they were willing to take him.

With regard to the man who chased me, if I saw him again, I would be able to say I think that is he. I could not identify the man who beat up ROBERT OSMAN. The man who chased me is described as follows:

Race	White
Sex	Male
Age	30 yrs.
Height	5'-8"–9"
Weight	145–150 lbs.
Hair	Dark brown, bushy
Complexion	Ruddy
Build	Slender
Clothing	Old sports clothes
Characteristics	Remnants of pock marks on face. Possible acne

"I have read this signed statement consisting of 11 pages including this one and it is true and correct to the best of my knowledge. I have initialed all corrections and other marks in this statement.

"/s/ MARIO ROBERT SAVIO

"Witnesses

"JOSEPH B. MC ALEER, Special Agent, FBI, July 23, 1964 Jackson, Miss.
"HAROLD F. GOOD, Special Agent, FBI, July 23, 1964 Jackson, Miss."

From observation and interview the following description and information was obtained from SAVIO

Name	MARIO ROBERT SAVIO
Sex	Male
Race	White
Place of Birth	New York, New York
Date of Birth	December 8, 1942
Address	MARIO SAVIO c/o RICHARD GOTARD-60 266th Street, Floral Park, Long Island, New York
Height	6 feet 1 inch
Weight	180 pounds
Eyes	Light Blue
Hair	Dirty blond, curly
Marital Status	Single
Relatives	RICHARD GOTARD, above, uncle
Education	Three years at University of California at Berkeley, California

Selective Service Data Number 50 63 42 1094, Classification 2-S, Local
Board
Number 63, Jamaica Avenue, Jamaica, Queens, New York

Arrest Record   Arrested at San Francisco, California, at the 2nd Sheridan
[Sheraton] Palace Hotel Civil Rights Demonstration on March 7 or 8,
1964 for disturbing the peace. Claims he was acquitted at trial about the
end of March, 1964

*Savio's statement offers an honest, vivid account of the attack. Since Savio had
initially fled from his assailants, he did not see the assault on Osman
in its entirety, so his account of Osman's injuries is incomplete. Savio*

witnessed Osman being beaten on his back, but Osman also reported to the FBI suffering "hard vicious blows from the club upon my right arm, right knee, right wrist, my ribs on my right side, and the right side of my back."

Osman's statement to the FBI offers a crucial detail that Savio's missed— or perhaps Savio avoided mentioning, since it may suggest that a slip on his part inadvertently helped to make him and his companions easy targets for these KKKers. According to Osman, "My companion Mario Savio . . . was wearing a button about an inch and a half in diameter bearing the inscription 'One man—one vote,' the motto of the voter registration drive for the summer of 1964." Osman believed that their "assailants identified [them] as civil rights workers through this button."[30]

Though wearing that button was for Savio clearly a point of pride while organizing in the black community, having it on when walking through downtown Jackson was dangerous. Since Savio was never asked about it, we can only wonder whether his wearing it was an act of carelessness—per-haps those tense, late nights dealing with threats at the Freedom House had left him too exhausted to consider the dangers and remove the button before leaving Holmes County. Or it may have been an act of defiance—a way of saying that, as a freedom worker, he was going to wear this button as badge of honor and a symbol of the movement's commitment to making a reality of the Fifteenth Amendment, irrespective of how racist whites reacted. It is also possible that since Savio did not know how to get from the black church on Farish Street to the COFO office on Lynch Street, he simply did not realize he would be passing through a white section of town, where wearing the button could be dangerous.

The most glaring omission in the FBI statement, however, was not Savio's but the FBI's, and it concerned the misconduct of the Jackson police in the immediate aftermath of the assault. Rather than being helpful to Savio and Osman, the police were threatening, insulting, and racist in their rhetoric. Savio tried to get the FBI agents to include this police misconduct in their statements. But, reflecting the antiradical politics of J. Edgar Hoover (who loathed the civil rights movement and Martin Luther King himself as dom-inated by Communists) and the bureau's close ties to Southern police, the FBI agents refused to record Savio's narrative of police misconduct and left all of his criticism of the police out of their reports. Savio was infuriated by this and wrote about it in his July 25 letter to Cheryl Stevenson.[31]

Having been pressured by President Lyndon Johnson to open up a Mississippi field office in the aftermath of disappearance of Schwerner, Chaney, and Goodman, however, the FBI did investigate the assault on Savio, Osman, and the black student, providing enough evidence for a rare trial and conviction of a Klansman. In the end, however, the assailant got off lightly on appeal, as one would expect in Mississippi in 1964, with a mere $50 fine.[32]

Mario Savio FBI file, 44–26027, part 1 of 5, obtained under the Freedom of Information Act, copy in editor's possession, published by permission of Lynne Hollander Savio.

DEPOSITION ON THE 22 JULY ASSAULT IN JACKSON

This deposition given to the U.S. District Court includes Savio's account of the racist misconduct of the Jackson police, which the FBI had refused to include in its report. It also better conveyed the seriousness of Osman's injuries than did the FBI report.

UNITED STATES DISTRICT COURT
FOR SOUTHERN DISTRICT OF MISSISSIPPI
JACKSON DIVISION

COUNCIL OF FEDERATED ORGANIZATIONS, et al. Plaintiffs
v. L.A. RAINEY, et al. Defendants
CIVIL ACTION No. 3599 (J) (M),
STATE OF MISSISSIPPI. . . .

MARIO ROBERT SAVIO, being duly sworn, deposes and says . . . I am a student volunteer doing voter registration work with the Council of Federated Organizations. . . .

On July 22, 1964 at about 3:40 P.M., Robert Osman and I were walking from the Farish Street Church, where COFO people eat lunch, toward the COFO office at 1017 Lynch Street. We were accompanied by a local Negro fellow whom we had met at the church.

We were on the corner of Amite and Gallatin when a gray car pulled up and stopped ahead of us. It was an old gray car. Two white men with billy clubs got out. The clubs were dark wood, and appeared to be regular police billy clubs. The men appeared to be about 30; they were dressed informally in old clothes. They were thin and one appeared to be about 5' 9" tall. We ran. They came after us. We all three ran down the street. Robert Osman ran into the grass at the side of the sidewalk; the Negro fellow and I ran down the sidewalk toward the intersection. The Negro fellow got away without being hit at all. I was struck one glancing blow as I ran.

I continued running until I had outrun the man who had struck me. I was by then in the middle of the street in front of the McKesson building. I turned and saw Robert Osman down on his knees and face, protecting his head as best he could, while one of the attackers beat on his back with a billy club. The other attacker had already started back toward their car, since local people were coming to the scene. As both ran to the car, I ran after them to get a better look. I saw that the car had 1963 Mississippi plates (light blue letters on a white background); the county designation was covered up with what was either a piece of cardboard or metal. I believe the license number was 501611.

I went back to Robert who was badly hurt and could not even rise at first. At the suggestion of a local Negro who had come to the scene I entered the McKesson building to call the police. Robert came in shortly thereafter. The people in the McKesson office were very cooperative and friendly, letting us phone both the police and the COFO office. In about ten minutes, while we were still waiting for a return call from COFO, the police came.

Despite the obvious cordiality of the people in the McKesson Building, the police rudely insisted that the former did not want us in the building; accordingly, the police said, they could not allow us to wait for the call from COFO, indeed they would not even let us tell the people in the McKesson office that we were expecting that call. In the course of our explanation to the police we became aware that they were hostile toward us. Robert Osman asked the officers where they were taking us. They said, "Down to the station." When asked what would be done there, they replied "We'll decide when we get there." Only after I asked them specifically whether we were being arrested did they reply that we were not. Because of the extreme evasiveness of the police in answering our queries as to why we were being taken to the station, we had become worried that we were under arrest, and that is why I asked whether we were being arrested.

The police said to us when we referred to the Negro young man who had accompanied us at first, but who had already escaped by running off, "We don't call them 'Negroes' here, we call them 'niggers'". On the way to the station they asked "When was the last time you guys took a bath?" At the station the police proceeded [preceded] us up the stairs saying "White people first." They repeatedly referred to "niggers." "Who was the nigger you were with" etc. The hostile manner of these policemen produced the feeling in me that in all likelihood they would try to complete the beating the attackers had begun; fortunately they did not.[33]

I hereby certify that a notary public is not available to me and that the above is true to the best of my recollections, this 28 day of July, 1964.

Signed Mario R. Savio
Two witnesses: Julius
Samstein, Denni[s]
Sweeney.

Mississippi Department of Archives and History, Jackson, Mississippi, published by permission of Lynne Hollander Savio.

TO GOVERNOR EDMUND G. BROWN

24 JULY 1964, MCCOMB, MISSISSIPPI

With white supremacists in control of Mississippi's Democratic Party and the official voter registration process, the obstacles to winning voting rights for African Americans were formidable. Over the course of Freedom Summer, civil rights workers—Savio among them—recruited some 17,000 Mississippi blacks to complete voter registration forms, but the state's white registrars allowed only 1,600 of them to become registered voters. To keep the pressure on for voting rights, the Mississippi movement built on its new tradition of Freedom Elections—mock elections open to the state's residents irrespective of race. Freedom Elections had started the previous fall, and in that first election, some eighty thousand blacks had voted for the

Mississippi Freedom Democratic Party's interracial ticket of Aaron Henry for governor and Edwin King for lieutenant governor, the largest black vote in the state since Reconstruction. During Freedom Summer, the Mississippi movement used this same tactic, but this time on a larger stage, seeking to get an interracial Freedom Democratic Party delegation seated at the national Democratic Party convention in Atlantic City in place of the whites-only delegation of the state's regular Democratic Party. In this letter, Savio seeks to convince California governor Edmund Brown to support this challenge to Mississippi's white supremacist electoral politics.

Dear Governor Brown,

I live with my family at 1216 E. Northridge Avenue, Glendora, California; I attend the University of California at the Berkeley campus. This summer I am joining with over 800 compassionate human beings— mostly, though not exclusively students—of both the Negro and white races, to help bring freedom to Mississippi. Doubtless you are very familiar with the Mississippi Freedom Summer Project which has been organized by the Council of Federated Organizations (COFO), a state-wide organization co-ordinating the activities of the major civil rights groups working in Mississippi (NAACP, SCLC, CORE, SNCC). The stands you have taken on questions of equality in housing and employment encourage me in the belief that you are a good friend of the work we are trying to advance in Mississippi. With this encouragement I write to you concerning something that *you* can personally do to help bring freedom to the oppressed of Mississippi.

A crucial part of the work of COFO is the strengthening of the Mississippi Freedom Democratic Party. It is well known that the regular Mississippi Democratic Party does not support the national party platform, and cannot be expected to do so in 1964. Furthermore—and intimately related to the first point—the regular *Democratic* Party is not a *democratic* party. The regular party represents the interests of the White Citizens' Council and the wealthy plantation owners. Negroes are systematically excluded from participation by disenfranchisement—and the handful who have been permitted to vote are excluded from participation in precinct meetings. Moreover, the yoke of oppression falls almost as heavily on the poor whites of Mississippi. The Mississippi Freedom Democratic Party is—

in vivid contrast—open to *all* the people. Its candidates discuss the real issues of vital importance to Mississippians—whose state is the poorest in the union; the candidates of the regular party vie with one another in primary races for which can attack most vitriolically the civil rights movement, the national administration, and the Negro citizens of Mississippi. Governor, I have personally met with the violence of Mississippi whites, and the encouragement of such violence by local police. You have the power to help seat the Freedom Democratic Party at the Democratic National Convention. Please help free Mississippi![34]

Respectfully,
Mario Savio

Edmund G. Brown papers, Bancroft Library, University of California, Berkeley, published by permission of Lynne Hollander Savio.

TO CHERYL STEVENSON

25 JULY 1964, MCCOMB, MISSISSIPPI

Savio's first letter to Stevenson upon arriving in McComb was his longest from Mississippi and offers the fullest account he would ever write of the Freedom Summer experience. The discussion of violence is by far his most extensive—from the threats to the Freedom House in Mileston and the defensive violence of well-armed black residents of Holmes County (shown in his admiring portrait of Hartman Tunbow, a local leader of their free- dom movement) to the attack on Savio and his compatriots in Jackson and the bombing of the Freedom House in McComb. The letter reflects Savio's deepening commitment to the movement and his growing radicali- zation, illustrated by his vehement denunciation of the FBI for covering up the misconduct of the Jackson police, his disgust with the two-party sys- tem, and his class analysis of the Jim Crow system linking black economic and political subordination in Mississippi.

Three decades later, when Savio spoke about the voter registration work described in this letter, he contextualized it poignantly as a maelstrom of danger and idealism, guilt and liberation. The guilt came because Savio

*was acutely aware that, though encouraging blacks to register to vote was
an important part of a historic democratic crusade, in a time and place of
immense racist hate and violence, "obviously I endangered people by
bringing them down to register," since they could have lost their jobs "or
worse." Savio recalled growing increasingly effective in his door-to-door
advocacy of registering by appealing to the local black population's knowledge of the state's dismal history of disenfranchisement and their hopes for
a better future. Savio recounted the conversation he would have with
blacks fearful about registering.*

"Did your father vote?"

"No sir."

"Did your grandfather vote?"

"No sir."

"Do you want your children to vote?"

*"That's all. I don't know where I got the nerve to say such a thing. . . .
When I came to the third question, they were ready to register. . . . Change
was in the air and they wanted to be on that freedom train. . . . It was
almost an effrontery to ask those questions. But I asked them. Nobody told
me to."*[35]

Dear Cheri,

I've come to roost at my final resting place—gad! That doesn't sound
too good at all. I mean final until the end of the summer. Amite County—
you'll be happy to read—has been judged "suicidal." So I'll spend the rest
of the summer in McComb, Mississippi. This is also in the Southwest of
the state.[36] The house I'm in right now was bombed about two weeks
ago. Lucky the Klansmen are such poor aims. No one was seriously hurt
though the garage and side of the house was badly damaged. The people
here are really great, some of those I most liked in Oxford including
Jesse Harris and Freddye Green (sister of George Green who would have
been our project director in Amite County).[37]

McComb is very different from Holmes County. Here we have hot and
cold running water and a regular indoor bathroom with a flush toilet and
a bathtub. The Freedom House where we are staying is a kind of lower,
lower middle class (Negro, need I say) community. I was initiated into
the commune tonight by cooking for all 12–14 of the workers. We had

baked spare ribs, potatoes, and onions. I never had cooked spare ribs
before, but I seemed to have done a good job—there were no more ribs
left when I was done cooking. . . .

Some time ago a report reached us that some whites in Mileston (the
place in Holmes County where we lived) were out "to break some heads."
That night a car came by on the road near the place we were staying. It
failed to give the proper signal with its horn. We turned on the flood
lights in front and escaped out the back to the barn, where we clim[b]ed
into the loft. On another occasion at the sign of possible danger we fled
into the woods to a nearby friendly farm house. In both cases it was false
alarm—fortunately. (It was with the second of these incidents—it
occurred after the first—, the escape to the woods and farm house, that
the "to break some heads" threat was associated). But perhaps the worst
night was the first night in Holmes County once we began living at the
Freedom House. It was a night of veritable paranoia. We crawled about
on hands and knees, fearing to be caught before a window. We kept
watches all night. We subsequently discovered that all the farmers round
about are armed to the teeth. Holmes County—as comparatively safe as
it may appear—is the peaceful exterior of a dangerously live volcano. If it
were not so very well known that the Negro farmers are not non-violent,
I seriously doubt that a non-violent student movement would be possible
in Holmes.

And that brings me to Mr. Turnbow. He is the leader of the Mileston
movement—an incredibly active man, a local independent farmer. The
independent farmers form the core of the Holmes County movement.
They do not have to fear that their income will be cut off if they take part.
Also, having to manage their own affairs has caused them to become
much more self-reliant than are the town-dwellers. Last year Mr.
Turnbow's house was fired into. He fired back—he's a very fine shot! A
white man was quietly buried shortly thereafter without incident and
without identification, so I understand. They then bombed Turnbow's
house setting it afire. He rebuilt it and became even stronger in the
movement. For an involvement in these incidents which is still not clear
to me, the Sheriff of Holmes County was brought to court. Things have
been quiet in Holmes County ever since and until just a couple of days
ago. Turnbow is the county registrar of the Freedom Democratic Party,

he's known throughout the County, has been to Washington, and is "respected" by the whites. It is men like Turnbow, and there are many in Holmes County, whose courage protects the non-violent movement. The Jeffersonian ideal of democracy based upon the independent farmer is classically exemplified in the Holmes County movement.

By contrast, the town dwellers are, as the saying goes, "scared shitless." They depend for their livelihood upon employment by whites. But it is these people who must be gotten into the movement, because sooner or later the interests of the independent farmers will come into conflict with the ideal of social and economic democracy. Alas, these town dwellers sometimes turn us away before we can even get in the door. They have been warned by the whites not even to speak to the "northern agitators." Still we make some progress, however slow. I have had the agonizing experience of sitting and talking with a family for fully an hour without convincing them they should go down to the court house to attempt to register to vote. And this hasn't happened once or twice but over and over again. And after all, what can you tell these poor people when they say to me they may (or *will*) lose their jobs or have their welfare cut off if they agree to do what you ask? You can't even say they will become registered voters because Negroes are not permitted to pass the literacy test no matter how well they can read or write. The literacy test requires that the applicant interpret a section of the Mississippi constitution chosen by the registrar to the satisfaction of the registrar. There are 285 such sections; one never receives one's paper back after the test; all registrars are white and "safe." Should people risk their lives and livelihoods because of [a] suit the federal government *may bring* if enough people try to register?

Dear Cheri, I keep adding to my list of things to write to you. I now have 24 items, one with 4 subdivisions. You'll have to wait for most of this till I see you—which I dearly desire to do soon.

While in Holmes County things were so peaceful—until this last week— that our gaurd [*sic*] had really slipped. That all changed when we reached Jackson *en route* to McComb. I was walking with a friend, Robert Osman, and a local Negro fellow down a main street in downtown Jackson—in broad daylight. We crossed the major intersection of Gallatin and Amite Streets when a car pulled up ahead of us and two white men jumped out

with billy clubs. We began to run as they came toward us. The Negro fellow
escaped without being hit. I was struck a glancing blow on the back. But
Rob, who ran to the side into the grass, instead of back along the sidewalk
toward the intersection—Rob was cut off in his flight. He fell to the ground
as we'd been taught in our non-violent workshops and he was viciously
beaten. As people started to come to the scene, the attackers ran to their
car. I ran after them to get the plate number. Downtown Jackson in broad
daylight! I called the police and our [COFO] office. The police then took
over. "We don't call 'em 'Negroes' down here, they're 'Niggers,'" and "go on
back where you came from, and stop causing all this trouble here, don't
you have enough up there?" And "you'll get in a lot more trouble before you
leave Mississippi," and "When did you take a bath last[?]," and on and on.
At one point both Rob and I fully expected the two cops to complete the
job the attackers failed to do well. The next day we spent arguing with the
FBI, who refused to accept in our signed statements anything concerning
the harassment by the police, but who insisted on including the willingness
of the police to take Rob to a hospital. Damned red-baiting bastards. I
don't care who reads this—and, believe me, there's a good chance someone
else will before you get it, Cheri. The FBI establishes a new office in
Jackson and then releases its figures—unexplained—"proving" that
Mississippi has the lowest crime rate of any state. Murder of Negroes isn't
a crime here. And what about crimes committed by the law itself[?]

You probably know a lot about the Freedom Democratic Party already.
We are preparing to challenge the seating of the regular Mississippi
Democratic delegation at the Atlantic City convention the end of August.[38]
I plan to be there, to button hole delegates and do whatever else I can to
bring about our seating. Already some northern states and California have
agreed to support us. Write to Governor Brown, he's a key man and very
friendly to our cause. Get others to write also—ask your father, please. The
Republicans have repudiated whatever of value they had left. This is a
golden opportunity for the Democrats to act responsibly. The recent *tete-a-
tete* between [Republican presidential nominee Barry] Goldwater and
[President] Johnson to the effect that neither will make civil rights a gut
issue can only be seen as the beginning of a sell-out.[39] The Democrats—or
some of them—may feel they can easily win against Goldwater without
courting the cause of equality for all citizens. Cheri, I've spoken to so many

frightened weary, nearly broken people who still had enough spirit left to
light up when I explained the convention challenge to the party of the
White Citizens Council. How can we let these people down[?] When the
different Democratic candidates down here run against one another in the
primaries, they win who attack the civil rights program the most strongly,
who do the most red-baiting, and who heap the most abuse upon the
Negroes. The candidates of the FDP discuss the real issues of poverty and
oppression. Mississippi is the poorest state in the union—though I'm fully
prepared to say one of the prettiest. But the poverty is abysmal, desperate.
The FDP holds out the only hope for the poor of Mississippi.

The reason I've not been asking for more of my money is that a group
of local citizens in Oxford, Ohio got together to aid, and those with
whom I've maintained contact have sent us money which I'll go in to
Jackson to pick up about 8 o'clock this morning—it is now ten of five. In
case I'm in further need I'll try Oxford first, and only if that well runs dry
will I dip into my own funds. I need the money.

Cheri, remember we agreed to work harder in school? What's
happened? You know how terrible exams can be if you've not studied.
There's too much pain, don't subject yourself without need (6 lines of
preaching. I'm sorry).

I took the 3 A.M. watch (3–6) tonight *in order to* write you this letter.
Every fifteen minutes, or whenever I've heard a suspicious sound (car, etc.)
I've gotten up to look around. At first I was opening the door, but then I
became fearful that I should be shot quite dead if I did that. But to look
through the door around the curtains is not enough because I can't see to
the sides where someone might be planting a bomb. And the reality of the
latter possibility is brought brutally home whenever I look up from this
letter to the wall across the room which is smashed at the corner from the
last bomb attack. That wall is covered with what looks like a floral tapestry
which covers the one-time picture window from which all the glass has
been blasted out. It was that drapery which kept those sleeping in this
room from being badly cut when the glass was shattered by the bomb
blast. I don't want to die, yet there is no place else I'd have rather spent this
summer. Knowing that the Negro people here daily live in this terror has
only served to strengthen my commitment. Mississippi was an abstraction
to me before. And I could only think of what some abstract "one" should

do—namely go to Mississippi to fight . . . for freedom. But Mississippi is no longer abstract—the fight is mine. The thing which moved me most was this: Bringing an old man down to the court house in Lexington to attempt to register to vote. Someone whose years alone should command respect. And then seeing the man treated like a dog—worse than a dog. And your [sic] powerless to do anything. It tears your insides. And then the poor little white children whose hearts are not yet filled with fear and hate. And the poor little black children who've not yet learned to cringe and shuffle and bend their heads and say "yasir" and "nosir" to every white they see. I've been called "sir" by an 80 year old woman. And the poverty—only in Mexico have I seen it as bad. Rarely in Mexico did I see it worse.

Mississippi has been making me do an awful lot of thinking about Mario Savio. Where do I fit in? I've decided at last to return to school in the fall. I won't change my major but I will take some courses in Sociology and History—I guess one in each. I believe that Physics, like staying over in Mississippi, would be a form of escapism. I'm going to take your advice and explore my motivations at great length with a psychiatrist.[40] But I think I shall try to prepare myself for some kind of public service, perhaps even—tho[ugh] I doubt it—politics. If there's one lesson to be learned in Mississippi it's that there is a crying need for honest men in the service of the common good.

I'll be seeing you soon, Cheri, that will be good.

Love Mario. . . .

Mario Savio correspondence: Mississippi, to Cheri Stevenson, Bancroft Library, University of California, Berkeley, published by permission of Lynne Hollander Savio.

TO CHERYL STEVENSON

1 AUGUST 1964, MCCOMB, MISSISSIPPI

Savio's voter registration work culminated in his participation in the Pike County convention of the Freedom Democratic Party, which he recounts in euphoric terms in this letter. He also discusses his transition from voter registration work to his new role teaching in a Freedom School. Educational

work in the black community through such schools, staffed by movement
volunteer teachers, was a major focus of Freedom Summer, which worked
to make up for the inadequate, badly underfunded schooling that black
Mississippians received in the separate and unequal educational system
during the Jim Crow era.

Dear Cheri,

I am so happy that I had to let you know. Last night I was present at
part of the county convention of the Freedom Democratic Party for Pike
County. The convention was held outside the Freedom House where I'm
writing now. People who had been denied the fundamental right of self-
government for so long, who did not even have the most rudimentary
education in the processes of a democracy, were learning as they needed
to, to elect representatives, pass resolutions, in short, to be FREE! That so
rare thing, guilelessness, was present in abundance. It was self-evident
that people conduct themselves fairly and justly. And at the end of what
was, after all, a political convention, everyone joined hands to sing *We
Shall Overcome*—and they shall! *we* shall! Someday white people will
thank Negroes for saving America from the historical trashcan. Freedom
and democracy are things to sing about, but what white northerner has
not at some time felt uncomfortable when singing about freedom. I have
felt that discomfort. Down here I do not.

Have you ever heard the recording of *In White America?*[41] I heard the
record last night. Tonight the play was performed outside the Freedom
House, with people from all over the area attending, hanging on each
word. The most enthusiastic one was a blind man—in McComb there is a
home for the *blind* with separate entrances for white and colored! I
won't make the slightest attempt to describe the performance. But I
plead with you, Cheri, to buy the record. It will tear at your insides, but it
will have been worth every moment.

I won't be able to go to the convention after all.[42] I don't have enough
money. What I mean mostly is that I will have to return to Berkeley as
soon as possible after the program down here has ended so that I'll be able
to find a job. It is absolutely essential that I have the money to go to school
this September because I have just received a notice today from the
University—a notice that I am officially on probation for failing to

maintain my average. Alas! I mean to earn that degree. Also, as I told you in another letter, there is something else for which I'll need the money. I'm finally strong enough to profit from a thorough probing of my aberrations. Oddly enough, it's an undertaking I am looking forward to with relish.[43]

How are you getting on, Cheri? Have you been keeping up with your classes? How has the work in Fillmore been going? KPFA?

Things have been going fairly quiet down here lately. Of course, five churches in the area were bombed in the space of about two weeks. But it's about par for the course (to coin a cliché!). I'm surprised that the Freedom House has not been bombed again. I'm no martyr, and so I'm not looking forward to any bombing. By the way, I'm doing Freedom School work now instead of voter registration [VR]. It's not that I prefer it particularly. But the need in McComb was for teachers. And while my preference was for voter registration, I've been doing it for about one month in Holmes County. The teaching is somewhat safer (a relative matter here) but I didn't choose it for that reason either. In fact, I'd thought to keep to voter registration lest the thought of the lessened danger be a subconscious inducement. What I really mean is, there was a certain attraction for the glamor of the reportedly more dangerous work. But the final decision came when I told the Freedom School coordinator here that I'd changed my mind and had decided to continue doing VR. He seemed so let down that I could hardly feed my ego on the rich diet of greater danger at the expense of starving the students here eager to eat up our instruction (to extend the figure into an all too hard to digest conceit!). I'm teaching Negro history (which I learn as I teach it), English and "citizenship" (the former three days a week, the latter two), biology (a course in heredity; which unit being soon complete, a former pre-med student will take over), Spanish (my favorite), and remedial arithmetic (which began as a course in physics, when I discovered that the 11th graders I was teaching did not understand ratio and proportion).

Freedom School ends on August 21. I will leave for Glendora on 22nd. I will see you before the 1st. Anticipating a long delicious kiss.

> *I remain, with love—*
> *Mario*

Mario Savio correspondence: Mississippi, to Cheri Stevenson, Bancroft

Library, University of California, Berkeley, published by permission of Lynne Hollander Savio.

TO CHERYL STEVENSON

4 AUGUST 1964, MCCOMB, MISSISSIPPI

Savio's enthusiasm about his Freedom School work, evident in this letter, was shared by his colleagues and students. Since the schools were voluntary, both teachers and students were there because they wanted to be, so the learning environment was ideal. And the combination of Savio's intellect and personal concern for his students made him, in the words of fellow Freedom School teacher Ira Landess, "an impassioned teacher. You saw that his kids adored him. . . . He was singular in his capacity to engage the kids and really gain their love—and it was more than respect. You saw that they loved him. . . . He was followed around by the kids as if he was the pied piper. . . . That was Mario as a teacher."[44]

This was also the last letter in which Savio discussed the Mississippi Freedom Democratic Party's attempt to get its interracial delegation seated at the upcoming national convention of the Democratic Party in place of the state's whites-only delegation. The skepticism Savio voiced in the letter about the national Democratic Party and the prospects for a successful challenge in Atlantic City would prove prophetic. President Johnson proposed a meager compromise in which the Freedom Democratic Party would be offered only two at-large seats at the convention. The high point of the convention for the freedom movement came when Mississippi FDP delegation member Fannie Lou Hamer, a movement heroine, testified before the credentials committee—televised nationally—of how her civil rights work had led to her firing, jailing, and beating in prison on the orders of Mississippi's racist police. Speaking for the Freedom Democratic Party, Hamer rejected Johnson's compromise, saying, "We didn't come all this way for no two seats!"[45] For many SNCC and Freedom Summer veterans, including Savio, LBJ and the Democratic Party's refusal to seat this delegation in place of Mississippi's white supremacists was a disgrace and a sell out—and for them, Atlantic City became a symbol of liberal hypocrisy.

Dear Cheri,

I'm not in the habit of answering letters the day after I receive them. This is a happy accident. Yesterday evening I found out there are $70 worth of books coming here COD. We don't have $70 on hand— surprisingly! I offered to lend the money, which will be returned in time for me to register. That's the reason I'm writing now instead of a bit later. Please send a money order.

So you knew about my little difficulty in Jackson before you received my letter—"Mike promised to let me (Cheri) know anything he found out about you (Mario)." You know it made me happy to read that.

Yes it is hard to just leave things here and go back to Berkeley. Especially my Spanish class. We started out with less than an hour. We have worked up to almost an hour and a half. The children are fully attentive through the whole class. They love it and I love it. They're really learning. In two and a half weeks the class will end—damn! So much to do, so little time.

I can't answer your letter in detail. I'm excited about the split in the Redevelopment Agency—thanks for the clippings.[46] Let me just say a word about the FDP: We do—so far as I know—have enough states for a minority report. But, to utter heresy, I'm not sure which would be better—that the FDP delegation be accepted or that it be rejected. I had the same mixed feelings concerning the anti-Rumford initiative.[47] It's the kind of thing you must fight for with all your strength. You can't gain anything if the opposition wins without a struggle on your side. But it's the sort of thing where you may gain more from a bravely fought defeat, than from a victory. By the way, there is being formed a Mississippi Student Union and a Mississippi Young Freedom Democrats. The first I think is a great idea, the second not so great. A way to domesticate the young potential radicals in Mississippi. After all, we don't have a "good" party and a "bad," but rather a "bad" and a "much worse." And I fear that the money which the nat'l Young Democrats will be spending down here may result in a measure of control—[the] same fear the conservatives legitimately have over federal aid to education! I don't know that the students here will be sharp enough (intelligent enough they are, but are they sophisticated enough?) to take the money but reject the "doctrine."

There's a *blue* letter of mine which you should receive before this one which says something about when I'll be back in Berkeley.

Pete Seeger was here last night, and at the Freedom School this morning—wonderful. He sang a song for us that he'd seen for the first time about five hours before—a new song. He gave us the words and music, he wrote them out of his head on one of the girl's notebooks. He's simply a great man. He told all about his trip around the world this past year, about the new nations in Africa. He was in N[a]irobi (?) on the first day of Kenyan independence. That was the Negro history lesson for today, complete with South African freedom song.

About my major, what I meant is I'm not committing myself to anything. I haven't studied any physics down here. I'm not sure why I suddenly felt the way I did about physics just before I left. But—you remember—it had something to do with changing my mind about coming down at all. My motivations are in all respects ambiguous. But you know that. As you know, my official college major is Zoology—you know about that. I won't bother changing it for a semester in any case.[48] I'll take the American Institutions course, German, maybe a Sociology course, I don't know what else. I guess because of my confusion it would be wise to sign up for Physics 4C and the next Math course. That's already too many credits so I'll have to cut somewhere—I'm not sure just where. In any case I'll have to make up the Chemistry. Matters are made even more confusing by my being on academic probation—damn!

But the important point is that I've gotten away from missing a semester every other semester. Despite its pain, last year was good for me. I'm on the way to wholeness. It's not uncommon that a thing like Mississippi should alter a person's life, give it direction. Perhaps I should follow the desire to want to know more about American history which I wrote you about. I'll be thinking about these things—maybe you can offer some suggestions as to how I should plan my fall program given my state of confusion. Course, the decision is finally mine. I'll register when I get back. The fact that I didn't study any physics this summer—and didn't miss it!—should be weighted heavily.

Yes, that was your third letter. Thanks for keeping track of them. I can tell, also, by what you say in them that you've received all of mine.

Please remember the $70 money order as soon as you can.

I wish you were right here in this room. Sorry about the trouble with your courses—we'll work harder in the fall. Be happy.

With love,
Mario

Mario Savio correspondence: Mississippi, to Cheri Stevenson, Bancroft Library, University of California, Berkeley, published by permission of Lynne Hollander Savio.

TO CHERYL STEVENSON

12 AUGUST 1964, JACKSON, MISSISSIPPI

In Jackson to testify at the trial of the Klansmen who assaulted him, Osman, and John in July, Savio writes of the start of the prosecution. The letter also captures the contrast between Savio's political dynamism, his efficacy in his movement work, and his tendency toward psychological depression, and it indicates the origins of these feelings can be traced to the tense relationship with his father.

Dear Cheri,

I reveal my weakness by writing. I'm reasonably safe from myself as long as I keep busy. But this week has been one of steadily increasing loneliness. I'm writing this on a bed I've been using in the home of a white family of Jackson. I've returned to Jackson to identify the suspects the F.B.I. agents believe were those who attacked my friend and me that last time we were in Jackson. Most of my time has been spent in the deathly silence of this air conditioned house. Mr. Hubbard, a psychiatrist at the University of Mississippi medical center here in town, is out most of the day. . . . I've spent so much time waiting around because there was real difficulty in observing the suspects. No arrests were made 'til just today. I easily picked one of the men out of a line-up this morning. Though my certainty was less that of Rob and John (the local fellow), still it was greater than I thought it would be. On Friday at two o'clock there'll be a hearing.

In the meanwhile I'll stay here, where three other CR [civil rights] workers, ones involved in the white citizen's community project, are staying. Being here doing virtually nothing—I've been reading Ignazio Silone's *Bread and Wine* (about an Italian atheist revolutionary disguised as a priest in Fascist Italy)—doing virtually nothing I feel returning all those old fears, the feelings I've had as a member of a family in which I always felt under foot, in my father's way. I feel the same dominance and hostility of Mr. Hubbard. Mrs. Hubbard seemed hurt when I tried to arrange the last night somewhere else, so I'm staying here. I almost never feel that I'm really one of the people in a room. I don't know *how* I affect others, nor do I regularly feel that I do—a crushing impotence. I play a little game with myself of trying to bring before my mind images of your appearance and gestures, the way you laugh, the way you hold a cigarette. It's a comfort to know you're alive.

> *Love,*
> *Mario*

Mario Savio correspondence: Mississippi, to Cheri Stevenson, Bancroft Library, University of California, Berkeley, published by permission of Lynne Hollander Savio.

TO CHERYL STEVENSON

16 AUGUST 1964, JACKSON, MISSISSIPPI

Savio's final letter from Mississippi attests that his work in the summer project had impressed SNCC staffers, who asked him to stay beyond the summer—a request Savio considered seriously. This is the only letter in which Savio mentions his parents' attitude toward his work in the Mississippi movement (since he was twenty-one, he did not have to get their permission to join the Freedom Summer project). Not surprisingly, they felt great anxiety about his safety. His parents' concerns helped lead to his decision to return to Berkeley and his academic work in the fall.

The letter also offers Savio's first attempt to set the Freedom Summer project into historical context. He fretted that the surge in racist violence against the freedom movement at the summer's end might represent the same kind of bloody backlash that the South's racist white "Redeemers" had used to overthrow the interracial democratic revolution initiated by Radical Reconstructionists after the Civil War. Savio's use of these historical analogies suggests that he had learned a great deal about the South's painful past while teaching black history in the McComb Freedom School.

Dear Cheri,

I've finally gotten away from that place, but not before beating my "father" at a game of chess. We won the court case, we've gotten a conviction, though I'm not sure of the sentence because only one witness was permitted in the courtroom at a time. In any case, the accused is either out on appeal bond now or soon will be. There are some interesting details to the case that I can't write in this letter, but which I'll tell you of when I see you in a couple of weeks. He had nineteen people testifying for him as to his presence someplace other than the scene of the crime. But their testimony did not hold together, and the friend with whom I was involved in this affair, overheard the attorneys speaking to the effect that their testimony held together better before the trial!

No less a person than Jimmy Travis was disappointed that I was leaving the state.[49] He will be organizing projects for all the coming year on the delta and in the southwest part of the state. The offer was very tempting, as you can guess. I've come to feel myself a part of this operation in a way I could never have guessed before coming to Mississippi. Though I didn't plan it that way, there's no question but that this summer was more valuable for me than for Mississippi. Of course I called home to gauge my parents' reaction to my spending a full year in Mississippi—their reaction was violently negative as I could easily have guessed. And I still believe they are largely correct, until I complete that college degree. Still, it was (perhaps overly) gratifying to know that I was being considered as a desirable candidate for the permanent salaried staff.

And now for the inevitable "note of sadness": Just as the barbaric elements in the South waited until the troops were withdrawn in 1877 (i.e., the infamous compromise that brought Hayes to the White House— see, I've been doing my homework!), so they have been biding their time until the withdrawal of the *new reconstructionists*. Last night there were many cross burnings all over Louisiana and Mississippi, there were at least 4 right here in Jackson—one only a couple of blocks from the office. Likewise last night there was a shooting in Greenwood, two here in Jackson, and a fellow here in Jackson was beaten over the head with a baseball bat—just try to imagine what that could mean—and was taken to the hospital. Also, a store not far from the Freedom Houses in McComb was bombed. We must show them that we're not frightened to the point of being immobilized, so we still have Freedom Days in McComb beginning Tuesday—for which purpose I'm returning there starting within the hour. You probably know, but Freedom Days are periods of massive voter registration when large numbers of local citizens go down to the court house to attempt to register to vote. The last Freedom Day in Greenwood resulted in mass arrest as you know. The stepped-up rate of violence which I have described in this paragraph has been going on for just the last week, and it has us all on edge. The growing fear is that when large numbers of us leave, there may well begin a period of blood letting as bad or worse than anything which has been seen yet. The summer project has been somewhat more peaceful than originally anticipated only because of the initial disaster, so that period of easier breathing is no indication that we have any reason to be hopeful for the coming year. An ominous note is that many of the crosses were burned on school property.

I tried to call you yesterday to ask your advice regarding Jimmy Travis' offer, but in view of the reaction of my parents'—as well as my understanding that although their concern for my education is a little-masked expression of fear for my safety, nevertheless, the argument holds its own weight—in view of the reaction of my parents, I will proceed as per my original plans: Leave for Glendora on the 22nd, and be in Berkeley about a week later.

Looking forward to seeing you—hope your hair has grown!—I remain,

> *With love,*
> *Mario*

P.S.: The sentence was $100 and 30 days.[50] A burly white gorilla just tried to rough up a couple of our people outside the office. Our friends next door in the cafe came over and punched him a couple of times—he got back into his car and left. It does our non-violent heart good.

Mario Savio correspondence: Mississippi, to Cheri Stevenson, Bancroft Library, University of California, Berkeley, published by permission of Lynne Hollander Savio.

3 Leading the Free Speech Movement

PROTEST AND NEGOTIATION, SEPTEMBER–
NOVEMBER 1964

Although Mario Savio never lived to complete his memoir, the outlines he developed for that book suggest how he thought the Free Speech Movement, and his role in it, ought to be remembered. He planned two chapters on the FSM, whose titles, "Free Speech at Last" and "A Free University in a Free Society," leave no doubt as to what he saw as the movement's aspirations and achievements. He later wrote that the FSM was "both moral and successful," and in analyzing the movement, he explored why this was so. Savio wanted it understood from the outset that he was not the leader of the movement but was part of a leadership team, and as a member of the FSM Steering Committee, "day by day I took part in the political leadership of the movement." He was aware that the media focused disproportionately on him, because of his oratory: "on a more visible level," he became " the principal spokesman for the FSM, with a major responsibility for selecting the language in which the movement would be defined."[1]

Savio's book outline indicated that the movement's story ought to begin with an exploration of the theme "of the civil rights origins of the FSM." The FSM was to Savio "the first great campus revolt of the nineteen sixties" and had grown "directly out of white student participation in the Civil Rights

Movement." In fall 1964 he had just returned from Mississippi, where he had witnessed free speech and voting rights violations, and when he learned of UC's ban on political advocacy, he thought back to that Lexington court-house where he had watched an "old black farmer whose simple brave act of free speech was repeatedly interrupted by ridicule" from a racist regis-trar.[2] Keeping faith with that farmer and others who had put their lives on the line in the Mississippi movement was something Savio felt morally obligated to do. That meant opposing the ban and keeping the campus open to the civil rights movement. In comparison to Mississippi, where he had seen people "risk their livelihoods and maybe their lives" to register to vote, Savio considered the risks puny in opposing Berkeley's free speech ban. "What was there to risk here? This was nothing."[3]

Savio realized that only a small number of Berkeley students had gone to Mississippi and experienced what he did during Freedom Summer. Yet he saw that many students "also in one degree or another" took offense at the closing off the campus to recruitment for the civil rights movement, since "the campus breathed the Civil Rights Movement. Those who had not gone south literally had gone there vicariously—in spirit" as they read of the dramatic, life-and-death struggle with white supremacists in the Jim Crow South.[4]

So the first crucial mistake the UC administration made in closing down the Bancroft strip (and one from which it would never recover) was failing to see how explosive this would be. The student body would not stand by while civil rights organizers were evicted. These administrators were, in Savio's view, "simply out of touch with the dedication and sense of mission, with the depth of commitment . . . a large part of the student body" felt about the civil rights movement and the need to protect its local activists.[5]

Savio connected the FSM's success and moral authority to the civil rights movement in that the Berkeley movement adopted its nonviolent ethos as well as early SNCC's hyper-democratic organizing style. "A hallmark of the Free Speech Movement," Savio wrote, "was a deep commitment both to dem-ocratic objectives and to scrupulously democratic means of achieving those objectives." The FSM's goal, like the Mississippi voter registration campaign, was not some extreme-sounding revolution but securing rights associated with America's constitutional tradition—the Fifteenth Amendment in the

Deep South, the First Amendment in Berkeley. "Yet in the style of the Civil Rights Movement, the FSM" pursued these moderate demands with forms of mass action that involved the forging of an engaged community whose political organizing was "characterized by fervor, militancy, and a deep sense of comradeship and solidarity."[6]

Just as his memoir would have stressed that the roots of the FSM went back to the civil rights movement that preceded it, Savio saw the protest movements that followed the Berkeley rebellion as having roots in the FSM. He credited the FSM with having "pioneered the forms of organizing which permitted the great scale and high militancy of anti-war demonstrations in the subsequent years."[7] The FSM's pioneering use of sit-ins on campus gave student protesters a powerful political tool—a great equalizer that offset the power of college and university administrations. It was a model for militant students, and it was so influential in defining the 1960s as an era of campus protest that the President's Commission on Campus Unrest would label it "the Berkeley invention."[8]

Savio planned to devote a second FSM chapter to the "educational objectives of the movement and its character as an anti-bureaucratic revolt. These were always subsidiary themes, but powerful motivators." "From immediate experience [with the UC administration's unilateral decisions and decrees] we learned," wrote Savio, "to appreciate the remarkably undemocratic nature of university governance." As in the South, the cure for undemocratic power seemed to be a community organized to demand, in a realistic, determined way, its right to self-government. "We began to formulate *in concerto*," Savio wrote, "the meaning of the central New Left credo: 'The people must participate in making decisions that affect their lives.'"[9] When the UC administration banned political advocacy, it inadvertently turned the attention of Savio and other Berkeley activists from off-campus civil rights work to the university itself—raising questions about what had gone wrong with UC, why the university suppressed political expression on campus. What resulted was an educational reform agenda that included, as Savio put it, "student opposition to education as mere training." Such narrow vocationalism bred student alienation where there should have been the creation of meaning and a community devoted to promoting egalitarian change, social criticism, and the pursuit of truth.[10]

Having come to political consciousness during the Cold War era, Savio was critical of how the anti-Communist crusade yielded antiradical, illiberal impulses at home that constricted free speech. America, he thought, could not be a free country until it liberated itself—as he and his fellow radicals had liberated themselves—from the garrison-state mentality and McCarthyite legacy of the Cold War, which is why he planned to title his memoir "Beyond the Cold War: The Education of an American Radical." Nor did he think that a university could be free or the FSM in a position to lead it toward free speech unless it rejected this antiradical legacy.

So in his FSM chapters, Savio wanted to address this Cold War context head on, discussing how the Cold War–tainted rhetoric of the UC administration, the press, and public officials yielded "red baiting . . . a problem for the FSM." Savio intended to be open about the Left's role in the FSM and about the fact that Bettina Aptheker, a Communist student activist, "was one of a handful of key FSM leaders" and that he and the FSM rejected any attempt to ban Communists. In fact, as Savio explained, "I grew to feel admiration and affection for Bettina, and respect for a number of others" in the FSM "who regarded themselves as (non-Communist) Marxists." So Savio and the FSM, in a way characteristic of the early New Left, wanted their movement and American society to be a participatory democracy open to all. Savio intended to stress in his memoir how "as principal spokesman, [he] learned to represent the FSM as the democratic, all-American campaign that it was, without contributing in the least degree to the poisoned rhetoric of the Cold War."[11] Thus, while the FSM viewed in a national frame is often depicted as a launching pad for the *new* (the New Left, new student militancy, new campus protest tactics), in a local Berkeley context, Savio and the FSM represented an end to something *old:* the antiradicalism that—through and beyond UC's Loyalty Oath controversy—had so traumatized the campus community in the Cold War era.

As to the FSM's evolution, dynamics, and chronology, Savio planned to embed in his narrative an analysis of the way the movement functioned internally and how this impacted its responses to the crises that emerged in battling a powerful university administration over the course of the entire fall semester in 1964. He thought that "all the perennial issues concerning the proper relationship of a movement to the leadership of a

movement can be studied in exquisite miniature as the FSM unfolds."
Here he was referring to the struggle of the student movement's leadership to not merely function democratically but make tactical and strategic
decisions that would seem reasonable and attractive to the masses of non-
radical students who the movement had to enlist if the FSM was to suc-
ceed. This was not always easy, because a mostly Left-leaning leadership
that had committed itself to full-time work in the FSM at times erred in
getting too far ahead of mainstream students with less knowledge of the
latest crisis, as it did momentarily in the aborted sit-in in November—
opting for a tactic that was too militant and too quickly adopted for most
rank-and-filers to understand or support. This is likely what Savio had in
mind when he pledged that his memoir would "express criticism of the
Movement . . . where such criticism seems fairly warranted."[12]

The FSM's commitment to nonviolence, its inclusive and democratic
leadership style, willingness to negotiate (though not to compromise on
free speech), civil liberties goal, building of community and solidarity
among its activists, linkage to a much admired civil rights movement,
attractive name, soaring oratory, and veteran political organizers made it
a force to be reckoned with. Still, it is important not to conflate the process
of organizing the movement with its outcome, to assume, just because in
the end the FSM triumphed and secured free speech on campus, that
Savio and the FSM's leadership were uniformly brilliant or preordained to
win this free speech fight. In fact, Savio himself, in one of his last talks on
the FSM—given at UC Santa Cruz in 1995, the year before his untimely
death—stressed that even to the "very last moment we could have lost the
whole thing," despite the FSM's having "beautifully" made the case for free
speech.[13] One could argue, and Savio and other FSM veterans have, that it
was less the movement's tactical brilliance than the UC administration's
persistent stupidity that made the victory possible.

This line of thinking came to be known in Berkeley as the "atrocity"
theory: if the movement flagged, all one needed to do was hang on and
wait for another outrage to be committed by UC's heavy-handed leadership.[14] Bringing onto campus a police car, for example, to arrest a free
speech activist on Sproul Plaza at lunch hour, the most crowded time of
day, was an act of astounding political incompetence. As Savio put it, to
"drive [that car] right in the middle of the Plaza, kaplunk! . . . You've really

got to be bereft of all sense to do that!"[15] The same could be said of the Greek Theatre fiasco or what appeared a vindictive administration attempt to discipline FSM leaders just as things seemed to be calming down over the Thanksgiving break. In fact, the most massive acts of civil disobedience during the FSM, the police car blockade and the occupation of Sproul Hall in December 2, were sparked when the administration compounded its unpopularity on the free speech issue by deploying what students saw as police-state tactics to punish free speech protesters.

Although in the pages that follow you will find the most complete collection of Savio's FSM speeches ever assembled, readers ought not to mistake them for a complete history of the Free Speech Movement. There were numerous FSM leaders who spoke eloquently during the protest rallies at Berkeley that fall, including Jack Weinberg, Jackie and Art Goldberg, Bettina Aptheker, Michael Rossman, Steve Weissman, Martin Roysher, Dusty Miller, and others. The tapes of the car-top rally include memorable speeches by rank-and-file protesters, undergraduates, and graduate students, as well as student and faculty critics of the movement (especially on tactical issues). There were also the speeches and press conferences UC administrators gave opposing the FSM. Savio's oratory, influential and important as it was, constitutes only part of this rich stream of oratory from Berkeley's free speech crisis. And there was more to the movement than rally speeches. A complete history of the FSM would include the proceedings of the committees established by the Pact of October 2 to assess the campus political regulations (the Campus Committee on Political Activity) and deal with the disciplining of movement leaders (the Heyman Committee), as well as the organizing by the FSM's faculty allies in the Academic Senate. Such a history would also spotlight what grassroots FSMers were saying in the various FSM "Centrals"—where movement volunteers did the essential organizing tasks—plus the FSM's leaflets and newsletters. Savio's oratory interacted with all of these other layers of the FSM experience, and so the more one knows about them (and the press attacks on the FSM) the clearer the context is for those speeches.

The Berkeley revolt was not one undifferentiated mass, but rather it evolved through distinct stages that influenced the quantity, tone, and importance of Savio's speeches. The initial stage of the movement was one of *polite petitioning* and emerged as Berkeley student activist groups responded to the September 14, 1964, letter sent to them by dean of students Katherine A. Towle, which banned political advocacy on the Bancroft-Telegraph strip of sidewalk adjoining the campus's south entrance. This first stage occurred well before the ban's opponents took for themselves the name Free Speech Movement (during the first weekend in October). The polite petitioning lasted a week—from almost the moment Berkeley activists learned of the ban though September 21—and was an interval of tactical moderation. At this stage, a broad, united front of student organizations, from Socialists to Goldwaterites, met with campus administrators in the hope of convincing them to lift the ban. During this time of relative hopefulness about negotiations it was not Savio but the established student leaders, most notably Jackie Goldberg, who played the central leadership role in the embryonic movement. Goldberg, an able leader, knew UC's administrators well, and her sorority and peace movement ties and moderate political style made her an ideal student to head this broad, Left-to-Right free speech coalition, known initially as the United Front. Goldberg led the determined but futile effort, via polite meetings, to get the deans to drop the ban.[16]

Goldberg arranged a meeting with Dean Towle for September 17. She and the representatives of eighteen student groups tried to convince Towle to end the ban on advocacy. It quickly became apparent that the dean lacked the authority to restore free speech on the Bancroft-Telegraph strip, but she did indicate a willingness to receive proposals from opponents of the ban. As a result of this meeting, Goldberg would submit, on behalf of the student groups, a petition calling for an end to the ban, offering to better arrange the political tables and posters on the strip in response to Towle's claim that problems with foot traffic had contributed to the decision to issue the ban. Towle liked neither the ban nor the way the policy had been formulated by Vice Chancellor Alex Sherriffs with no student consultation, and the students sensed this. At a follow-up meeting with Goldberg and the student groups on September 21, Towle tried to be conciliatory and had been authorized to make some empty concessions, among them that students could staff tables on the Bancroft-Telegraph strip and use them to distribute "informative" but not "advocative" literature. Recruiting for political action and causes or soliciting funds for them was still banned.[17]

Savio, as head of University Friends of SNCC, had attended these initial meetings. Though not leading the delegations to Towle, Savio asked searching questions that helped demonstrate that—once you removed the transparently misleading claim that the ban came about because the political tables caused traffic problems—Towle had failed to offer any convincing reason for the ban. Towle tried to make the case that, once it was clear that the Bancroft strip was on university property, advocacy had to be banned there to accord with UC policy. But Savio pushed back, making distinctions (facts vs. reasons) that reflected his work in linguistic philosophy, arguing against her claim that the ban was enacted because the strip was university property: "That's not a reason. That's a fact. . . . Does the law require the University to forbid these tables here? Show us that." Towle admitted that there was no specific law forcing UC to adopt the ban. Savio replied that this was therefore "a matter of discretion" and the administration had adopted a policy barring advocacy on campus. He asked, "What's your justification for it? You need a reason. If you exercise discretion, you need a reason, and we insist on getting a reason." Towle could not come up with any reason for the ban, that, as Savio observed, "could really stand muster." Savio and the other delegates had insisted on a reason, and neither Towle nor any of her fellow UC administrators had one. "That was really decisive."[18]

Savio was right. This question about the reason for the ban was of great importance. Goldberg, Savio, and many Berkeley students had started to answer this question themselves, in ways that were unflattering to UC's administration. This helped pave the way for the second stage of the free speech conflict, the shift from polite petitioning to public *demonstrations and defiance* of the ban, which began on September 21, shortly after the second Towle meeting. Students had come to suspect that the ban had come about because UC administrators had caved in to pressure from right-wing forces outside the university to close the campus to civil rights organizers. Towle had inadvertently contributed to this suspicion when she said something privately to Goldberg "tying [William] Knowland," the *Oakland Tribune's* Goldwaterite publisher, to the ban. Goldberg reported this back to the United Front, and the story resonated powerfully, since Knowland had editorialized in favor of punishing student civil rights protesters, and his newspaper was being picketed by students demanding an end to the paper's racially discriminatory hiring policies. Berkeley's student newspaper, the *Daily Californian,* reported that Towle admitted that the frequent use of the Bancroft strip for recruiting students for picket lines and demonstrations had been a concern, and the story left the impression that the ban was motivated by animus against Berkeley's civil rights activists.[19]

Given that the meetings with Towle failed to end the ban and that there seemed evidence that political pressure had played a role in the ban's creation, Berkeley's free speech activists concluded that their only hope of lifting the ban was to generate political pressure of their own. They started doing so at noon on September 21 with a picket line outside Sproul Hall, where some two hundred students marched, carrying such signs as "Bomb the Ban." Some three hundred students participated in an evening free speech vigil outside Sproul Hall, about a third of whom stayed overnight, sleeping on the steps. A new spirit of defiance took hold as the students ignored the ban—risking suspension or expulsion for breaking campus rules—first by staffing political advocacy tables on the Bancroft strip on the edge of the campus, and then by moving their tables to Sather Gate, brazenly defying the free speech ban smack in the middle of campus. On September 28 the protesters held their largest campus rally yet, by Wheeler Oak—without obtaining permission—and at the rally's end more than one thousand students marched to a welcome-week meeting to picket while Berkeley chancellor Edward Strong spoke.[20]

In the midst of this second phase of the free speech struggle, demonstrations and defiance, Savio emerged publicly as a leading voice of the movement—and the timing of this makes perfect sense. As the students moved toward mass protest, Savio's gift for oratory would become evident and begin to set him apart. Savio was one of the speakers at the unauthorized Wheeler Oak rally of September 28. Unfortunately, radio coverage of the free speech dispute had not begun yet, so no tape (or full text) has survived of this first Savio free speech oration. Students recalled its eloquence in highlighting "the importance of the civil rights movement and student involvement in the issues of the day."[21]

The closest we can come to the text of that first speech is what Savio recalled of it in his court testimony during the FSM trial in 1965, which focused primarily on one part of it, where he rebutted President Clark

Kerr's condescending put-down of student activism. In defending the ban on advocacy, Kerr had made a dismissive statement on the educational value of political action—telling the press that pickets and fundraising for dissident causes "aren't high intellectual activity" and are not "necessary for the intellectual development of students." "If that were so," he said, "why teach history? We can't live in ancient Greece." Savio found Kerr's statement "preposterous" and reflecting "no understanding of [either] the need for student political activity" to promote democratic change or the value of such activity in teaching lessons (as Mississippi had for him) about society not covered in their degree programs. He charged that Kerr lacked any "understanding of the need for the study of history," and cited Thucydides's conviction that even though future generations could not take part in the conflicts discussed in his *Peloponnesian Wars*, they would still benefit from such history through its lessons on the nature and "actions of war."[22]

Savio's speech invoked UC's own history in making the case for an end to the ban on political advocacy. He stressed that "rights students had exercised for years had now been taken away." Savio urged that students not be fooled by phony concessions made by the administration "since they did not include the right to advocate specific political and social action."[23]

A paper and audio record of Savio's free speech advocacy began in the aftermath of this speech at the Wheeler Oak rally and the escalating conflict between the protesters and administration over the next three days. The paper trail began because Savio, in giving this speech at an "unauthorized" (i.e., not approved by UC's administration) rally and in advocating a free speech picket of the chancellor at an official university function, broke campus rules and generated administration correspondence concerning his being disciplined. Radio coverage of the free speech struggle and Savio's speeches began on September 30, when the conflict's escalation drew the news media. The deans summoned students to their offices for violating the ban, and protesters responded by staging a sit-in at Sproul Hall, the first such mass civil disobedience on campus in UC's history. It is in this late September period of escalating conflict that our first FSM chapter opens, with Savio en route to becoming the Berkeley rebellion's leading voice and the most famous student radical in the United States.

CRITICIZING AND DEFYING THE BAN ON POLITICAL ADVOCACY

28–30 SEPTEMBER 1964

Written to document Savio's violation of university rules for disciplinary purposes, this memorandum by dean of men Arleigh Williams shows that from the start of his involvement in the free speech conflict, Savio saw his defiance of UC's ban on political advocacy (and other university restrictions on speech) as a defense of constitutional rights, and that he justified his actions by invoking the First Amendment right to freedom of speech and the Fourteenth Amendment's equal protection clause. As Williams makes clear, Savio was neither apologetic about this defiance nor evasive about his having violated UC rules (or at least the latest version of those rules as interpreted by the deans), but instead he argued the moral case for opposing unjust, unconstitutional regulations.

The Williams memo narrates, from the administration perspective, Savio's involvement in two pivotal early events in the Free Speech Movement's history: the large rally at Wheeler Oak on September 28, at which Savio gave his first speech, and the sit-in at Sproul Hall two days later. This sit-in was a remarkable event, because it was the first time UC protesters used on campus the sit-in tactic that the civil rights movement pioneered off campus, and it also embodied an extraordinary spirit of solidarity. When the dean cited five students on Sproul Plaza for defying the ban on advocacy, hundreds of students immediately signed a petition of complicity indicating that they too had violated the ban. This refusal to allow a few students to be singled out for punishment continued in Sproul Hall, when between three hundred and five hundred students (estimates vary), including Savio, marched with the cited students to the dean's office, demanding that Williams meet not just with the five but with the hundreds of students present who had also violated the ban.

October 12, 1964
MEMORANDUM TO: Faculty Committee on Student Conduct
RE: Mario Robert Savio
Violation of University Policy on Use of Facilities
On Monday, September 28, Mr. Savio addressed a pre-announced (*Daily Californian,* September 28, 1964) and unauthorized student rally at the

oak tree in line with Sather Gate and within the broad areas of Dwinelle Plaza. His apparent purpose was to urge students to join in picketing the University meeting (11–12 A.M.) which was in progress in the Student Center Plaza.

I talked with him during the rally and at a time when he was not speaking to the group. He was informed by me that this rally and his conduct were in violation of the University Policy on the Use of Facilities. In addition, I told him that I had no alternative but to initiate disciplinary procedures against him and that if a student organization was involved that the disciplinary authority of the University would be invoked against the organization. I stated that individual students were free to picket as long as they did not interfere with or disrupt a University exercise. I urged him to listen to the Chancellor's statement of clarification relative to the privileges of student organizations, and I informed him that the Chancellor was to make his statement at the University meeting then in progress. He replied that he was aware that he was in violation of University rules and that he as well as others had violated the University policy during the week. Further, he emphasized that he couldn't stop the plan to picket the University Meeting. Again, I informed him that he was in violation of the Use of Facilities policy and that I would have to initiate disciplinary action against him.

In my conversation with Mr. Savio on Tuesday afternoon, September 29, 1964, he acknowledged his conduct as reported above. He explained his actions in terms of his conviction that University policy violates the guarantees to free speech and equal protection under the law contained in the spirit of the first and fourteenth amendments of the Constitution of the United States. He stated his belief that any person, student or non-student, inherently possesses the right to speak on any subject (other than advocating the violent overthrow of the Government) at any time and at any place upon the campus, and that both groups or individuals (student or non-student) have the right to set up tables in designated areas to collect money, to solicit membership, to advocate any position or course of action, and to distribute literature. This reasoning prompted him to be a leader of the unauthorized rally and to take an active part in exhorting the listeners at the meeting to join a picket line and march upon the University Meeting. Further, purposefully and admittedly in violation of University policy, he set up a table at Sather Gate in the afternoon of September 29, 1964, on behalf of S.N.C.C. for the purpose of demonstrating his belief in the rights of students and non-students.

Mr. Savio identified the "principle of double effect" as further justification for his actions. This principle appears to state that when one is seeking an end which is morally sound (quite apart from its legality or illegality), the selection of the means employed must be governed by the judgment that the probable good effects outweigh the potential bad effects which are inherent to the method under consideration. In his judgment, his actions had satisfied fully this philosophical requirement.

On Wednesday afternoon, September 30, 1964, Mr. Savio brought three hundred or more students to see me in my office. I met him and them at the entrance door of the Dean of Students Office. He identified himself as the spokesman for the group and described their purposes, i.e., that they knew of several students who had been directed to make an appointment with me for violating the University Policy on Use of Facilities and that each person with him acknowledged violation of the same policy and was desirous of making a similar appointment. My first response was to request five students who had been observed violating University regulations (Elizabeth Gardner, Mark Bravo, David Goines, Donald Hatch, and Brian Turner) to go into the Dean of Students Office and talk with Dean Murphy and Dean Van Houten about their conduct. The purpose of this request was to inform them that they had the choice of appearing before the Faculty Committee on Student Conduct or that the report of their violation could be forwarded directly to the Chancellor. This request was not accepted by Mr. Savio, the specific students noted, or by the group in general. Savio again spoke for them. He indicated that I misunderstood apparently his statement of position. He repeated it and suggested clearly that I would have to talk with each member of the group if I wanted to talk with any of them.

I repeated the direction to the five students named, and then informed the group that it would be impossible to talk to all of them at that time. I requested each to leave his name with me if he wished to do so, and I stated that I would determine if and when appointments would be made for them. I informed the group that I was concerned only with observed violations. I reminded them that upon the request of students, arrangements were made to meet with the leaders of each organization actively involved in the protest, that the advisors of each organization had been urged by us to attend this meeting, and that the meeting was scheduled for 4:00 P.M. that date. I declared that we wished to hold this meeting, but that we would not conduct it unless it could be held in an environment conducive to good exchange of statements. I concluded my remarks with the request to them to leave the building.

Mr. Savio responded

1) That equal protection under the laws was at stake;
2) That the group was prepared to leave only if I would guarantee that the same disciplinary action would follow for each person in this group and,
3) Without such assurances he would urge everyone to remain right where they were.

I spoke again and told them that I would not make such guarantees, that I was committed to support University policies and that I had every intention of doing so. To the best of my recollection I believe that I told them again about the scheduled meeting of student leaders and their advisers and of my hope that this meeting could be held. I asked them again to leave the building because they were interfering with the ability of neighboring offices to continue their University work.

At the termination of my remarks Mr. Savio organized the sit down.

At approximately 4:05 P.M. I approached the group again and requested Elizabeth Gardner, Mark Bravo, David Goines, Donald Hatch, Brian Turner, Sandor Fuchs, Art Goldberg, and Mario Savio to see me as each was involved in a personal disciplinary problem. Further, I announced that the scheduled meeting of the presidents and advisers of the groups was cancelled. I should note none of the students listed above responded to my request to see them.

Arleigh Williams
Dean of Men AW:je

Mario Savio disciplinary file, UC Berkeley, Mario Savio archive, copy in editor's possession, published by permission of Lynne Hollander Savio.

REPLY TO DEAN ARLEIGH WILLIAMS' MEMO ON SAVIO'S
ROLE IN THE FREE SPEECH RALLY AND PICKET OF
SEPTEMBER 28TH AND THE SPROUL HALL SIT-IN
ON SEPTEMBER 30

CIRCA MID-OCTOBER, 1964

Embodying the hyper-democratic spirit of the Berkeley rebellion, Savio's response to Dean Williams was iconoclastic, utterly lacking in deference to constituted authority, and insistent that the protests were an expression of mass student sentiment and not the invention of himself or some small group of leaders. The reply exhibits the sarcastic edge to Savio's discourse with the administration and, especially in its closing lines, the way he made use of humor during the FSM. Savio's discussion of his work for SNCC and his reference to "Dixie's Cotton Curtain" underscores the way he connected the free speech struggle to the civil rights movement, and his citing of Thomas Aquinas typifies how he drew on his studies in philosophy, history, and religion in his FSM discourse.

Commentary on a Memorandum Prepared by Dean of Men Arleigh Williams Alleging that Certain of my Actions Have Been in Violation of University Policy on Use of Facilities:

1. The first two paragraphs of Dean Williams's memorandum are substantially correct.

2. In his third paragraph the Dean states that I acknowledged my conduct as reported in the first two paragraphs: namely that I performed certain actions in violation of University policy on the use of facilities, whereas I made it quite clear that I at most violated certain interpretations made by Deans Williams and Towle (and possibly Chancellor Strong) of some policy which the latter Deans told me was set by the Board of Regents, but of which it can be said that if such a policy indeed existed, then it had not been enforced for years.

I did not say any person is bound not to speak upon the subject of advocating the violent overthrow of the government, but only, as I understand the law, that a person may not advocate a specific action aimed at the violent overthrow of the government—a considerable distinction.

I must say, the Dean is talented in choosing provocative forms of expression. I exhorted students peacefully to picket a University meeting;

Dean Williams has it that I exhorted the listeners to "march upon the University meeting."

The final sentence of the Dean's third paragraph states: "Further, purposely and admittedly in violation of University policy, he set up a table at Sather Gate in the afternoon of September 29, 1964, on behalf of S.N.C.C. for the purpose of demonstrating his belief in the rights of students and non-students." In the first place, my action was at worst in violation of certain obscure "interpretations" of an alleged policy; second, the table was for University Friends of SNCC (of which I was the chairman); and finally—most significantly—it must have occurred to the Dean that at least in part I set up the table simply to conduct the ordinary business of Friends of SNCC, to accept donations for the South, to advocate certain off campus political and social action, to recruit members for SNCC and Friends of SNCC, and to disseminate information concerning the plight of certain of our fellow citizens held captive behind Dixie's Cotton Curtain.

3. Dean Williams's fourth paragraph shows a remarkable grasp of the principle involved; his case is by no means hopeless.

4. In his fifth paragraph Dean Williams states that I "brought three hundred or more students" to see him in his office, whereas it would be more correct to say that more than four hundred students, among whom I was included, came to see the Dean. So far from my identifying myself as spokesman for the students I was by consensus chosen by them to serve as their spokesman. None of us acknowledged violation of a certain policy, rather we all subscribed to a statement that we had performed that same act which it seemed was the one for which disciplinary action was being considered.

This fifth paragraph is indeed clever, for although Dean Williams did request the five "observed violators" to come into the Dean's office, he was no where near so clear on September 30, as in this paragraph of October 12 that the purpose of the visit was to inform the five "that they had the choice of appearing before the Faculty Committee on Student Conduct or that the report of their violations could be forwarded directly to the Chancellor." Perhaps Dean Williams should have informed us of this "purpose" but at the time he simply did not.

5. Concerning paragraph six: Dean Williams states that he was concerned only with "observed violations." Well it turns out that about 50 to

100 students were prepared to replace one by one each of the students initially sitting at the Friends of SNCC table. Thus suspendee Brian Turner was replaced by Donald Hatch, and Hatch by Mark Bravo.[24]We tried to keep the "little deans" Murphy and Van Houten from leaving, but they had no intention of taking 50 or more names. If I may say so, they knew what they were in for. These two deans ran on back to the Dean's office. So we had no choice but to do for them the task they were unwilling to do for themselves. Aquinas observed 700 years ago, that an unenforceable law is a mockery of law; and a law which no one will obey is obviously unenforceable. The deans realized this instinctively, and made their hasty retreat.[25]

And concerning the manner of disciplining all of these students: We would have been glad to leave with a clear statement from the Dean of Men that all would be treated identically. It didn't have to be done all that day. But the Dean states that he would determine "if and when appointments would be made for them." It's the "if" part that was unacceptable. After all, an acceptable procedure would be to see the 400 five at a time—starting from the bottom of the list!

Then the Dean implies that we made impossible the meeting at 4 P.M. Well, we didn't ask to be in there for disciplinary action. We were summoned by the Dean's office, or at the least had performed actions for which we would have been summoned had the "little deans" had the courage to take down all of our names originally. It's hardly our fault if the Dean found himself in the embarrassing position of having to enforce unconstitutional "interpretations" of some ill-defined and possibly non-existent policy of the Board of Regents, a policy which if we admit existed, was at least not enforced for years.

6. It is gratifying that Dean Williams has credited me with having "organized" the sit-in although I must say there was little to "organize." For students who had shown themselves to be well-apprised of their constitutional rights—and the attempted abrogation of these—the act of crossing one's legs and reclining was a relatively simple matter.[26]

Mario Savio

Mario Savio disciplinary file, UC Berkeley, Mario Savio archive, copy in editor's possession, published by permission of Lynne Hollander Savio.

SPEECH AT THE SIT-IN, SPROUL HALL

30 SEPTEMBER 1964

Since the sit-in itself had not been planned but was a response to Dean Williams's refusal to meet with the protesters, Savio's speech was completely improvised. And so was his role as spokesperson for the sit-in. As Savio later explained: "We all marched into Sproul Hall and there we were . . . just a glob of people. . . . And then there was Dean Williams at the other end of the hall. And so I just started talking for all these people, across the hall. It was a very emotionally-packed scene. There was no formal legitimacy for my talking in that fashion [since no leaders had been selected or spokespersons designated by the demonstrators], but it was and continued to be clear that a lot of people were feeling what at the same time I was expressing, and it was a very useful thing."[27]

Of this first Savio speech at the sit-in, David Goines, who, as one of the cited students, was in Sproul Hall that day, has written, "Had I been in the shoes of the administration, I would have trembled at this oratory, and carefully examined my motives and what I hoped to gain and what I stood to lose. This is not the speech of willful fractious children deprived of a glittering toy. This is the speech of the Americans who dressed up in war paint and threw taxed tea into Boston harbor."[28]

This started out as a completely spontaneous response of students at this University against arbitrary action taken by the dean's office here against certain students who thought they had the right to free expression at this University. Well, free expression, for the University, means that you can talk about lots of things, but as we just heard in the statement from Chancellor Strong, those things you can't do are the taking of action on various ideas that you discuss.

Now, I'd like to connect that, right here, very, very clearly, with statements that have been made by President Kerr in his book on the multiversity. President Kerr has referred to the University as a factory; a knowledge factory—that's his words—engaged in the knowledge industry.[29] And just like any factory, in any industry—again his words—you have a certain product. The product is you. Well, not really you. And not really me. The products are those people who wouldn't join in our protest. They go in one side, as kind of rough-cut adolescents, and they come out the other side pretty smooth. When they enter the University, they're dependent upon their parents. That kind of dependency is the sort of thing that characterizes childhood and adolescence. When they're in school, before they enter the University, part of that dependency is shifted to the various schools that they're in. Then they come to the University. And now, instead of suckling at their mother's or at the breast of their schools, they suckle at the breast of Holy Mother University. So here they are. Now they're dependent upon the University. They're product. And they're prepared to leave the University, to go out and become members of other organizations—various businesses, usually (and I hope I'm not offending anyone in this, but I'm speaking my mind)—which they are then dependent upon in the same way.

And never—at any point—is provision made for their taking their places as free men! Never at any point is provision made—you know, someplace in society, some things you can do which in some ways can be expressive of your individuality. You just can't do that unless you have no intention of making it in this society. You can be poor and have dignity, but if you have any intention of making it in any way, you're just completely out of it! You've got to be part of a machine.

Now, every now and then, the machine doesn't work. One of the parts breaks down. And in the case of a normal, regular machine, you throw that part out; throw it out, and you replace it. Well, this machine, this factory here, this multiversity, its parts are human beings.[30] And, sometimes, when they go out of commission, they don't simply break down, but they really gum up the whole works! That's what we're all doing here. We've kind of gone out of commission. We won't operate according to the way the parts of this machine should operate, and the machine started to go out of commission. But the remedy is the same! In the case of a regular machine, in the case of this machine, you throw the parts out! And that's what they decided to do. That's what the statement says. They're on indefinite suspension. I presume that's close to the words he used—of those students who went out of commission, those students who weren't good enough parts, who didn't function well enough.

For one brief moment, there were lots of people, lots of students, whose imaginations were fired. Maybe we would not have to likewise be parts.

Maybe somehow we could take our place as free men also! So those students said, "We're with you! We stand right with you! Not behind you. We're next to you! We're brothers!" They signed that sheet! That sheet said, "We want you to treat *us all the same way*." Now, you know it was an unreasonable demand. It was unreasonable in this regard: it's not a demand the University could have met without completely dropping any kind of disciplinary action against anyone. And they knew it! And . . . we knew it.

Well, they've decided, instead, to disregard your protest and to assume that you had never come in here, nothing like that had happened, that instead what it is—the eight students, they refused to speak with the proper authorities, and they've been axed.

We can do various things. I suppose that's really what we want to talk about. . . . We can—and this is what I would hope the group here would want to do—we can make as the issue of our continued protest three things. First, whatever action has been taken against these particular individuals singled out by the administration, this action be dropped, completely! *[cheers and applause]*

Are there any abstentions? *[laughter]*

The second thing is that we here, all of us, the committee of the whole, we demand those particular demands I read to you from that yellow sheet earlier today concerning freedom of expression on this campus. We are putting our weight behind those demands. *[applause]*

In particular, our protest is demanding a meeting with Chancellor Strong—none of these little guys, we're done with that. *[laughter and applause]* We're demanding a meeting with Chancellor Strong to discuss those demands.

Third, we demand that, at least until that meeting has taken place, if there are any groups on campus who exercise what they believe to be their rights of free expression, there will be no disciplinary action taken against them, at any time! *[cheers and applause]*

I presume that, from the basis of the response [i.e., the crowd's cheering for each demand], in the name of all the people assembled here, and hopefully in the name of the University of California, we can make these demands public and make them to the administration, to the chancellor. Is this something we can do? *[shouts of "yes!" followed by applause]*

Transcribed from audiotape, Mario Savio archives, published by permission of Lynne Hollander Savio. Also available online at UC Media Resource Center at www.lib.berkeley.edu/MRC/FSM/fsmchronology1. html.

RESPONSE TO ASSISTANT DEAN THOMAS BARNES, AT SPROUL HALL SIT-IN

30 SEPTEMBER 1964

This first Sproul Hall sit-in was one of the few demonstrations in which UC administrators proved willing to debate the free speech protesters. Assistant Dean Thomas Barnes, who was also a history professor, spoke to the protesters in the corridor outside the deans' office on the second floor of Sproul Hall. Barnes claimed that the administration's ban on political advocacy was necessary to preserve the university's political neutrality. Several protesters replied that UC's involvement in developing nuclear weapons and in research for agribusiness showed that it was not neutral.

One protester charged that the timing of the ban was suspicious, that after years of allowing advocacy on the Bancroft strip, suddenly it was banned. This gave the appearance of yet another departure from neutrality, since the university seemed to be "responding to outside pressure" to silence student activists—and yet would not even explain "why they're giving" these activists "the axe."

Savio told the crowd that he would "definitely like to hear from" Dean Barnes "on that very question" of the ban's timing. Adding evidence suggesting that the ban's origins were political, Savio cited Dean Towle's retreat from her initial claims that the free speech area had been closed due to traffic problems.

> *She said the following to the second meeting of the representatives of the political organizations. She said, after she had decided, "No, traffic violations wasn't the thing," and, "No, tables in the wrong places, it wasn't any of that," someone asked her, "was it the fact that we've been asking people to come down to [do civil rights] picketing? Did this trigger this action [the ban on advocacy], this new enforcement [on the Bancroft strip]?" And she said, "Yes, that definitely had something to do with it." With that as a preface, we'll let Professor Barnes speak.*

Barnes admitted that he "could add nothing" to what Savio had just said on the origins of the ban but again defended the university's regulations on behalf of political neutrality.

The crowd asked for Savio to respond to Barnes, which he did with a searching critique of his claims about UC's neutrality and a rebuttal to Chancellor Strong's written statement claiming that free speech protests at UC were totally unjustified since, with regard to political expression, students enjoyed "the fullest privileges in the history of the university."

There are three main things. . . . First, the remarks of Chancellor Strong that the open-forum policy will be maintained and that that policy will include no acceptance of donations and no recruitment of people to take part in direct action, nor recruitment . . . of people to join off-campus political organizations. Oh, yes! Now let's for a moment try to clear our minds of legal cobwebs and try to see just what that means in terms of facts. Most of the groups affected are of such a character that if they couldn't do these things they just might as well do nothing at those tables. Now that's a fact we ought to consider. . . .

But I understand that it does not address . . . the legal questions involved. So I'd like to move very quickly to what Professor Barnes said concerning the neutrality of the University of California. The university wants to maintain itself, he said at one point, politically neutral. And then he amended that—I was very careful in my notes—to legally neutral, and there is a very big distinction. Because I agree it is legally neutral. Now let's see how politically neutral it is. . . .

He said the university is run as a trust by the Board of Regents. Okay. They have quite a bit of control over what goes on at the university. We ought to ask who they are. . . . Who are the Board of Regents? Well, they are a pretty damned reactionary bunch of people! . . .

There are groups in this country, like laborers, for example, like Negroes—laborers usually—like educators, sometimes, when they don't act as Uncle Toms for administrations. These people, see, I don't think have a community of interest with the Bank of California. . . .

On the Board of Regents, please note, the only academic representative— and it's questionable in what sense he's an academic representative—is President Clark Kerr. The only one. There are no representatives . . . explicitly, of faculty—because they don't need it. . . . So [the] question is, is the university in fact neutral politically? And it obviously is false. Obviously. . . .

When someone brought up the issue of the kinds of things we do here, like the building of newer and better atom bombs, there was a lot of booing. . . . The people here don't want to discuss this matter. I think that it should be discussed. . . . Let's consider for a second the degree to which in this country we have democratic control over our foreign policy. I'd like you to consider this, please. I think it is extremely important.

One day after that Tonkin Bay incident, the very next day—remember this was an action of a Democratic administration—one day after this action was taken, the two representatives of the Republican Party, Miller and Goldwater, said, "As of now, Vietnam is not an issue in the campaign."[31]

What did that mean to you as voters and to me as a voter? It means that when we go to vote in November, we can't choose on what kind of foreign policy we want, because they [Democrats and Republicans] both have the same kind of foreign policy. Part of that foreign policy involves doing various things like building newer and better atom bombs. . . . We have no say in choosing . . . between that foreign policy and some other policy that someone else may want.

Now note—extremely important—the University of California is directly involved in making newer and better atom bombs. Whether this is good or bad, don't you think . . . in the spirit of political neutrality, either they should not be involved or there should be some democratic control over the way they're being involved?

I would like to raise now some genuinely legal issues, to which maybe some people will want to respond. There are several ways in which we can look at a university from a legal point of view. We can look at it as a private organization run by a small group of people. And in the past, on occasion, the regents have taken a position that they have virtually unlimited control over the private property which is the University of California. That's one way.

Another way is [that] we can look at the university as [a] kind of little city, and then we could ask ourselves, is there any part of this so-called open-forum policy which contradicts the ways in which we do things in little cities? Okay? I say there certainly is.

Let's say that the mayor of Berkeley announced that citizens of Berkeley could speak on any issue they wanted from the steps of the fire building. . . . But let's say that they placed the following restriction upon non-residents from Berkeley: that they could not do so unless they obtained permission from the city of Berkeley and did so seventy-two hours before they wanted to speak. You know there'd be a hue and cry going up: "Incredible violation of the First Amendment! Unbelievable violation of the Fourteenth!" . . .

Well, now, look at the university here not as the private property of Edward Carter. . . .[32] Let's say, instead, that we look upon it as a little city. Well, then, how come I—before I was expended (all right, before I was expelled, suspended)—I could get on the steps of Sproul Hall and say anything I wanted as long as I didn't start giving arms to people. You know, I could say anything I wanted without notifying anybody. But a nonstudent would have to obtain permission from the university and do that seventy-two hours before he wanted to speak, and the university might just not like what he had to say and might well deny the permission.

Now, consider the analogy with the city. Consider how gross—how gross a violation of the spirit of the First and Fourteenth Amendments that is. Here's the legal principle. I think it's more a moral principle.

We hold . . . that there ought to be no arbitrary restrictions upon the right of freedom of speech. Now what does an arbitrary restriction mean? An arbitrary restriction is one based upon an arbitrary distinction, for example, as between students and nonstudents. Now, note . . . sometimes the distinction is very material. If, for example, you consider [who is allowed in] classrooms . . . perfectly reasonable, material distinction. . . . But now the issue is freedom of speech. We have people out in Sproul Hall. There's not a class going on there. . . . What, therefore, is the material basis for the distinction in this instance between students and nonstudents?

Why seventy-two hours for nonstudents and no time for students? Let's say, for example—and this touches me very deeply—let's say that in McComb, Mississippi, some children are killed in the bombing of a church. . . . Let's say that we have someone who's come up from Mississippi . . . and he wanted to speak here, and he had to wait seventy-two hours in order to speak. And everybody will have completely forgotten about those little children, because, you know, when you're black and in Mississippi, nobody gives a damn. . . .

Seventy-two hours later and . . . the whole issue would have been dead. Or let's say that some organization here . . . objects to some action of the administration in Vietnam . . . and has to wait seventy-two hours to object. By that time it's all over. You know, we could all be dead.

I'm suggesting legally, therefore, that the distinction that they make between students and nonstudents has no basis except harassment. . . . Furthermore, they claim that the university is neutral. A lot of hogwash! It's legally neutral. It's the most un-politically-neutral organization that I've had personal contact with. It's really an institution that serves the interests and represents the establishment of the United States. And we have Clark Kerr's word on it in his book on the multiversity.

As I said before, the purpose of the university is simple: it's to create a product. The product is to fit into certain factories. You go out and take part in the Establishment, and that's why there is a university!

Anybody who wants to say anything on this campus, just like anybody on the city street, should have the right to do so—and no concessions by the bureaucracy should be acceded to by us, should be considered by us, until they include complete freedom of speech!

Savio's role as spokesperson for the protesters was so central that he was the leader quoted most extensively in the Daily Californian's *coverage of the sit-in. The sit-in would turn into a sleep-in, as the protesters stayed on, demanding that the dean meet with and discipline all of the hundreds of protesters there or none. "We want equal action," Savio told the student newspaper. "And that's no action, because they can't take action against all these people who are here. They're scared. We're staying."[33]*

The sleep-in would end at three in the morning, when the protesters voted to disperse and renew their defiance of the ban on political advocacy the next day on Sproul Plaza.

Transcribed from audiotape, Mario Savio archives, published by permission of Lynne Hollander Savio. Also available online at UC Media Resource Center at www.lib.berkeley.edu/MRC/FSM/fsmchronology1.html.

OPENING SPEECH OF THE CAR-TOP RALLY,
SPROUL PLAZA

1 OCTOBER 1964

As the students sat in at Sproul Hall on the evening of September 30, top UC administrators, including President Clark Kerr, Chancellor Edward Strong, and Vice Chancellor Alex Sherriffs, worried that "a revolution ... now ... is happening," held a strategy session up at Alumni House. They decided to hold off on having the police come to campus to end the sit-in but to place on "indefinite suspension" Savio and the other seven student protesters who had been cited for defying the political advocacy ban. "We have clear cases on the eight.... Pick off one at a time.... Hold out on throwing the [student political] organizations out at this time.... Do not do everything at once.... Important to get the opposition to a minimum as we build up friends from the students and faculty." Their most fateful decision was that, going forward, they would initially make outsiders the focus of their attempt to suppress the protests: "Avoid police action—except non-students.... Have police remove non-students."[34] This is why Jack Weinberg, a vocal CORE activist and a nonstudent, would be arrested on Sproul Plaza just before noon on October 1, where he was brazenly defying the ban.

This decision to escalate the conflict with police power was to be implemented by Deans Peter Van Houten and George Murphy. At 11:45 A.M., they came to the campus police station and requested that Lt. Merrill F. Chandler "accompany them to the west stairs of Sproul Hall where tables were set up in violation of University Rules," which Chandler did. Sgt. Halleran would accompany Chandler and the deans but "remain at a discreet distance and if an arrest was imminent" call the police "station via ... portable transmitter and request a patrol car to transport the person under arrest...." When Murphy came to the Campus CORE table, Weinberg refused to leave the table or identify himself. "When it was obvious" to Chandler that an arrest would be made he signaled to Sgt. Halleran, who "called to direct the police vehicle to proceed to the west side of Sproul Hall." Chandler informed Weinberg that "he was under arrest for violation of section 602-L of the California Penal Code (trespassing)."[35]

The police car arrived with two officers in it. But the arrest was slowed down as Weinberg went limp, making it "necessary to forcibly carry" him to the car. As the police "were lifting" Weinberg to the car, shouts of "sit down" rang out and "approximately fifty persons laid [sic] down in front of the car," and then more protesters surrounded it, "making it impossible to drive the car from the place of the arrest." [36] *The crowd around the car grew quickly, as this was the busiest time of day on campus, and the car was in the middle of Berkeley's main plaza.*

Savio sat on the police car's hood soon after the blockade began and decided he would use the roof of the car as a platform and podium from which to explain the protest and urge more students to join the sit-in. Of this moment, when he ascended the car-top and began what would be a thirty-two-hour rally around the blockaded car, Savio recalled:

> *When I do something I feel is a little bit questionable, a little bit risky, my heart beats faster. I wouldn't have been surprised if people had hooted me down. I had some feeling of embarrassment. But it . . . had a kind of poetic rightness to it. Sometimes you're just . . . gripped by the moment, and you have a feel for what's poetically right. . . . What was correct? Free speech or police taking away this person who was sitting at a table? It was a question of what thing would prevail. What deserved contempt and what praise. You somehow feel those things.* [37]

We were going to hold a rally here at twelve o'clock. And we were going to have to shout our lungs out to get people. I'm so grateful to the administration of this wonderful university. They've done it for us! Let's give them a hand. We must really feel very, very sorry for these poor policemen here, you know. Good men. They're family men, you know. They have a job to do. That's right, they have a job to do.

[A voice from crowd yells, "Just like Eichmann."]

Yeah. Very good. It's very . . . like Adolf Eichmann. He had a job to do. He fit into the machinery.

We are asking the following. We will not stop direct action against . . . the administration of this university unless they accede to the following very simple and reasonable demands.

Number one: they must immediately, that is, the chancellor—Chancellor Strong, seeing as he's the one who did it—must immediately say that no students have been suspended from the university. [38]

Figure 8. Savio atop the police car, October 1, 1964. Note that he removed his shoes so as not to damage the car. Photograph courtesy of Steven Marcus, Bancroft Library collection.

Number two: Chancellor Strong ... must agree to meet with representatives of the off-campus political organizations to discuss with them reasonable regulations governing freedom of speech on this campus, which means no arbitrary restrictions of any kind on freedom of speech on this campus! He must agree to such a meeting. That's demand number two.

Number three: the final demand is [that] the chancellor must agree that no disciplinary action will be taken against anyone setting up tables or speaking here until, at the very, very least, that meeting is held.

And I am right now publicly serving a notice of warning, and—I should say—a threat to this administration, that they . . . will be subject to continuous direct action by us, and it's going to be damned embarrassing for them. We're going to get foreign press; we're going to get domestic press; we're going to get all sorts of organizations against them until they accede to these legitimate demands.

Now, folks, here's what it is. A fellow who said that on his own initiative, which I have reason to doubt, [he] has been acting as a go-between between the administration and us. This fellow has now gone up to his friends in the administration, and he told us he's going to see if he can get them to drop charges against this student [Weinberg, though he was actually a *former* graduate student] who stood up for all of us. All right? Now, let us suppose that does not happen, and there's a good likelihood that it won't happen. All right, if that does not happen, I propose that everybody at this meeting—or as many as can fit—get into that damn building, get into Dean Towle's office, into Dean Arleigh Williams's office, into the offices, and just sit at the desks, just sit right in the chairs, just sit right on the floor, and make it absolutely impossible for them to conduct their work.

We can't really ask for too much more, can we? . . . We can't tell who was arrested, because he has refused to give his identification. I'd like to explain that, because there is really some legitimate difference of agreement as to whether the person should have given his identification. And I think there is a perfectly legitimate rationale for his not having done so. And it's this: . . . by general agreement, people have . . . been acceding to the demands of the university to identify themselves. Yesterday we did that. Over at Sather Gate, people sitting at a University Friends of SNCC table identified themselves in accordance with the demands—perhaps ill-considered and unjustified [demands]—of the administration. And do you know what they did? They used that as a tool, as weapon to take eight [protesters and initiate disciplinary procedures against them]. . . . They ignored 409 others who said they were doing the same thing. And so to protect ourselves—it's a simple matter of self-protection—we cannot accede to this demand that we identify ourselves until this administration is prepared to deal with us in a nondiscriminatory manner. . . .

All right. Now the question is, why was he arrested? All right, we can answer the question in two ways—at least! The police say he was arrested for—for violation of a trespass ordinance. All right. See? I'll tell you why he was arrested in my opinion. He happens to be a person . . . who has been quite outspoken in his disagreement with what the administration does. Furthermore, the people that they axed the other day were likewise people quite outspoken in their disagreement with what the administration does. . . . Other people, both today and yesterday, who were violating the same regulations and laws. They happened to pick upon those people who are the most outspoken.

You know there's a story told—it appears in one of the tales that Herodotus tells . . . about the Persian Wars. He said . . . this: a person wanted to know, "how can we take over a particular city or country in the most effective way," and the following . . . parable was told. Have you ever seen a wheat field? You see how there are some stalks of wheat that stand up above the others? It's very simple. Don't cut them all down; just cut down the ones that stick up the highest. And you've won! Well, that's precisely what they did. They're smart to that extent, at any rate. That's why they arrested him. . . .

[Someone in the crowd demands to speak.]

We believe in freedom of speech. I don't know what this fellow wants to say, but I'd like to have him say it.

Transcribed from audiotape, Mario Savio archives, published by permission of Lynne Hollander Savio. Also available online at UC Media Resource Center at www.lib.berkeley.edu/MRC/FSM/fsmchronology1.html.

REPORT ON MEETING WITH UC BERKELEY CHANCELLOR EDWARD STRONG, CAR-TOP RALLY, SPROUL PLAZA

1 OCTOBER 1964

Less than an hour into the police car blockade, ASUC student government president Charlie Powell spoke from the car-top and offered to serve as an

intermediary between the protesters and the administration. The crowd suggested that he go but have Savio represent the protesters. Powell agreed to do this. Savio replied, "fine. I love to talk with people, I really do, and . . . I'll be glad to go . . . with Charlie Powell to see these people. All right, but—I want it understood that until this person in this car is placed . . . out of arrest nobody will move from here," which the crowd responded to with applause and cheers.[39] About an hour later, Savio returned to report on his tense meeting with Chancellor Strong (and other administrators). The report typified Savio's devotion to transparency in leadership, as it narrates the most important exchanges in this meeting and does so in more detail than the chancellor's own internal memorandum on this meeting.[40] What follows is an abridged version of Savio's report on what he and the chancellor said to each other.

I'll just tell you exactly what happened, just precisely what took place in the meeting. I was introduced by [ASUC president] Charlie Powell, and then I spoke. . . . And I said exactly what I said to you, exactly the same demands that we agreed to support here we asked of the chancellor there. We asked that the person [in the police car, Jack Weinberg] be released. That those eight have their suspensions removed, that they be reinstated. That was the first demand. Second, . . . that a meeting . . . [of] the chancellor with a representative of the off-campus political organizations be held to discuss what are legitimate restrictions upon the use of freedom of expression facilities here, and that from now to such a time as such a meeting has ended, no disciplinary action be taken against any student for exercising the rights that we have been exercising for years at Bancroft and Telegraph in a place. As a matter of fact, I said, "It will be fine. I think it would be acceptable to us here that during that period of waiting for this meeting that they should specify a place by Sather Gate, we'd be willing until the meeting was over to do those things." Those were the demands, just those. He rejected *every single one of them, every one.*

His basis? I'll tell you. Precisely the basis that Dean Towle finally had to retreat to. Namely, "It's a regulation of the university. I am bound to enforce it. These people were violating regulations of the university willfully. I am bound, therefore, to take this action against them and cannot have a meeting with you under these or any conditions. I can have a meeting, an unconditional meeting, namely that the following takes place: that you suspend all activity, all protest. This person goes to jail. Those eight remain suspended. I will gladly meet with you under those circumstances." *["No," shout protesters around the car.]* You know what's going to happen if we ever, *ever* to agree to such incredible demands? I'll tell you. . . . He'll find a convenient time to meet with us after a little time has elapsed, during which we are not exercising rights we've been exercising for years, and then he'll say, "No, I'm just enforcing a regulation which has always existed. I don't see what your gripe is. I'll be glad to explain it to you." And he will. Again.

It was really an interesting thing to see. Chancellor Strong, aside from stating this position, took *umbrage* that we were misrepresenting [the issue]. He said it was not a freedom of speech issue. "Why, what are you doing misrepresenting my position? I feel that I have been personally done a wrong." And he said "Can you name one instance—one instance— in which this Open Forum policy [of UC Berkeley, which regulated campus political expression] is in any sense a violation of freedom of speech?"

So I told the following. I said, "you know, of course, about the First and Fourteenth Amendments. The First Amendment . . . provides, among other things, . . . for freedom of expression. The Fourteenth, in its first section, provides for equal protection of the laws. Now freedom of expression is a reciprocal thing, a complementary right is freedom to hear arguments expressed."

So I gave him the following instance, which I will describe, which is part of their regulations, which violates the First Amendment in that it restricts students' rights to hear and violates the Fourteenth in that it makes an arbitrary distinction on the rights of people to express their opinions. This is one of the regulations that we're trying to get rid of. It's the following. "Any student at all can speak from the steps of Sproul Hall, at any time, on any subject—providing he doesn't cause a traffic hazard, such as we're causing right now." All right, any student, any time, without any prior notification. A nonstudent—that's like me, for example [because of his suspension]—a nonstudent must obtain permission seventy-two hours in advance. . . . And [this] obviously [is] placing restrictions on the First Amendment guarantees of the hearers, because they obviously cannot with equal facility hear students and nonstudents. And presumably some nonstudents, for example, the chancellor, might have something important to say. *[laughter]*

It places a Fourteenth Amendment restriction on the right of speakers, because they're treated in a discriminatory manner. There's an arbitrary distinction made between students and nonstudents. Let's explain what we might mean by . . . an "arbitrary restriction." A reasonable restriction is something of the following kind. Students . . . should have the first right to the use of a classroom, because they signed up in the course. And after that, privileges can be extended to those who want to audit. There there's material basis for nonarbitrary distinction. But consider the following arbitrary distinction: let's say the city of Berkeley decided that residents of Berkeley could speak from the fire department any time they wanted. But nonresidents would have to obtain from the city seventy-two hours prior notification and permission in order to speak. It would be quite arbitrary. There would be a tremendous hue and cry, the First Amendment and Fourteenth unbelievably violated. Well, I claim the right to speak here. I presume we're all claiming this—the right to speak here. That there does not exist the material basis for the distinction between students and nonstudents.

Well, I told him this. I don't know if he understood the issues involved. Presuming that he did, he didn't agree with me anyway. He would not accept this as an example. I don't know what to say. So one of his points was that the issue was not freedom of speech. I think we've cleared that up.

I said further, "it's not just a matter of freedom of speech. We're protesting something else. It's freedom of speech, to be sure. Acceptance of donations is not exactly a question of freedom of speech. But we've been doing it for years. . . ." And I suppose that we have to distinguish—and he did understand the word in this case—between de jure right and de facto right. We've had the right de facto for years. What's the rationale for taking it away on the basis of *his* interpretation of some de jure ruling of the regents? And he had not been able to give any, except that it *is* the regulation. Okay.

We're just where we were before. Just exactly where we were before. We're here, some of us sitting in front of this car and behind this car and around it. They [the police] can't get through. It's very, very difficult for them to put this person under arrest in an orderly way without their getting through. There are lots of us right here maybe two thousand, maybe more [*a voice from the crowd says "five thousand"*], thousands who think is not such a good thing which the chancellor is doing. . . .

Transcribed from audiotape, Mario Savio archives, published by permission of Lynne Hollander Savio. Also available online at UC Media Resource Center at www.lib.berkeley.edu/MRC/FSM/fsmchronology1.html.

EXPLAINING AND DEFENDING CIVIL DISOBEDIENCE, CAR TOP RALLY, SPROUL PLAZA, LATE NIGHT

1 OCTOBER 1964

For Savio and the crowd of protesters around the police car—which had swelled to several thousand at the protest's peak in the afternoon—their nonviolent human blockade around that car was among the most dramatic and exhilarating political acts of their lives. They saw themselves as taking a bold stand for freedom and, through their collective effort, halting a blatant injustice (the arrest of Weinberg for defying an illiberal ban on political advocacy) and demonstrating against both that arrest and the suspension of eight students for defying that ban. "Collective" was the operative word, for what made the blockade and car-top rally possible was solidarity. Every demonstrator around that car was, as Savio later put it, "needed. And they were needed to stay there all night.... They had a job to do . . . night and day—namely, to keep this car." That common work in the face of common danger shaped a profound sense of community whose free speech mission was, in Savio's words, of such "importance" that it "touches the deepest part of you. . . . We felt a very personal responsibility for the well-being of all. That's something which must be described as beautiful."[41]

This sense of community was reinforced by the fact that this was not a silent sit-in, but an immense, open-ended rally, one in which Savio and speaker after speaker discussed the free speech conflict and the first principles of democracy, academic freedom, the civil rights movement, and engaged citizenship. Since the protesters were risking suspension, arrest, and their physical safety by blockading that police car, the speeches from the car-top and dialogue with the crowd were not merely academic, but of

*immediate and practical import, almost a matter of life and death. As
FSM leader Michael Rossman later recalled, they discussed civil liberty
and the ideals of the French Revolution and ancient Greek philosophers
with an unprecedented sense of urgency, "as if they had meaning."*[42]

*This sense of community was put to the test late at night as a rowdy
crowd from Berkeley's fraternities—some of whom seemed fortified by
alcohol—appeared on the scene, attempting to use the threat of violence to
end the blockade. Outraged that a police car had been immobilized by protesters, the hecklers shouted for the car's release and hurled rotten eggs,
fruit, vegetables, and lighted cigarettes at those who spoke from the car-top.
Throughout the day, the car-top podium had been open to opponents of the
blockade, and some had gotten up and debated the protesters. These late
night hecklers were invited to speak as well, and some did. But it soon
became apparent that most of the hecklers had come not to debate but to
forcibly evict the protesters.*

*As the hecklers began throwing things, Savio urged those who are "part of
the demonstration for freedom of speech on this campus" to remain calm. He
sought repeatedly to explain the protest but was interrupted by heckling.
When he asked what they wanted, some replied "the car. . . . Let the policemen
have their automobile. . . . Give up the car! Yes or no?" Savio replied, "It's not
as simple as that," and he urged that they "think a little more deeply" about
the principles at stake in this free speech struggle. The hecklers responded by
telling Savio to get off the car and show his UC registration card, and quipped
that if he did not "like Cal" he should just "go someplace else!" Savio replied,
"Look—the only reason that I took part in this is that I like Cal very much.
I'd like to see it better. I'm not here to destroy something. We're here to try to
build something." As the heckling continued, Savio managed to get the floor
long enough to explain the meaning of civil disobedience and link the police
car blockade to the history of such dissent, dating back to Thoreau.*

I would like to explain—please, would the people here at least keep quiet.
I would like to explain the principle—as I said before, and see if you're
willing to accept it—on the basis of which we took the action. Are you willing to listen? *[Hecklers shout, "Get off the car!"]* . . .

Have you ever heard of a man named Thoreau? *[A heckler jeers.]* The
man's name was Henry David Thoreau. Part of his life was during the time

the United States engaged in a war with Mexico. At that time, there was no slavery in Mexico, and there was in the United States. This man believed that he could not in [good] conscience support a war to extend slavery into Mexico. And so do you know what he did? He disobeyed the law. He refused to pay any taxes. He disobeyed the law. He believed that there were certain matters of conscience which exceeded any legal matters in importance. We likewise, in this instance, we believe that there are matters of conscience which greatly exceed the question of disobedience to law. Do you recognize that there at least could be circumstances ... *[Hecklers chant, "We want Thoreau! We want Thoreau!"]* ... I wish I could give him to you! That's a start! You'll be on our side in a little while if you keep chanting that!

What I'm asking you is this, if you would just keep quiet and think for a moment on the principle. Do you agree that there are times when questions of conscience exceed in importance questions of law? That's the question.

[A heckler hurls an object at Savio.] You missed me, fortunately. Alright, we're going to sing for a while. Maybe that will calm us.

An impassioned condemnation of violence and appeal for calm by Father James Fisher of the Newman House and Dean Louis Rice's call for the hecklers to go home finally got them to leave. Savio also credited those sitting in for preventing serious violence by remaining calm during this tense scene, which he saw as evidence that "the demonstrators had greater internal resources than those who were heckling us."[43]

Transcribed from audiotape, Mario Savio archives, published by permission of Lynne Hollander Savio. Also available online at UC Media Resource Center at www.lib.berkeley.edu/MRC/FSM/fsmchronology1.html.

ENDING THE POLICE CAR BLOCKADE, CAR-TOP RALLY
EVENING OF 2 OCTOBER 1964

While on the night of October 1 the threat of violence came from the fraternities, the next day a much more ominous threat came from hundreds of

police officers who were assembling, ready to use force to end the blockade.
But under pressure from Governor Brown, who "feared there would be
bloodshed" and "didn't want another . . . Mississippi" (where people had
been killed during the desegregation crisis at the University of Mississippi),
President Kerr stepped in and did something his recalcitrant subordinate,
Chancellor Strong, had refused to do: he entered into negotiations with
Savio and a delegation of the protesters.[44]

The negotiations were tense, and the students resented the way Kerr
used the threat of a police invasion as a lever in the negotiating process.
Savio debated Kerr and, as in his prior meeting with Strong, refuted
administration claims that there was no free speech issue at stake in this
conflict. Savio was initially opposed to ending the police car blockade by
signing the settlement Kerr was offering, which he thought gave the pro-
testers too little. By the terms of this settlement, the Pact of October 2, the
students agreed to end the blockade and in exchange won only UC's agree-
ment not to press charges against Weinberg, while essentially postponing
settlement of the free speech dispute by setting up committees to consider
the cases of the suspended students and the campus's regulation of political
speech. Savio insisted upon and obtained a modification of the settlement's
language. Under intense pressure from his fellow delegation members, who
feared tragedy would result if the police were unleashed against the pro-
testers, Savio reluctantly joined them in signing the pact. Ten minutes
later, at 7:30 P.M., Savio returned to the police car to read and explain the
settlement, which would end the police car blockade.

I would like to request that we have silence. I want everyone here to
understand very carefully, very, very completely, the seriousness of the circumstances in which we find ourselves here and now. You all see how
many are assembled. The demonstrators know the nature of certain of the
people who are assembled here who are not demonstrators [the hecklers],
and likewise, I'm sure we're all aware of the presence of large numbers of
police. Until this time we have tried our very best to submit all statements
to a vote of those present. However, let us consider what a vote means. A
vote should be the result of an intellectual decision. Such a decision, if we
have respect for our dignity as free men, cannot, I believe, be made under
the circumstances of a meeting of this sort, with the police present, as they

are, with our knowing full well the kinds of things they—or hecklers—may do. However, as a preface to these remarks, and because I have a very deep respect for popular process, I would like to call a meeting for Monday, twelve o'clock, to be addressed from the steps of Sproul Hall. At this meeting, all those with a vital interest in these proceedings will have an opportunity, one with another, to discuss the nature of the document which I'm going to read here. This will give adequate time for the free men involved to consider carefully the very serious issues involved in this matter.

I would like to read the statement through once. Then I would like to call special attention to a change which was made in the wording of one of its provisions, in order to protect all of us who have engaged in this demonstration. I want to make it very clear that, as representative of University Friends of SNCC, I could not have in good conscience subscribed to the statement before that change. And I think you will clearly understand why. I should now—*[noise from hecklers]*. Please maintain silence! I appeal to you, please maintain silence! Retain your dignity and self-respect in this matter, please! I think you're aware of some of the pressures we're under, so please! I implore you! Maintain your composure, please.

I should now like to read the document. The first provision: the student demonstrators shall desist from all forms of their illegal protest against university regulations. *[cries of "No! No!" from the protesters]* Please, please.

Number two: a committee representing students (including leaders of the demonstration), faculty, and administration will immediately be set up to conduct discussions and hearings into all aspects of political behavior on campus and its control and to make recommendations to the administration.

Three: the arrested man will be booked, but released on his own recognizance, and the university, which is the complainant, will not press charges. *[cheering and applause]*

This is four: the duration of the suspension of the suspended students will be submitted within one week to the Student Conduct Committee of the Academic. Not to the administration! *[cheering and applause]*

Five: *[heckling from the fraternity members]* Please, please be silent! Please! Please be silent! Five: activity may be continued by student organizations in accordance with existing university regulations. That is, in other words, none of the groups originally involved have had their privileges suspended. *[applause]*

Sixth and last, and then I should like to explain the first, as I said. The president of the university has already declared his willingness to support deeding certain university property at the end of Telegraph Avenue to the city of Berkeley or to the ASUC. Now, do you understand what that means? You will be able to do there—if this goes through—*[from the crowd: "How about here?"]* One minute. A committee will be set up immediately to discuss what we may do here. You will be able to do there—if this goes through—what has been done there for years. *[cheering and applause]*

Now, I have only two more points. The first, I should like to briefly explain article one. The original wording of that article was as follows: "The student demonstrators promise to abide by legal processes in their protest of university regulations." This, I felt, would have been an impossible bind upon the consciences of those who, perhaps at some time in the future—and this was my opinion as representative of just one organization, but there were others who joined me in this—this we felt would have had the effect of binding for an indefinite period of time the freedom of the protesters to engage in actions which they may feel at some time, though technically illegal, are the only ones they can take. We could not have accepted that provision. *[applause]* Instead, we accepted the wording that I read the first time, with the understanding that this would not indefinitely bind anyone, and it was, "The student demonstrators shall desist from all forms of their illegal protest against University regulations." I would like that those who have taken part in this protest will agree, by acclamation, to accepting this document, and as soon as they have done so, to rise, quietly, and with dignity, to walk home. May I please have that decision? *["YES!" from the crowd; cheering and applause]* Will you please then rise at this point, and will you please follow me away from this area quietly and with dignity, please! *[The crowd dispersed.]*

Transcribed from audiotape, Mario Savio archives, published by permission of Lynne Hollander Savio. Also available online at UC Media Resource Center at www.lib.berkeley.edu/MRC/FSM/fsmchronology1.html.

INTERVIEW WITH MARIO SAVIO IMMEDIATELY AFTER
THE END OF THE POLICE CAR BLOCKADE

2 OCTOBER 1964

Question: Mario, would you say that you backed down or that the university backed down?

Savio: I would say that really no one has as of yet backed down, especially when you consider provision 1. We're willing to wait. I think this is an expression of good faith on the part of the demonstrators. We're willing and *anxious* to be sure to conduct the discussions not with guns at anybody's head. I think that we understand what could have happened tonight. And neither we nor the president wants those to be the conditions under which discussions go on.

Q: Is this cooling off period till Monday part of the concession?

Savio: No. This is simply a meeting which the leaders of the demonstration have called for the following reason. I have been in many situations in which action being taken is decided by a small elite without even adequate information being given to the people involved. It has been my feeling that in this matter that *everything* should be done completely in the open. And I feel that all the people involved should have a right in an open forum to discuss these matters. However, I think it clear for those who are aware of the power circumstances involved in this particular situation that this agreement could not possibly have been submitted to a vote.

Q: So is it [the Pact of October 2] actually accepted, or what is the situation?

Savio: The agreement was accepted by representatives of the off-campus political organizations provisionally, in the name of the demonstrators. But it's clear we cannot bind the consciences of those who have not themselves agreed today so.

Q: Will Monday a vote be taken?

Savio: Monday a vote will not be taken on this agreement. Some other things may be decided by the group on Monday. We must leave now. It absolutely essential that we leave.

Q: One more question, Mario. Can you continue to collect funds on this campus in this area or not?

Savio: In accordance with this agreement, we cannot.

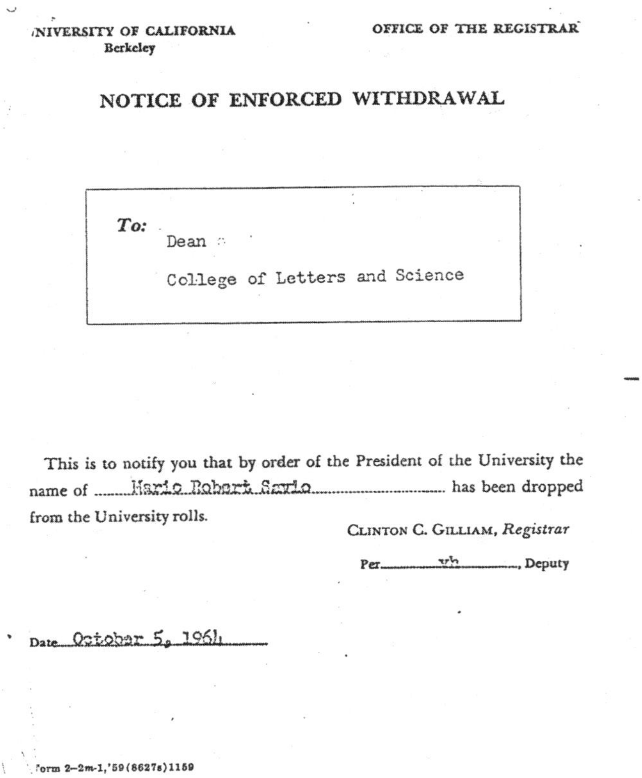

,NIVERSITY OF CALIFORNIA   OFFICE OF THE REGISTRAR
Berkeley

NOTICE OF ENFORCED WITHDRAWAL

To:
   Dean

   College of Letters and Science

—

This is to notify you that by order of the President of the University the
name of ....Mario Robert Savio........................... has been dropped
from the University rolls.

CLINTON C. GILLIAM, *Registrar*

Per............vh............, Deputy

Date....October 5, 1964........

'orm 2–2m-1,'59(8627s)1159

Figure 9. The price of activism: Savio's notification of
suspension from the student body, October 5, 1964. Mario Savio
disciplinary file, Mario Savio archive, image courtesy of Lynne
Hollander Savio.

*Transcribed from audiotape, Mario Savio archives, copy in editor's posses-
sion, published by permission of Lynne Hollander Savio.*

SPEECH AT FREE SPEECH MOVEMENT RALLY, SPROUL HALL STEPS

5 OCTOBER 1964

*On the weekend after the police car blockade the protesters met, named
their struggle and organization the Free Speech Movement, and adopted a*

highly democratic structure. The FSM would be led by the elected Steering Committee, which included Savio, and the Executive Committee representing every student group as well as unaffiliated students.

The first official FSM rally on campus occurred on the Monday after the police car blockade. The holding of this rally itself became a free speech dispute since Chancellor Strong—still smarting from Kerr's intervention in promulgating the Pact of October 2—was again leaning toward a hard line, indicating that if Savio sought to speak at this rally, he would be arrested, since he had been suspended and, technically, had lost his right to speak on campus. Fearing that such an arrest would yield confrontation, faculty interceded and convinced Strong to back down on the arrest threat. In his speech, Savio discussed all this, the issue of red-baiting, the Pact of October 2, and the FSM's struggle to have students treated as equal partners in negotiations and university governance.

The only surviving record of this rally—and Savio's speech at it—is an amateurish transcript made by the campus police for President Kerr and Chancellor Strong—the first of several made as the administration monitored the FSM. It is published here, as these administrators read it, complete with that transcript's garbled patches, applause marks, and curious paragraph structure.

As you say [sic] today, by the remarks that were made by at least one person, we're subject to a great deal of pressure from both sides. I'd like in part to respond to that pressure not as pressure, by indicating among the things I'd like to say here the reason I think we've won a substantial victory. . . .

There was some question up until 20 minutes ago as to whether I should be permitted to speak here at all, and we had people on this matter who were going to bat for us—people on the faculty as well as people from the organization of political organizations that's been kind of steering this, and the following statement came out this morning over Dean Towle's signature—you probably have heard it already, but I'd like to call special attention to it because it's not precisely our position on the matter, and you ought to know that. It says, "we are honoring the spirit of the President's agreement and therefore have granted a special waiver for this meeting today so that leaders of the demonstration may discuss the written agreement of last Friday."[45] Now, we acknowledge our right to speak today, obviously, but we don't acknowledge this as a special waiver covering only today's meeting. (applause)

In case there are some here who will question our prudence in not making that acknowledgement, I should like to motivate it by reference to the agreement that we signed. It is very uncommon in any form of negotiation, for one side to allow the other to act as arbiter in specifying the interpretation of the agreement. The interpretation, in our opinion, which the administration would like to make of this agreement is now unlegalistic. On the other hand, for today, they've been very wise in deciding to put that aside. I'd like, if I may, to motivate their original position from the agreement and then to motivate ours from the agreement, likewise. As you know, provision one of the agreement was as follows: "The student demonstrators promise to abide by legal processes in their protest of University regulations." Now, if you think about that, you'll realize that it has a kind of indefinite time sense on it. You know, as though we're binding ourselves from now and for all time not to do things which might be construed as civil disobedience. At the time that this agreement was under consideration with Clark Kerr, I indicated to him that at least I personally, and there were others there, could not put their signatures to such a document. Accordingly, we agreed upon the following re-wording: "The student demonstrators shall desist from all forms of their legal protest against University regulations." This does not have the indefinite time sense on it, and we interpret it, and likewise it was the understanding of the meeting we had with Clark Kerr, that it was put in there specifically so as to get rid of any notion that there was an indefinite time sense put upon that provision. All right. Now, the position of the administration regarding article one is that it binds us in the following way: that suspended students are not students and are subject to the 72 hour prohibition against speaking, for example here. They had to budge on that today, and I think that they have acted in good faith though there's a difference between the reason for an action, obviously, and the motivation for it. Now, our interpretation rests upon a combination of provision one and provision two. We feel it's a total document, and we don't hold that only the first provision is meaningful, which I think they would like us to hold. Provision 2 says the following: "A committee representing students (including leaders of the demonstration), faculty and administration will immediately be set up to conduct discussions and hearing into all aspects of political behavior" and so forth. Now, if there is knowledge in provision two that the leaders of the demonstration are to act as representatives of the students and if, as I think will be highly unreasonable, they could construct that to mean I am not one of the leaders of the demonstration, you know, then they would have a case. I don't think that they can possibly put that construction upon it. In other words, I don't think that it would be acceptable to any of us if, for example, I'm not one of the negotiators. (applause)

No one is suggesting for a moment that the university is considering not letting me be on the premises. But ~~they're~~ we're [they were] thinking about it. All right, now if as is reasonable, I am one of the leaders of the demonstration, therefore in the wording of section two, I am one of the leaders of the students, you see of the representatives, to use their word, of the students, then it's not simply a matter of saying this is a non-student who is getting up to speak, but a very particular non-student, and that good faith in interpreting this particular declaration, we feel, must be that during the negotiations, those who have been suspended must be granted on this campus the same speaking rights as are granted to students. (applause)

Now, as concerns whether this was a victory or not. It obviously was not the whole war! Very obviously! But, it's the biggest battle. It's the battle for jurisdictional recognition—you know, just like with unions—they negotiated with us, and they said that absolutely under no circumstances would they do so. Let me explain just what that meant in terms of the particular negotiations which we conducted—and they may want to call them talks, but after the explanation I give of what occurred, it will be clear that this is a matter of words which are more convenient to them but less substantive in their reference. Here's what occurred. They didn't want to budge at all on the original four provisions which very hurriedly were presented by a faculty committee, I think in a very wise act on their part, to avoid violence. However, I indicated to them at the time, as I've said here, that we absolutely would not budge on provision one, and Clark Kerr at that point, when he realized what was at stake, had to leave the room to confer with people from whom, I suppose, he could get some kind of understanding concerning power to change provision one. All right. So far from not negotiating, we were not only negotiating, but I would suggest negotiating with other forces besides those explicitly represented at the meeting. (applause)

Very well. What were—those were the kinds of pressures that were upon Clark Kerr and I must say, though we obviously disagree very substantially, he had a good deal of cool. (laughter and applause) Now, the kind of thing, seems to me, that it comes to—we have to consider what would have been gained by other action at that meeting. I think this is very, very important. There were different reports in the papers saying that there were various numbers of policemen there running from 500 to over 900. Some of these policemen were . . . Oakland policemen. At the meeting we were told the following by Clark Kerr. He said, I have requested them not to do anything to disturb the meeting you're having until negotiations have ended. (The mike seemed to go out for a moment here) He said that he had requested of the police—and this includes obviously the Oakland ones—not to do anything to disturb the meeting until negotiations were over. And I requested upon him to find out what that meant. And it meant—and he was honest about this—and to him it meant until we arrived back at the meeting. But, he said, in fact they may judge at some time, depending on how dark it is, or other matters—you know, they're pretty trigger happy—they may decide at some point to overrule my request. All right. Now. Notes were taken on the meeting. He has the notes. I'll be perfectly happy for him to use his notes, you know. This really occurred at the meeting, and I want to say that again, he acted with a good deal of strength. Now it's a question of seeing whether that will also be a matter of negotiation of acting in good faith. But certainly with a good deal of strength. Now, what would have been gained. All right. We had, one, the jurisdictional dispute, which was a big thing. One, the right to further negotiations in this matter. Furthermore, we are now in the position of having acted with the utmost and, I would say of our side, the only one to have acted, with complete moral responsibility in that situation. (applause)

Now, there are some people whom you've heard speaking here to whom that may not mean anything or not mean much. I can't say that's true. I just have that feeling. All right. I hope that in that question of our having acted with great responsibility, I do hope that we will continue to have the support of the vast mass of students. (applause)

Now, it should be clear that if these negotiations are not conducted in good faith, and we have every belief that they will be so conducted—in good faith—should be perfectly clear that if we are again put into similar circumstances and have been treated unfairly in the past, we will consider differently how best to act. (applause)

Right now, I'd like to turn to a matter which—well, we'll leave that for a little bit later—let me read a beautiful statement of support which we received. This statement is the expressed will of 2,400 State of California college professors, executive committee. (applause) This is an indication of other reasons why I really feel that we should wait on any kind of pro-vocative action and we should, at least, negotiate completely in good faith. We are rallying in support of the following kind and we really ought to try to do so. Perhaps at some time in the near future there will be other people besides one professor from our own campus up here on the platform with us. (applause)

So let me read this brief but very, from our point of view, optimistic statement. "News release on UC student demands from Executive commit-tee of the Association of California State College Professors, October 4th, 1964. In the press of October 3, it was reported that the administration of the University of California at Berkeley has prohibited students from 'col-lecting funds on campus for political purposes, from recruiting for political groups and from organizing off-campus demonstrations. It was evident from the report that some student organizations which are not affiliated with political parties but are generally dedicated to various types of social action, have been prohibited under these rules from fund raising, recruit-ing and organizing activities on the campus. The California State Colleges and the University of California have a mutual interest in academic free-dom for students and faculty, (we're fighting their fight too; I hope they'll join us in it) and in freedom of speech in general. The Executive Committee of the Association of California State College Professors believe that stu-dent participation in social action is consistent with our constitutionally guaranteed freedoms and contributes to the educational process. (applause) Therefore, whether it is political or non-political, it ought not only to be permitted but actively encouraged, (applause) so long as it does not inter-fere with the regular instructional program (in other words, this question of traffic disturbances and so on on campus) even if it involves persons from off campus who are invited to participate by students and faculty members. (applause) Consequently, the Executive Committee of the Association of California State College Professors supports all University of California students and student groups, whatever their social or political commitment, in their efforts to bring about the repeal of these rules against political action. (applause) (And there's this final note of irony). The Association of California State College Professors is in complete accord with the eloquent words of university president Clark Kerr, to wit, 'when freedom of thought and expression have died on a university campus, it will be dead everywhere.' (applause)

It was subscribed to by 43 economics and political science t.a's on Friday. Again, in support of us, indicating that some people who are almost faculty are starting to break. (applause) ["]To the Regents and administration of the University of California, we wish to add our protest to the many that you have received during the present controversy over the rights of students to solicit funds and recruit others for political and social action. We urge you to restore the student rights that have traditionally existed on the Berkeley campus, including the right to solicit funds and recruit members. In this way, the University can maintain its highly commendable position of political neutrality, by allowing all political positions to be freely heard.["] (applause)

["]We further urge that in the interest of re-opening channels of communication with the students, the disciplinary action against the eight students be lifted. The undersigned."

Now, and I have some static from our friend[s] on just whether this should be raised, but I think that we have to raise it inasmuch as we've insisted thus far on keeping all kinds of problems that we've been having before all the students who are involved. I think we have to continue doing that. And, it's kind of like this—30 years ago, just about, in that period of time, there were a lot of people who in my opinion, and I'm sure there'll be people in the audience who disagree on this and I don't think that it affects the substance but it's a good preface, a lot of people involved in trying to effect progressive changes in the social and economic structure of the country. Now, at that time and since then at various subsequent times, a great bogey man has been raised. And this is the one of subversive infiltration and control of these activities. (laughter) That may be the bogey man.

(laughter) Now, as we all cannot help knowing, we are now in the sixties involved in another great movement being led at the present time by the negro people in their desire for freedom—another great movement for political and social liberality and fairness. All right. And again, again, the same phantom is being raised. Last summer, last summer—well the summer that's just past is what I mean—I was working in Mississippi, and almost every day the Jackson papers had some article showing how the activities in which we were engaged—in showing conclusively beyond any doubt—how the activities in which we were engaged were designed, were being carried out in accordance with a long-standing plan, according to one report, originally drafted in 1928—a long-standing plan to infiltrate and subvert the United States. Now, the issue has again been raised, and has been raised specifically with reference to the students on this campus. No one wants to admit that large numbers of people are damn sick and fed up with the way things are. (applause) Now, there was a statement—and I hope in view that we're going into negotiations, we'll treat this statement with a certain amount of personal dignity in our response to it—there was a statement issued by President Kerr. The statement must have been reported in several ways, but was reported at least in two ways and I have the two papers with the different reports. One of the reports is substantially more provocative than the other. I called the President's office in University Hall this morning and I indicated to the secretary that I could not responsibly be silent on that issue at this meeting. And I wanted to know which of these two reports—if either—in fact was an adequate reflection of the President's words. And the President was on the way to Davis at that time and they stopped him at the airport to find out. And the secretary called back and said that the less provocative of the two was an adequate expression of his words. (laughter) And we have no reason at all to suppose that's not the case inasmuch as there were plenty of people who could very easily have influenced that article—the more provacative [sic] one—and would have been very happy to do so. I don't know. Perhaps that's enough said. Maybe I don't even have to bother going on reading them. (laughter and talk) All right. First let me read the more provocative of the statements and then the one which I think in honesty we have to acknowledge on their word as being the a reflection of Clark Kerr's sentiments. This appeared in the San Francisco Examiner, Monarch of the

Dailies, of Saturday, October 3, 1964. It's on the front page and the head-line is "'Reds on Campus'—UC's Kerr." All right—there is a pun there but I . . . OK. (laughter) I'd like to read just the first part of it which contains the allegation—no need to read a long article—you'll see just what I mean. This has a by-line of a person you might want to contact. His name is Ben Williams. "University of California President Clark Kerr yesterday declared flatly that a hard core of 'Castro-Mao Tse Tung-line Communists' were in the crowd of demonstrators gathered in front of Sproul Hall on the Berkeley campus." (Obviously, we're in favor of all kinds of people speaking here and I would defend under any circumstances [the right of] Fidel Castro to speak here. (applause) But that's not the issue obviously that's being raised. It continues . . .) Kerr told an Examiner reporter that very few University students were actually involved in the hard core lead-ership. (It continues, and this is the only remaining part I'm going to read) "'There is an extreme left wing element there', he said, (this is all in quotes, but in fact it's not a quotation from him) "'49 per cent of the hard core group are followers of the Castro-Mao line.'" Quiet please. Now, we are going into negotiations, but I want you to please—it's very, very impor-tant—to keep on the look out for this kind of thing. Now, this Saturday, October 3—the same date—in the San Francisco Chronicle which has treated us a good deal better, I must say. (applause) Here, and these are the words which Clark Kerr officially acknowledges, "I am also sorry to say that some elements have been impressed with the tactics of Fidel Castro and Mao Tse Tung. There are very few of these, but there are some." I must say both those gentlemen impress me; I'm sure all are impressed by Fidel Castro and Mao Tse Tung. All right. I'd like to cut off my remarks now; there are a lot of people who would like to speak and we were going to go from 12 to 1 and I don't really see how we'll be able to adhere strictly to that. Let me just say that the organization which we have begun to set up—we are making specific provisions and will soon be announced in a very, very widespread way on campus for we are bringing as many independent students as possible on to the steering committee. (applause)

There's a question that I would like to take and then I would like to turn the microphone over to someone else.

(question not audible)

Oh, the committee—The question is who is choosing the committee which will decide upon the length of the suspension of the eight students. And this as originally an administration matter, but in accordance with the agreement we signed, it is now a faculty matter being handled by the— is it the committee of the Academic Senate? Faculty committee on student disciplinary matters, and the Academic Senate will choose the committee. Now, I'd like to turn the matter over to someone else. (applause)

Records of the Office of the Chancellor, University of California, Berkeley, CU-149, The Bancroft Library, University of California, Berkeley, published by permission of Lynne Hollander Savio.

SPEECH AT FREE SPEECH MOVEMENT RALLY,
SPROUL HALL STEPS

12 OCTOBER 1964

This FSM rally was designed to appeal for student and faculty support in pressing the UC administration to end its ban on political advocacy and to explain the first steps the FSM was taking in preparing for the imminent negotiations on the campus rules governing free speech. While no verbatim record of the rally exists, a detailed summary of the rally and Savio's speech at it was made for UC vice president Earl Bolton by someone close enough to Bolton to have simply signed it with his first name, Bruce. The account conveys not only the content and tone of Savio's speech and the rally itself— whose other speakers included Dusty Miller and Bettina Aptheker—but also the attitude of its author, who was clearly not enamored with the FSM. Thus the account of the rally opens, after offering an estimate of the crowd size at 250 to 300 students (and noting that the crowd's "enthusiasm was no doubt tempered by the weather"), with the claim that "the crowd was largely made-up of the sandal set"—a caricatured beatnik image of the protesters that was common among the FSM's detractors. The writer also was not well acquainted with most of the FSM's leadership, referring to Bettina Aptheker as "Pettine." But he did get Savio's name right, and his account, despite some garbled sentences, conveys Savio's critique of the administration accurately, even while reporting on it sarcastically.

Mario Savio (with his New York type accent): He attempted to place FSM in perspective, to tell what it stood for—free speech rights like those enjoyed on other state campuses (SF State figured prominently in all examples). Very dull. Then he asserted that the University has once again taken the initiative, and thus will give the general public, as well as other interested segments the feeling that it has gotten down to work on the issue, while the students merely mill-about in an emotional state. He further pointed out that a mire of University regulations exist concerning student political activity and free speech, and that many were contradictory, some dovetailed, etc. He said the regulations are bonds upon freedom of speech and freedom of expression because the people who are affected (students) cannot change them. He said the 14th Amendment is violated here. He said these new rules (new Communist speaker rule, 72 hour rules) are harassments.[46]

He stated that the Study Committee cannot be considered legitimate until it has been examined (as to structure, composition, frequency of meetings, method of decision-making, and strength of its recommendations), and then it will be decided whether FSM joins at all.[47] He wants a Peaceful Settlement, that will give all three sides (students, faculty, and administration) peace and a settlement. He said at the present time the National Student Association is conducting an investigation of the ASUC since it is really only a tool of the administration and does not have its own voice.[48]

Next brief topic was the Eli Katz case—Savio railed against the bureaucrats who cause all these troubles, and use[d] the Katz case as a rallying point for the faculty to join the students (his type) for freedom.[49] He said the faculty senate is indeed regarded and treated like the ASUC senate.[50]

He called a meeting of the FSM executive Committee for 6:30 P.M. upstairs in Westminster Hall. Also a meeting of the non-students would take place at the same time in the great hall of Westminster House.

Stressed that Thursday will be the "last ditch" appeal to the Regents. Pointed out that matters cannot be handled by demonstration, but only by sitting down and talking these things out with Strong, Kerr, or someone who has credentials and can speak for Kerr.

Mario Savio archive, copy in editor's possession, published by permission of Lynne Hollander Savio.

SPEECH AT FREE SPEECH MOVEMENT RALLY, SPROUL HALL STEPS

16 OCTOBER 1964

This would be the last FSM rally and Savio speech on campus until November, because the movement was shifting from a protest to negotiating stage. But, as Savio alludes to in this speech, this shift was almost short-circuited by flaws in the Pact of October 2 and by Chancellor Strong's attempt to control the composition of the committees charged with resolving the free speech disciplinary cases and assessing the rules governing political activity on campus.

The pact had provided for the Academic Senate Committee on Student Conduct (a faculty committee) to adjudicate the disciplinary cases, but it turned out that no such committee existed. So Strong appointed his own committee to hear these cases, which was unacceptable to the FSM, since it wanted a committee independent of the administration. Similarly, Strong appointed the four members of the faculty, four members of the administration, and two of the four students to the Campus Committee on Political Activity (CCPA), the body charged with resolving the dispute over the free speech regulations. This too was unacceptable to the FSM, which refused to participate in the deliberations of these committees until these representational issues were addressed.

Just as it looked as if the negotiation process was going to break down before it could even start, Kerr stepped in and made concessions acceptable to the FSM. He agreed to have the Academic Senate establish an ad hoc committee (independent of the administration) to handle the disciplinary cases. He also enlarged the CCPA. Half of the faculty delegates would now be chosen by the Academic Senate, and the number student representatives was increased to six, with four selected by the FSM, doubling the FSM's representation.

While these representational issues may seem merely technical or narrow, they were for the FSM a significant part of the struggle to have student rights and representation taken seriously. It meant ending the administration's monopoly of power, having independent faculty presiding over fair disciplinary reviews, and launching a serious review of the campus's antiquated political regulations. In effect, they embodied a radically dem-

*ocratic ethos the FSM was promoting in order to reform (or even revolu-
tionize) university governance. That ethos was reflected in Savio's remarks
at an October 12 meeting with Strong: "We don't respond as children
toward their parents; we respond as equals; this is a new situation and it
should be dealt with in a new way."*[51]

*The only surviving record of this October Savio speech is a police tran-
script sent by Captain Woodward to President Kerr and Chancellor Strong,
which is printed here verbatim, with only some badly garbled sections
repaired (with bracketed inserts).*

Before, not too long ago, we had fully intended to have this meeting enti-
tled this way: "One hour Informational Meeting; Please Bring Sleeping
Bags." Fortunately . . . we have not had to do it that way. I would like to
describe this to give a kind of feeling of what we have been in: A dream
which a friend of mine, formerly a member of the Steering Committee
until he found out that he just didn't have the time to do it, Dave Friedman
(?) had the following dream.

Clark Kerr was on the edge, on the very brink, you see, of a huge chasm.
And he was standing there, and he didn't know just where to go . . . He
was just wavering right on the edge. And here was the Free Speech
Movement running headlong toward him ready to grab hold and jump off
with him! And let me tell you, that's the way we felt a couple of days ago.
We've been accurately described as practicing brinkmanship, and I am
glad, in fact, that we are still standing on the edge and haven't gone over.
I think that probably President Kerr had a similar vision because the dispute was resolved just two hours before the five P.M. Thursday deadline
that *we* had set on any form of mediation for the dispute. (Applause)

And I would like now publicly to thank Professor Arthur Ross of the
Institute of Industrial Relations who served as a mediator. (Applause)
Professor Ross, who's had a great deal of experience. . . . with labor relations disputes, met with the Steering Committee at our meeting Wednesday
night at about 10:00 . . . and we talked until about 2:00, and then he went
across to meet with the administration, and the administration came
across with substantially what we had asked Professor Ross for with a few
face-saving changes in the wording, but nothing in the substance. So . . .
we've turned what was a partial defeat into a very substantial victory, and

we have gained a lot of experience in the art of bargaining from a position of weakness—and winning.

I would like now to describe briefly the substance of what we've got that is absolutely clear what it is. First of all, eight students were supposed to, according to that pact [of October 2] we signed, meet . . . before a subcommittee of the Academic Senate to have their cases . . . reviewed. And then came down a statement on high, that, in fact, they would meet before the Faculty Committee on Student Conduct, which was appointed by the Chancellor, and we said they would have to meet alone—we're not coming . . . And instead in our place went_____ Bethick . . . [Enrest Besig], who is deputy director of [the] Northern California ACLU, and their general council, Wayne Collins, [. . .] who challenged (1) the jurisdiction of the Committee (2) whether or not we had been granted our rights in the due process rule, and (3) most important, the constitutionality of the regulations we were accused of violating, see.

And well, that committee now has had the cases taken out of its hands completely. By unanimous vote of the Academic Senate there has been set up an Ad Hoc Committee of the Academic Senate by the members appointed today by the Committee on Committees to try this pattern. We will, of course, be represented by counsel; once again we'll question the constitutionality of the regulations—that's what we're fighting over—violating the first and fourteenth amendments and doing it pretty blatantly. And then . . . we had the right to record the meeting, and so on, and it will be both recorded and will make very good material for any future meetings of various kinds. Now, that concerns Point 4 of the original agreement.

Point 2 is the question of setting up a board for the [ad]judication of the entire dispute, and that board, you know, on Monday was unilaterally set up by the administration as a study committee. Well, it's not going to be called the study committee anymore, and it's not going to do study anymore. The following thing: The FSM has been officially recognized as the legitimate body to . . . negotiate the dispute____ ____ ____[Our position has been] strengthened. We will have present as negotiators—or disciplined negotiators—that means they will have a chairman; they will decide who talks when; they will have their policies set up; they will have the right to caucus; they will have five student observers appointed by our executive committee who will caucus with us; we will have a counsel present; and recordings will be taken in a way agreeable to the entire body.

Likewise, we . . . [won] something for the faculty, and I hope they will . . . be appropriately grateful, that the faculty contingent of this committee, two of its members will be added by the *Academic Senate* instead of by the Administration.

Now, concerning structure: [of the CCPA] . . . The administration wanted to have . . . equal numbers, so look what they've done. We now have 6 and 6 faculty, students. They put in two from the statewide university level which means, in fact, we're no longer negotiating for Berkeley, we're negotiating for the *University of California!* (Applause). There was . . ., in the original agreement it said hearings and discussions, and we kind of had a feeling those hearings might drag out indefinitely. So we said meetings of this Committee've got to be split into two parts, the hearings first—they will take now more than two weeks—and these will be at the rate of about 2 or 3 meetings a week. This is in the statement that Chairman [Robley] Williams will make. Now at those hearings . . . we'll have people in [the] civil rights movements, for example, come and say, "Look, you're destroying us." There'll be public hearings, and we'll scrap the whole business, so we're going to get really a great show.

Now, two important things remain, and they are these: We were *very* interested to know that these be resolved in a way favorable to us . . . . First of all, the question of who can submit evidence and . . . rule the evidence either in or out of order. We can't have the chairman doing that. Well, in fact, any one of the three bodies can submit any evidence they consider to be relevant to the proceedings, and it cannot be ruled out of order. (Applause) As concerns weight of recommendations, both parties understand that shortly, which means within one or two days, President Kerr will indicate how strongly he intends to take . . . the recommendations of this committee.

And now the most important point, how does it make decisions? We can't have it deciding by majority vote; we wouldn't buy that. Its decisions are made by consensus. What does that mean? It means there are three parties that have a vote apiece—no agreements without three votes. They didn't agree, because that's a face-saving thing—they didn't agree to officially disband the committee. Instead, they've changed its name and radically reconstituted it.

I want to indicate that this cannot be the end of the Free Speech Movement, because we have only . . . [won] one very, very substantial thing: We have a committee that can do the job, and we only . . . [won on] procedural matters—that's got to be understood. They've been decided . . . in a way completely favorable, but only [regarding] procedural matters, and there's a possibility that when the third comes along that might decide, well, enough of the procedure and then all just won't show up. So they've got to understand—and only a broad base of support on the campus can make them understand—that if something like . . . [that] can be pulled, or an attempt can be made, that once again . . . we will be out on the pavement with our sleeping bags. And if they're foolish enough to send a police car out, you know, the whole bit. (Applause).

Now you can see, in a way the Free Speech fight has been started. Now we really have to do the hard work of seeing to it that this committee, hands down, strongly consider[s] recommendation[s] concerning the kind of things we'd like to see on this campus as concerns . . . political activities, political rights. Now, that concerns the substance; I'd just like to make some general observations. Yesterday, right down, not too far from Sather Gate . . ., there were several professors, and they were talking about how intransitant [intransigent] and how unreasonable the Free Speech Movement was being handled, and I happened to walk up. And we got into a kind of debate. And I suspect that some of the people that are here . . . were probably . . . around, as a large crowd gathered around, cause I love to talk. What they were suggesting is the following: If you really mean to get free speech on the campus, you're going to have to send your two delegates to this committee cause it's obvious the administration can't back down any further. You're going to have to send your two delegates to this committee and then just . . . hope upon the good graces of the Berkeley administration members that they won't disband the committee in a manner which will be [un]acceptable to the Free Speech Movement.

Well, all right. They judged wrong. A lot of people who have been giving us advice during the last three weeks have really judged wrong at just about every turn. Their position was as follows, and one of them argued very passionately for it: First, of course, that we could change the committee from the inside. That may be true, but we've dealt with these people long enough not to want to take those kind[s] of chances. They represent, they say, some kinds of legal points, and they were as follows: That, legally, students at a university in the United States are recognized in terms of the administration as *children*. This is what the man said . . . . And, I said, well, that may be legally so, but it's, in fact, not the case now, at the University of California. (Applause) And so I asked, after the debate had gone on for awhile,—it turned out to be just between this person and myself after awhile—I said, "Are you suggesting, therefore, that the tactic we should use this time to obtain freedom of speech on this campus is complete capitulation?" And he said, "Yes." Imagine! . . . . [But we have seen to the contrary, that] the University does, in fact, unilaterally, capitulate. We should be very happy about what we have achieved.

Now there stands one more brief kind of comment. The pact of October 2nd was very loosely worded and very ambiguously worded. And, if the circumstances were not what they had been, it's well known by now we'd never have agreed to it. However, we have not permitted a certain wily negotiator, Clark Kerr, to make that agreement be what I imagine he had intended it to be—(1) a way to end a demonstration, (2) a way to get the students off his back, and (3) a way to pretend that, after all, nothing special had occurred in the first place. By refusing to meet with any committee set up by the University in unilateral violation of the agreement [the Pact of October 2] . . . and by [insisting that] the students who submit the case of our suspension[s be heard by a committee appointed by the faculty not the administration, . . . we] start . . . [with more fair and independent] proceedings [than the administration sought to impose. We] have made the University admit that something new, something extraordinary, has occurred and that has to be treated in an extraordinary way—not by the ordinary channels.

We have bent lovingly over the baby being born. The question of who governs on the campus, you know, that it be kind of pregnant. And by our courage, . . . by dignity in the face of unprovoked violence, by the insatiable adherence to principle of the students on this campus . . . we've shown ourselves guilty of one thing—of passionately entering into a conspiracy to uphold the first and fourteenth Amendments. (Applause).

The question has been asked . . . until this thing is over, what rules we'll go by. Well, they're flexible today; they haven't questioned us on this; as you know they made a public statement yesterday in the Daily Cal. We've decided that we really need to make negotiations, of course, and that we're going to hold to the regulation, exactly as set down, give themselves such time as the committee does hold its meeting[s] . . . [until] . . . a deadlock, which I hope that won't happen. I think that it's a kind of show of good faith not to . . . [defy rules] of this kind [while they are being negotiated].

Records of the Office of the Chancellor, University of California, Berkeley, CU-149, The Bancroft Library, University of California, Berkeley, published by permission of Lynne Hollander Savio.

COMMITTEE ON CAMPUS POLITICAL ACTIVITY,
MINUTES OF MEETING

7 NOVEMBER 1964

Contrary to the stereotyped image of 1960s rebels as perpetually manning the barricades and agitating, the Free Speech Movement pulled back from protesting for an extended period—mid-October through early November—and entered a second negotiating phase (the first period of negotiations had lasted a week in mid-September). The primary focus was on the Committee on Campus Political Activity, where the FSM, over the course of the CCPA's seven meetings, sought to win the faculty to its side. This attempt proved unsuccessful, since the administration insisted—with the support of the CCPA's faculty delegation—on retaining the right to discipline students if their advocacy on campus led to illegal actions off campus. This was unacceptable to the FSM on the principles of both free speech and due process and because the "unlawful" advocacy UC sought to bar included civil rights sit-ins and other protests involving civil disobedience.

What follows is an excerpt from the last CCPA meeting, which offers a view of the issues being debated as the committee reached its final impasse.

[Dean Frank] Kidner: . . . The fundamental principle upon which the vote of the administration will go is that if the University modifies its

present regulations and thus permits organization, planning, recruitment
. . . for off-campus political and social action, then participants who are
students who are involved in unlawful acts on or off campus and the
organizations . . . may well be subject to the internal discipline of the
University. This is a fundamental principle. . . . I propose to read to you . . .
an amendment. . . . "If acts unlawful under California or federal law
directly result from advocacy, organization, or planning on the campus,
the students and organizations involved may be subject to such disciplinary action as is appropriate and conditioned upon a fair hearing as to the
appropriateness of the action taken." . . .

Savio: Concerning the first part of the amendment, "unlawful under
California or federal law", by what means will it be judged if these acts are
unlawful?

Kidner: I am not prepared to say. . . .

Savio: Would you consider an act not to be unlawful unless it has been
so judged in a court of law?

. . . First, where no one is in fact arrested but there was some action
which has been judged by some persons to be unlawful. The second case
is one for which in committing the same acts some of the participants are
convicted but others are acquitted, in those two cases what would be the
criterion by which unlawfulness would be decided?

Kidner: My understanding of the position of the administration would
be that, with respect to the individual student, an unlawful act could not
be determined to be unlawful by University sources. If the organization
could be shown to have organized and be responsible for this, I think the
organization might be subject to disciplinary action by the University.

Savio: How would one determine that the organization was indeed
responsible? Would this be determined in a court of law?

Kidner: I think it would not necessarily be determined in a court of law.
. . . Let us suppose that a recognized student organization organizes,
plans, recruits, as under these regulations it could, off-campus political
action, specifically a lawful act of picketing some place. At this point there
is no problem. Let us suppose that . . . if that group then were to change its
tactics at that time and commit an unlawful act, and if these facts could be
shown, then I think that organization and students directly involved
would be held responsible with respect to University discipline. . . .

Savio: In the example you have just given then we incur nothing unlawful on the campus. . . .

. . . You brought up the example of a picket line being advocated on campus, which subsequently off campus turns into something else and then by some procedure is decided to be unlawful. It seems to me that the original advocacy could fall within full legality, with no violation of solicitation or conspiracy law. I understand that you would reserve the right in any case to hold those who advocated the original picketing to be responsible.

Kidner: . . . Mr. Savio, if you insist upon a straight yes or no, then I would have to answer yes. I would say that this has to do with the direct result and with the finding of some sense of direct responsibility by the organization concerned. It is difficult to determine this.

[Professor of history and economics Henry] Rosovsky: . . . We spoke before of a case in which some participants, say in a picket line, engage in common action and that 50% of the people are convicted and the other 50% are acquitted. Then you imply that the organization collectively might be held responsible for illegal action. Am I correct so far?

[Professor of law Sanford] Kadish: Yes. . . .

Savio: I would like to ask an even more carefully constructed version of Mr. Rosovsky's question. What if, for a variety of reasons, one of the several participants has been arrested, one of them pleads guilty and the rest are acquitted, do I understand that the University would under such circumstances reserve the right to take disciplinary action against the sponsoring organization?

Kidner: I believe if the responsibility could be traced to the student organization that would happen. . . .

Savio: . . . I turn now to the question, which is really the crucial one, the question of who decides unlawfulness of acts whether committed on or off campus and who decides this question of responsibility which is the one, as I understand it, on which you are basing disciplinary action. Can the University, in your understanding, under some circumstances itself find off-campus acts to be unlawful?

Kidner: I believe not.

Savio: Then it seems to be to be an inconsistency. Can the University itself find acts committed on campus to be unlawful?

Kidner: I think that answers itself; I think they cannot.

Savio: Can the University take disciplinary action against students who have not been found by courts of law to be involved in any unlawful act any place?

Kidner: I would say the University could take action where acts on the campus are in violation of University regulations.

Savio: If the kinds of things the students are doing fall under the general area of speech or organization in political matters, can the University take disciplinary action against such students if they have not previously been found guilty in a court of law? . . .

The last sentence on the blackboard I think now is the point we have come to—"fair hearing". Do we understand this to be a trial in a court of law? If not, why does the University insist upon prior right of judgment in these matters? What is a fair hearing?

Kidner: I mean a hearing which the University would conduct. It would be a hearing by the University. . . .

Savio: . . . The thing we are seeking is that genuine neutrality which the University is not prepared to grant. . . .

I would like very briefly to state three points which give the reasons for our position concerning this. Under the first sentence of the original proposal it is the advocacy which is protected. Advocacy of unlawful acts is in fact protected by the law. If it is the advocacy which is to be protected, this does not do it. We can advocate illegal acts under certain circumstances. Advocacy of not paying income tax is a very political thing. There is the question of intent versus wording. We are voting on the words, not the intent, that Mr. Kidner has said is his understanding regarding fair hearing. Because of the kinds of external pressures to which the University is subject I doubt very gravely that the University would be capable of giving a fair hearing. The FSM position must be that in both instances in this amendment where acts of speech are involved the only criterion we will accept for illegality or unlawfulness is determination by conviction in a court of law. . . .

Savio: I would likewise like to introduce an amendment. . . .

[Bettina] Aptheker: . . . We were instructed to make this amendment by the Executive Committee of the FSM. . . . "In the area of first amendment rights and civil liberties the University may impose no disciplinary action against members of the University community and organizations.

In this area members of the University Community and organizations are subject only to the civil authorities." . . .

Savio: The crucial difference between our position and the administration position has been stated ad nauseam. We hold the only set of authorities, the only body competent in all senses of the word to judge upon the legality or illegality of acts in the area of 1st amendment rights is the civil authorities. . . .

The question is not a legal one. The University is not bound to interpret anything here in the impartial legal way you interpret at this meeting. It is therefore not equipped to conduct a fair hearing, is not equipped to decide these questions of law. We must insist that, as our position, the only authorities competent in this matter of deciding questions of law are the civil authorities. . . .

Free Speech Movement Digital Archive, Bancroft Library, complete transcript of this and all the CCPA meetings are available online at www.oac. cdlib.org/ark:/13030/kt9g5006z8/?brand = oac4.

SAVIO'S REMARKS AT FSM PRESS CONFERENCE

9 NOVEMBER 1964

With the breakdown of negotiations on the CCPA, Savio and the FSM announced that movement activists would end their moratorium on exercising their free speech rights on campus. This meant a return to defying UC's restrictions on advocacy by staffing of political tables on campus and resuming demonstrations on behalf of free speech. The FSM was now entering its final stage, shifting from negotiation to protest. To explain this shift and the breakdown of negotiations, the FSM held a press conference at which Savio spoke.

Question: Wasn't this proposal of the administration to really tighten the restrictions rather than lift them that you objected to, don't you think that was in the nature of a ploy for collective bargaining purposes possibly? It's common to ask for a lot more than you're going to get in the hopes that you won't have to give so much in the end.

Savio: I wish we were in a situation where the words "collective bargaining" would be applicable—that would be fine. That would be a great improvement upon the present situation. But you see the committee [the CCPA] makes recommendations to the university [administration]. So what we would have, in other words, would be a collective bargaining situation where the firm sets up the collective bargaining apparatus in order to make recommendations to the firm. No, it's not that.

Furthermore, this proposal was not made by the administration—this final proposal. It was made by the faculty members on the committee and is considerably more liberal than the administration up until then had been willing to accept, [it] embodied, nevertheless, the very principle to which we are unconditionally opposed to. It was in other words, an attempt by the faculty members to package in a sufficiently appealing form—in terms of nice words—the principle that the administration insisted on, namely, that in certain areas of political rights at the discretion of the university, and at its own determination, if abuses of political rights occur then the university reserves the right to take disciplinary action. This principle, as I say, was nicely packaged in this final faculty proposal. But the principle is totally unacceptable. We maintain—and shall continue to do so—that in the area of political rights, the civil authorities and *only* the civil authorities may (1) determine if there has been an abuse; (2) take such action as is appropriate and with regard for full due process of law. So it was not, as a matter of fact, what you maintain that it was. . . . We embodied the principle I've just stated in one form or wording, and it was rejected by the committee. That was the final vote.

This was the wording we adopted for simplicity in the committee. I'll read that, and then I'll read a more complete legal statement, which we have made with the help of counsel. This was rejected by the committee: "In the area of First Amendment rights and civil liberties the university may impose no disciplinary action against members of the university community and organizations"—not just students, note. "In this area members of the university community and organizations are subject only to the civil authorities." They rejected that principle. I think that makes it clear. I don't think there is any need for a longer statement. . . .

Question: Assemblyman [Don] Mulford first raised this question of disciplinary actions on civil rights cases [and punishing students arrested in the Sheraton Palace sit-in]. Dr. Kerr [in his UC Davis speech in May 1964] took a stand rejecting the Mulford position, that this would be double jeopardy, and the university would not take disciplinary action against students who were involved in that outside community activity. Dean Kidner's proposal [at the CCPA]—which I assume you are referring to now—if adopted, would seem to me [to] constitute a complete reversal of Dr. Kerr's initial position and a bridge towards Mulford's position.

Savio: We must, of course, distinguish between rhetoric and positions of universities. There *has* been a change in the position of the university for the worse.

The position of the university to which Mr. Coleman refers was originally this: that the university does not follow students off the campus, and in their role as citizens, as they've put it, they are subject only to the civil authorities. In order to take that position, the university instituted regulations which denied students the right to advocate off-campus political and social action from the campus. So in other words, they would not follow us off campus provided we did not propose anything on campus which they would want to take action against when it occurred off campus.

Well, they've changed their position, yes. Now we can advocate on campus. But in exchange for that, they want to follow us off campus and take disciplinary action against us if something occurs there that they don't like. So yes, there's been a reversal for the worse instead of being for the better. . . .

We conceived of . . . [the] pact [of October 2] as setting up the machinery to do two things, at least. (1) To study the regulations [regarding political expression], because perhaps they were unclear to the faculty and to the administration. . . . What we were being restricted from doing was quite clear to us, though I must say that exactly which regulations were doing the restricting, *that* was unclear to us also. So the committee [CCPA] has that valuable purpose. It had an addition[al purpose]—and that was why we subscribed and the only reason we did—and the only reason we agreed to a self-imposed moratorium on the exercise of political rights. We thought that it might likewise serve as one means to help us secure our rights. It's now clear that it simply does not serve that function. . . . This Committee on Campus Political Activity is simply incapable of helping us at all to secure our political rights. It can still serve again . . . as a forum in which the faculty can come to understand exactly what's at stake. And I would hope that that does occur. In other words, we were going to go there Wednesday and meet with them. And as I say, I hope that the faculty can learn from the give-and-take on that committee, now that we have no illusions concerning its power, . . . can learn just what the problems are. However, because it is absolutely clear now . . . that the administration does not mean this to be a committee which can serve to get us our rights, we can no longer maintain the self-imposed moratorium. And so, as we have today, we will continue *every* day to exercise our constitutionally guaranteed political rights [by defying the ban on campus political advocacy].

Q: Could you describe what you consider to be the results of today's [Sproul] rally [the first to be held since the CCPA meetings began in mid-October, since the FSM had agreed to a moratorium on such defiance of the ban while the CCPA negotiations over the campus free speech regulations were proceeding]? Big success for your folks?

Savio: I would say so. While deans were sent down to take students' names, and did so—approximately twenty, I think—we exercised our political rights. And that's what we're after. So, if I may say so, the Pact of 1789 [the Bill of Rights] was upheld by this meeting, and that is precisely what we had started out to do. . . . In the past, this [the deans taking down of the names of protesters] has resulted in indefinite suspensions, . . . "a species of suspension invented at the time for the purpose" [of suppressing the Free Speech Movement]. . . . This is what has happened in the past. It may happen again.

Transcribed from audiotape, Mario Savio archives, copy in editor's possession, published by permission of Lynne Hollander Savio.

SPEECH AT FSM RALLY ON SPROUL PLAZA BEFORE THE MARCH TOWARD UNIVERSITY HALL, THE SITE OF THE UC BOARD OF REGENTS MEETING

20 NOVEMBER 1964

The high point of the FSM's new phase of protest came in connection with the UC Board of Regents meeting, when the movement sought to bring its

*free speech demands to the university's highest governing board. The FSM
organized intensely for this day of protest, planning first a rally on Sproul
Plaza, a march down to the large grass lawn on the campus's western edge,
across the street from the meeting of the regents in University Hall, and an
FSM delegation to speak to the regents. As an added draw, the FSM had
invited folk singer Joan Baez, who would play at the rally. A crowd of three
thousand to five thousand (estimates varied) attended the rally, and the
FSM leadership, including Savio, dressed up for the decorous march to
University Hall, which would be captured in that iconic photo (see frontis-
piece) of FSM leaders—including Savio, clad in jacket and tie—and faculty leading a march through the Sather Gate, holding aloft a banner
emblazoned with the words "FREE SPEECH." Savio's address at this rally,
which oddly has never before appeared in print, offers his most searching
critique of Kerr's position on political advocacy, a philosophical defense of
the FSM's more democratic vision of the university, and his most explicit
comparisons yet between the FSM and the civil rights movement.*

I'd like to speak very briefly—no, I'd like to speak briefly—about some topics which were opened up already by Martin Roysher and by Professor
[Morton D.] Paley.[52] And they have to do with a theme that President
Kerr took for his ninety-sixth Charter Day Address [that he] delivered at
[UC] Davis. In that address, he set down what I suppose might be considered the philosophy of the administration's point of view. The philosophy
behind the actions they've taken and the positions they've adopted. That's
where it was clearly stated . . . this dichotomy between people as students
and people as citizens, where the dichotomy was really set out clearly and
was likened to the corresponding dichotomies between citizens and members of religious groups, citizens and members of labor unions. All these
different roles, as President Kerr put it, have about the same logical
status. They're next to one another. No real hierarchy obtains among
them. This conception has a name. Sociologists, with no offense to one on
the platform, have a way, spend their time making up fancy names
for things which, if they were laid out right before us, we'd get rid of right
off. This is called the "pluralistic society." This conception of all of these
different interest groups and all of these different roles having the same
status, more or less, and being parallel to one other logically—no hierar-

chy. That's the view that President Kerr presented in the Charter Day speech.

And from that point of view, from that philosophy, he derived a response to Don Mulford, who had recommended that those students who had taken part in the Sheraton Palace demonstrations should be expelled from the university, at very least should come under severe punishment from the university. And President Kerr's response was "No, we'll not do that, because they were acting as citizens not as students off the campus," you see, "and therefore we have no right to apply any kind of punishments. We have no right to apply separate penalties and separate trials for activities that already came under, that come under, some kind of censure of law." That was the position—the philosophy and the position.

Now for us, that means if you're on a picket line, you're a citizen but not a student. Then if you're standing on Sproul Hall steps advocating joining a picket line and happen to be a student, then you're a student but not a citizen. Or at the very least, . . . if you're a student, you're subject to university discipline. And the university is not institutionally concerned with the fact that you're subject to other kinds of discipline as well. And it tries to apply its own discipline, because you're acting in your role as a student. It sets up a lot of dichotomies and separations. Martin Roysher was talking about . . . a world that's dead and one that's powerless to be born. A lot of dichotomies are set up like this—dichotomies set up within the human being himself, between what he knows and what he does, between what he studies and the actions he can perform, dichotomies set up between inside the university and out, between inside the human being and out. All these dichotomies. They likewise have a fancy sociological name. It's called "alienation," and we have a damned lot of it!

The word *know* is used in two senses that we're going to distinguish. One here at the university: you know what you learn, what you read in your book. But in the Bible there's another sense: the sense that you "know" a woman. In that sense, you can't separate knowledge from action. Well, the same is true of knowledge of political science, knowledge of sociology, knowledge of history. You separate the knowledge from the action, there is no knowledge. There is none. All right.

Fortunately, or unfortunately, some of the people on the other side haven't closed their eyes to the fact that no such dichotomies exist. The powers that have exercised extralegal pressure upon the university—which pressure the university acknowledges—those powers don't recognize a dichotomy between students and citizens. They know that student citizens on the campus can do quite as much damage and, in many instances, more than student citizens off the campus, where the things being damaged are certain powers which have been usurped by extralegal authorities. I'm talking about the civil rights movement. I'm taking about the pressures which have been exerted on the university to stifle civil rights ferment on campus. William Knowland doesn't recognize the distinction—and we don't either, but for different reasons.[53]

What we've been disciplined for—it seems to me—has been . . . our lack of hypocrisy in setting up these artificial distinctions. We've been disciplined for insisting on being citizens *all the time,* whether we're on campus or off. And in doing so, there is a kind of implicit philosophy in what we've done, which is exactly counterposed to this notion of a pluralistic society. It's a notion of a kind of hierarchical, organic, democratic society. Hierarchical, what do we mean? Well, that certain values, certain roles take precedence over other roles. You're always a citizen, but perhaps you're not always functioning as a worker in a particular plant. You're always a citizen, even when you're in that plant regularly. When an employer censured by firing their workers for taking part in political activity, we look upon this as an horrendous violation of the spirit of the Constitution. Well, certainly so for the university, when the university censures its students for taking an active role as citizens—citizens they are, whether on campus or off—we should look upon it in the same way as a vile and pretentious usurpation of powers of the courts and likewise as a complete flaunting of the ideals of the First, the Fourteenth Amendments, of the whole constitutional tradition, because we're not . . . citizens just off the campus, we're citizens right now. Right now we're acting as citizens. Right now we're confronting . . . the same powers we're confronting when we're on picket lines, only they're more nicely packaged here—the same powers. They understand that. We do.

Twenty-five centuries—more or less—ago, this conception of hierarchical structure, of an organic view of society was written down in Plato's *Republic.* What was Plato afraid of? Well, he was afraid that the aggressive, irrational element in men should rule men's actions. And he saw that this imbalance—this putting next to one another and giving equal weight to one another of things not naturally equal—was mirrored in society itself. So he went to see what justice in a man meant by looking to see what justice in society means. He found that it meant, again, a hierarchical structure where what is properly first takes precedence.

All right. Take a look at the university. Very parallel. There was a tripartite soul, the tripartite state, there's a tripartite university. It has a head. It has a heart. And it has bowels. Just the same as in Plato's *Republic*. There are some things which properly should take precedence. Knowledge, embodied in the faculty, should take precedence. It should rule with the heart of the university, you know, the students. Servants [i.e., the administration] definitely, definitely servants should be what remains.

In a book called *The Open Society and Its Enemies*, I think that's the name—yeah, by Karl Popper, right? By Karl Popper (I just asked Professor [John] Searle, who should know). . . . Plato and a lot of the things that have come out of him have been opposed to this pluralistic conception as totalitarianism, as opposed to a pluralistic conception.[54] Well, it's a kind of simple-minded view. There's a third camp, at least, namely an organic but democratic society where the structure in society corresponds with a sense of value which comes right out of the nature of the thing. That those who know that their points of view should in some way take precedence, but that, of course, they should not be the ones completely to the side who are the ones who know.

This is the kind of thing that we want here at the university. And this is the kind of thing that we want in the society outside. Those who've taken part in the civil rights movement are trying to, it seems to me, bind up the wounds which separate society, which have put rents in its fabric, bind up the wounds that put next to one other things which should be one subordinate . . . to the other. This is the kind of thing . . . that we want to do here. And we're demanding the tools to do it. Those tools are certain procedural rights, rights to the First and Fourteenth Amendments. We demand the tools to bind up this wound. Citizens, students traditionally have been the ones who most keenly feel the way in which society's fabric is rent. Therefore, students *certainly* should be the ones who have the tools in their hands, the tools of freedom of expression, the tools whereby these wounds can be bound up, whereby what is first in nature should be first in law, should be put first in law. This is precisely what we're asking for.

Before I finish, I'd just like to draw attention to two things. First of all, it's not just political and social action organizations whose rights have been trampled upon. There is an organization here which represents intellectual freedom in the scientific community—namely Particle Berkeley. The university, in order to impose certain restrictions upon political expression and because of a certain lack of proper discrimination, has simply said, "no free student expression." We're fighting for genuine academic and intellectual freedom on the campus for all. The issue *is* broadened. And it's been broadened precisely because of the arbitrary acts of the university.

And finally, I'd like to say somehow the atmosphere of today compared with the atmosphere around that [police] car [on Sproul Plaza in October]. It's kind of like the March on Washington as compared to Birmingham. One would be impossible without the other. But one represents a kind of progress upon the other. Here we're going to, we have demonstrated our strength, we're going to again demonstrate it. Now that I think the cause that we represented has made its justice so manifest, we can represent that cause in another way—a way which *we hope* will be able to make more of an impression upon those who right now have the power to bring freedom to the campus of the University of California.

Transcribed from audiotape, Mario Savio archives, copy in editor's possession, published by permission of Lynne Hollander Savio.

SPEECH AT FSM RALLY ON THE WESTERN EDGE OF THE BERKELEY CAMPUS, AFTER ATTENDING THE BOARD OF REGENTS MEETING IN UNIVERSITY HALL

20 NOVEMBER 1964

To say that the FSM was disappointed with the regents meeting would be a vast understatement. After two months of struggling to get their free speech demands considered, FSM activists were appalled that the regents refused to allow an FSM delegation even to speak at the meeting (Savio and the FSM delegation were permitted only to watch the proceedings from the gallery), and the regents refused even to consider the movement's call to end university restrictions on political advocacy. The regents also disregarded the recommendation of UC Berkeley's faculty—the Heyman Committee—which, after careful deliberation on the student suspensions, had criticized the administration's disciplinary procedures and vacated most of the suspensions. Reporters on the scene at the FSM vigil on the lawn wrote that students sat there in "stunned silence and co-eds burst into tears" upon learning of the regents' decisions.[55] Savio's speech after the regents meeting reflects this FSM shock and anger and contrasts dramatically with his more hopeful and upbeat speech before the meeting.

The faculty proposal which was put before the Board of Regents in this question of advocacy of off-campus political and social action gave the students far weaker protection than are guaranteed them by the United States Constitution. The Board of Regents didn't think that was bad enough. So they took Clark Kerr's recommendation, which we have evidence was cooked up by their [UC] general counsel, [Thomas] Cunningham—and we presented that in the *Daily Cal* already, evidence that it was cooked up by . . . Cunningham before the . . . middle of October, at least. The . . . same wording, this insertion of the word *lawful*, the same wording which Clark Kerr read had been recommended by the general counsel, and we documented it.[56]

And the reason the general counsel gave was that the regulation as then in effect could not be defended in a court of law, because it clearly is unconstitutional. That's documented likewise. So he recommended "insert this word, change the structure of the wording a little bit so that they will be a little bit more defensible so we'll have some chance in a court case."

So Clark Kerr made a recommendation today to the Board of Regents, and I'll read the recommendation. First, it's in two paragraphs. (1) "The regents restate the longstanding university policy as set forth in regulation 25 on student conduct and discipline that 'all students and student organizations . . . obey the laws of the state and community.'" That's fine. (2) "The regents adopt the policy effective immediately that certain campus facilities carefully selected and properly regulated may be used by students and staff for planning, implementing, or raising funds, or recruiting participants for lawful off-campus action not for unlawful off-campus action."

That is far stricter than anything any faculty member has proposed. It's exactly the policy that the president decided to adopt and decided to recommend to the regents back in the middle of October and has the effect of putting students in the university who are advocating these things, putting them in a situation of prior restraint. It's against the law! It violates the Constitution! And here it is—the regents just passed it. A bunch of "wise men."

Last week I said . . . that if the regents don't come down with too horrendous restrictions, then I guess—for a while anyway—we're going to have to fold up shop. And I didn't say that with regret, because I'm damned tired. I think that most people who have come out to demonstrations and have been at rallies, . . . we're all awfully tired of having to spend our time defending the Constitution because the regents are too busy deciding whether dividends on stocks the regents hold are coming through well enough! They read a whole report on just that matter. They'd just got done with that, and they're quite happy, because they really have a going concern. Business is . . . shooting along just fine. But here they are, they set down their unconstitutional restrictions on *our* freedoms.

But courts are not enough, according to them. It's not enough that laws already exist against illegal speech. It's not enough that it's a crime to advocate crime under certain circumstances—no, worse, it's got to be, likewise, against university regulations far stricter than would hold up in any court of law. They're not prepared to indict you on the crimes of solicitation to crime or criminal conspiracy, no, they'll leave that to the district attorney—they know he's anxious. No, they want something stronger. They want to decide when you've abused your freedom of speech. They want to decide, not the courts, not the Constitution.

And then when they've made the decision in their administrative hearings—and you know what that will mean. They'll probably appoint some faculty members—it's got to look respectable—who will then, you see, make recommendations to the chancellor, just like the Heyman Committee made recommendations, which were *not* accepted, that's what they're going to do. Administrative hearings are going to decide when you've abused your freedom of speech, and then the university is going to decide what should be done about those abuses, what kind of disciplinary actions should be taken.

Well, now, negotiations [on eliminating racially discriminatory hiring practices] have broken down at the *Oakland Tribune*. We're going to start advocating that people go down there. You know what's going to happen? Might just turn out that, in somebody's opinion, unlawful acts have occurred. They don't even leave it up to the courts, the way the faculty does.[57] I suppose they're going to decide if the acts that occur there are unlawful. Let's say, for example, there are sit-ins that may occur. Let's say that some people may be convicted, others acquitted, hung juries may result in some cases. But the actions will be the same, and the university, according to this, has the power to decide that *all* were committing unlawful acts and that whatever advocacy took place on campus was not legitimate advocacy—that it was an abuse of free speech. And then, when they decide it was an abuse of free speech, Campus CORE is axed, its leaders are axed, whatever other groups took part, likewise. This is what they want to do. Well, pretty soon they're going to have a chance to enforce it. And I'm serving public notice on them now, we're going to be ready for them. We're not going to take it sitting down. If they try to enforce these unconstitutional regulations, they're going to suffer for it!

Transcribed from audiotape, Mario Savio archives, published by permission of Lynne Hollander Savio. Audio also available online at www.lib. berkeley.edu/MRC/FSM/fsmchronology1.html.

SPEECH BEFORE THE ABORTED SIT-IN

23 NOVEMBER 1964

The question of what to do in response to the regents meeting proved divisive for the FSM leadership. All were appalled by the arrogance of power displayed by the regents. But the Steering Committee, even after a forty-eight-hour meeting, could not reach a consensus about whether to stage a sit-in to protest the regents' refusal to end UC's restrictions on free speech. Savio strongly advocated such a sit-in as a moral statement, but others on the Steering Committee felt that, bad as the policy decisions were, no new actions had yet been taken to implement them, and the matter was too abstract to use as a justification for mass civil disobedience.

The Steering Committee narrowly approved sitting in but, in an act of hyper-democratic idealism and tactical foolishness, also took the extraordinary step of airing these divisions and the arguments of both sides on Sproul Plaza right before the sit-in. It was a striking act of candor to be so open about the lack of a leadership consensus on the sit-in, but, obviously, not a way of inspiring protesters to go in and take the risks involved in such an act of civil disobedience. The sit-in drew only a few hundred participants, and so the Steering Committee decided—with Savio objecting— to abort the action at Sproul's closing time, since courting arrest in such an ineffective protest did not seem worthwhile.

Since the sit-in proved a failure, Savio's speech before it has been forgotten. But the speech offers one of Savio's most able explorations of the free speech and due process issues at stake in the FSM, and it also captures his transparent style of leadership as he candidly discussed the movement's internal divisions over sitting in.

There are five things that I'd like to say. First, we haven't, on the report of faculty members, they've asked me not to reveal their names. That the problem with saying it's the original faculty proposal which has been accepted is the following. President Kerr . . . never presented . . . the [faculty] report to the regents before asking them [to approve his less liberal motion]. . . . I was there and I saw that. . . . Because he knew that they would not accept it [the faculty report]. That's the first thing.

Let's argue to what they say the policy is. There are two acts you must consider. . . . The act of advocacy which takes place on campus and acts off campus, some of which may have been advocated from on the campus. They tried to obscure the issue by saying something is going to be decided by the courts. But what that is, is the lawfulness or unlawfulness of the acts off the campus, not the acts on. There already are laws which govern speech as to whether it is abusive or not. The courts already provide safeguards. It's illegal speech. There is such a thing as illegal speech. The administration proposes to set up its own standards to decide if speech has been an abuse of free speech. And then, by their own administrative hearing after its finding, make a judgment as to what should be done about that. That they've admitted. That's what we're against.

The question of prior restraint. If I get up to speak, I take into account the fact that I may well be violating the law by speaking. But if I further have to take account of some action the administration may take, depending upon some future action over which I perhaps have no control and in which I'm going to take no part, then I don't know the extent to which my speech is abusive or not. I don't know if it's a violation of law or not. And the question of whether it violates the law is not the only criterion which determines whether I shall be disciplined. But, likewise, whether in an administrative hearing it's decided my language was abusive because the administration decides it was not appropriate. This is what we're against. Again, they admit they want this right.

The important thing is what kind of charges will they bring in these hearings and how will these hearings be conducted. Now, if they mean to bring the same charges that could be brought in a court of law and mean to give the same kind of due process as would be given in a court of law, there's no excuse for not putting it in a court of law in the first place. And I presented . . . this very question to Dean Kidner in the statewide administration . . . at an ASUC [Student] Senate meeting.

He refused to answer the question. And he said the following at that meeting. And then, when he found that KPFA was recording the meeting, he insisted the recording be turned over to the senate for its editing. He said the following at this meeting when he presented that position. He said, "I am not here to defend either the wisdom or the justice of this position, but only to present this position." That's all. That's what Dean Kidner said. He could come here and tell you in his own words if he wants. That's what he said. Those were the words: "neither the wisdom nor the justice."

What they're going to do is present charges that are weaker in these hearings than any charges that could be brought in a court of law. They're going to present charges that they say are your accountability. Now in administrative case law, accountability comes to this: that the principal (in this case, the one who advocates) is held accountable for the acts of his agents (those who go out and, say, have a picket line of something). That's not strong enough to bring indictment in a criminal court. And in a First

Amendment case, due process is far stricter than in an ordinary criminal case. They don't want even to give you the protection that you get in a criminal trial.

And we have, we have evidence. . . . We can only base things on past experience. First one thing they said, then one thing they did. First [the] thing that they said. They presented one and only one argument in that Committee on Campus Political Activity on behalf of their point of view, one and only one. And it was Vice Chancellor Searcy who first presented it and who repeatedly presented it—that the university is subject to external, extralegal pressures, and that it must have some way of responding to these pressures so that it'd be protected. That means to me that the due process you get or the consideration given the hearing by the chancellor—or both—will vary roughly inversely with the external pressures. Totally unacceptable!

That's what they said. Now a question of what they did. The Heyman Committee—a more sympathetic administrative hearing I don't think we could find. They couldn't accept its findings, very sympathetic. In that committee, the administration had to prove our guilt. At the same time, we had to prove our innocence, first. Second, the rule for burden of proof was not as in an ordinary criminal case, let alone a First Amendment case. It was not "guilty beyond a reasonable doubt and to a moral certainty." No, but by the preponderance of the evidence. Not even as strong as in an ordinary criminal case. That's the past experience. There's the past experience of the administrative hearing which tried Griffith, you know that star chamber. We know the kinds of things they've done in the past. We know the only reason that they've given for wanting this power is to respond to external pressure. Can we let them have this power? And we let them take away our rights? I say "No!"

And I say the following. That this was well planned. They're smart. They know the kind of things of which we are capable, because they've seen us do provocative things in the past. They know what we're capable of doing. And I know what they're trying to prevent. They've read our leaflet. We know what they were trying to prevent. And there are some people here who got up and walked away, because they're confused. And this has been their tactic from the beginning, to confuse, and by confusion, to divide. But faculty members have stood with us here. It's not a matter . . . of just some rabble-rousing students. I wanted to continue my classes this semester. I didn't have a desire to start this thing. You know I didn't have a desire to get together with the people who started this thing. . . . But we haven't stood alone. Now faculty members are with us also.

I say we can't allow them to divide us by confusing us. I say we can't allow them to prevent us from doing the kind of act which will bring them . . . to a change in their policy. We can't let the freakin' policy stand. I don't know. Some people will be with me, some not. The decision by a close vote of the Executive Committee of the Free Speech Movement was to sanction everything up to and including a sit-in. The decision of the Steering Committee, the majority decision—seven to four—was to have a sit-in. That doesn't mean we can bind anyone's conscience. But I say that we've got to do what they want to prevent us from doing. And I advocate here that some people here with some of us sit in today at Sproul Hall!

Later in the rally, Savio read the front page Oakland Tribune *editorial, "Who Runs UC?" denouncing the FSM and the UC administration for "capitulating" to the mob of anarchist student rebels.*

The controversy is: should there be a sit-in or should there not be a sit-in? We've never in the case of an action like that taken a genuinely majority position. There have always been a minority of people who have done sit-ins. On the other hand, if someone does take part in the sit-in, . . . they will not consider those who have not taken part [in the sit-in] to be somehow out of the movement—just to have a different appraisal of the situation. And I would ask that if such a sit-in does occur, that those who don't take part should at least recognize the legitimate feelings and judgment of those who do take part. I don't know of any faculty members who support our having a sit-in. I'll tell you that right now. I don't know of any. No, no. . . . That statement they read supported certain principles. [Someone suggests there was faculty support for sitting in, but Savio refuses to use this false argument to support his advocacy of a sit-in.] See, at this time . . . I want to make it clear so that no one is deceived. I don't know of any faculty members who support the sit-in now. . . .

All right. It's a question of tone. We're a little bit beyond anger, beyond tears now. It's a question . . . of a moral protest, a question of having people . . . look upon your bodies as they try to take part, . . . carry on the activity that they daily carry on, have to look at those bodies and consider what they mean. That's the kind of thing that I have in mind. It's that kind of protest that I'm advocating. We don't have a voice. They'll have to look at us there until such time as the chancellor's ready not to tell us what it [the UC policy restricting student advocacy] means but to talk to us about whether it should be that way at all. . . . When they're serious about that. On the last page of the *Daily Cal* today, the chancellor said, concerning this policy, "it cannot change and it will not change." It's right in there. We want them to have to see us . . . to have to look right into our eyes and keep going, daily, with their activities after having told us that this policy which affects us, which affects the faculty, cannot change and will not change, that we can't have the rights guaranteed us by the Constitution, that the abridgment of those rights cannot change and will not change. And it's that kind of moral protest, a sit-in with that tone that I am asking people to take part in.

Later in the rally, just before the start of the sit-in.

I just want to say we're not, not planning to . . . prevent passage. We'll sit along the walls [of Sproul Hall] and we'll wait.[58] And that's all I'm going to say.

Transcribed from audiotape, Mario Savio archives, published by permission of Lynne Hollander Savio. Audio also available online at www.lib. berkeley.edu/MRC/FSM/fsmchronology1.html.

SPEECH INSIDE SPROUL HALL DURING THE SIT-IN

23 NOVEMBER 1964

Savio stubbornly clung to his desire to continue the sit-in after Sproul Hall closed at 5 P.M., and thereby risk arrest in an act of moral witness, even though the protest would have no real political impact. The speech below was made before the Steering Committee's decision, by a 6–5 vote, to abort the sit-in; it shows how few political options there were and how lacking in promise they seemed. The months of protest and negotiation had been exhausting, and with the sit-in's collapse and the Thanksgiving holiday approaching, the FSM leadership would leave the campus having experienced its first ineffective act of civil disobedience and uncertain if anything could overcome the administration and the regents' refusal to end UC's restrictions on free speech.

There are a few things that we have to think about—all of us—concerning when we should leave [Sproul Hall and end the sit-in], because that's the kind of decision that those who made the commitment to come in here have to make. As we did when we first started this thing, if a majority says stay in, that doesn't bind the minority. If the majority says leave, that doesn't bind the minority. On the other hand, again as we did before, consideration should be given by the individuals involved to the expressed views of the majority. But the way that consideration [is given?] depends on the individual conscience of those involved.

Now, there are reasons for leaving when the building closes, there are reasons for staying on. I can give only some of them. You'll think of others. Both members of the Steering Committee who are here, and that includes some who were tactically against this but, because of solidarity, are with us here nonetheless—I'm talking about Art Goldberg and Steve Weissman—will be discussing these matters likewise. Later on, close to that time when such a decision probably should be made, . . . we'll let you know some of the other things that we thought of as reasons both for and against—some reasons that you have. Likewise, members of the Steering Committee are now speaking with people here, Mike Rossman . . . Goldberg, . . . group to group, in that way finding out what the sentiments are here now.

Things which we are aware of now. I've spoken to Lt. Chandler. I asked him, . . . "what do you think of this?" . . . And he said that "as such time as the building closes, you will have to leave." And I said, "well, what if it turns out . . . that that doesn't happen?" That doesn't mean . . . that everybody stays, but even if some stay. I said, "what if turns out that that doesn't happen?" And he said, "Appropriate action would be taken at that time." And, of course, I'm not sure what that means. But that includes, I presume, everything up to and including possible arrest. That's something we should consider. What would the charges be, for example? Would it be a

First Amendment case? And, therefore, could we test something? It's not clear. At the Sheraton Palace . . . the charge was breach of the peace. Some were convicted on that charge. Those who were acquitted, which included me and Jack, were [acquitted on the grounds of free speech], the expression we were making there. But I can't—I wouldn't want to guarantee or hold this out . . . as a substantial reason for considering for sitting in, but just as a reason, . . . just as something to think about in terms of what the charges might be in the event that arrest occurs. And there's no way to know . . . that, but that would take place, that's part of it.

So that would be one terminus on us staying, namely, when the building closes. Another possible terminus, at the meeting downstairs, Professor Zelnik and Professor Levine talked about the Academic Senate meeting that is going to take place tomorrow. And they said . . . that we should wait upon that.[59] Well, we might consider waiting here patiently upon that. Going to take place tomorrow in the afternoon and we might take the end of that meeting as an appropriate terminus of this. That's another possibility. Again, one that we'll all have to consider.

Likewise, we're going to send down a couple of people at a time downstairs to the rally there so long as this continues to explain to people why we're here. That the people here . . . feel that all channels have been closed to them. We've come up . . . against a bureaucratic stone wall. And, . . . there being no official channels, at least we want by our presence to make it clear to the people outside, both on campus and off the campus, to the administration, that there is something seriously, drastically wrong with the University of California. And that we're committed to seeing that it's changed. . . . They will try to explain that, explain that we're not here . . . to seize the building. But we are here so that the people who are working here have to see us. That will be expressed outside. . . .

[question from the crowd]

The question was if the police [instead of the UC administration] press the charges then we couldn't have a test case against the university. And that's not so clear. It depends upon a couple of things, the following: Which police? The police of the University of California or Berkeley police? That's one question. The other is at the Sheraton Palace, the police gave the hotel the opportunity to press the trespassing charges, and they did not. Accordingly the . . . police brought a breach of the peace charge.

Now people who . . . got acquitted were acquitted for First Amendment reasons. At the same time, understand it didn't constitute some kind of test case against the Sheraton Palace Hotel. In this case, the issue can be drawn the following way. That on university property we were exercising First Amendment rights, and these were upheld in the court. And I don't know what effect that would have legally accordingly later on—very complicated. I am trying to lay as much of it out as I understand, later on Malcolm Burnstein, one of the civil rights lawyers that is helping us, and possibly other attorneys, will be here to give their opinions which will be much more adequate.

[question from the crowd]

The question that has been asked again concerns a test case but from a different point of . . . view: the Art Goldberg case with the *Oakland Tribune*. The question that's been asked is: Art advocated going to the *Oakland Tribune* to a picket line. He was subsequently arrested. He's on probation, so the university is free to expel him. Could that be a test case on the advocacy issue, I believe you meant, right? And the answer is—and I hope I'm not giving the administration ideas—it's very easy for them to discipline him for the arrest off campus rather than his advocacy on campus. And I'm sure that they'll do that, which is the strongest thing for them in court. So I would say, in all probability, no. If they make the mistake—very unlikely indeed, if the thing they discipline him for is the advocacy, you know—then yes, but I think the chance of that is very, very small. . . .

Transcribed from audiotape, Mario Savio archives, copy in editor's possession, published by permission of Lynne Hollander Savio.

4 "No Restrictions on the Content of Speech"

SAVIO AND THE FSM WIN, DECEMBER 1964

Over the Thanksgiving holiday, the UC administration made a colossal blunder. Instead of letting things cool off and hoping that the aborted sit-in was a prelude to the FSM's collapse, the administration took the offensive. Chancellor Strong sent letters citing Savio and fellow FSM organizers Jackie and Art Goldberg and Brian Turner for violations of university rules, initiating disciplinary proceedings against them. The administration also announced disciplinary action against Campus CORE, University Friends of SNCC, and four other leading student activist groups.

Though angered by this disciplinary offensive, the FSM's leadership immediately realized that, politically, it was a gift from heaven. As FSM Steering Committee member Bettina Aptheker recalled, "I knew that was it. That was what we were waiting for—the final atrocity."[1] Or as Savio put it, "We used to say, you can always count on the administration for an atrocity."[2]

With regard to the disciplinary process, the UC administration, from the outset of the crisis, had a reputation for a basic lack of fairness. That reputation extended well beyond the FSM. In fact, the Heyman Committee—the faculty's ad hoc Academic Senate committee (chaired by law professor I. Michael Heyman) charged with reviewing the initial sus-

Figure 10. Savio speaks at FSM Executive Committee meeting. Photograph courtesy of Michael Rossman.

pensions of protesters near the start of the free speech crisis—had criticized the administration for "gratuitously" singling out movement leaders in late September and early October for "heavy penalties." These penalties on FSM leaders were "summarily imposed," even though many other protesters had committed these same infractions. The Heyman Committee report, in scathing language, noted that the administration had seemed to be out to "make examples" of these movement organizers, treating them "almost as hostages."[3]

Many students saw in the new round of disciplinary actions this same pattern of unfairness, this same impulse to make examples of prominent movement organizers so as to intimidate others and thereby quell the free speech protests. FSM supporters viewed the new citations as a sign of bad faith, because the citations were for violations of campus rules committed on October 1–2, violations that the Heyman Committee had already reviewed. The administration seemed to be disregarding that committee and unilaterally imposing its own new round of disciplinary proceedings. It seemed especially inappropriate to discipline Savio and Jackie Goldberg for causing trouble during the police car blockade when both had signed the Pact of October 2 ending that protest peacefully.

With its Thanksgiving letters, the administration inadvertently provided the FSM with the same kind of catalyst for mass civil disobedience that it had served up on September 30 when it issued citations against five ban violators on Sproul and with the arrest of Jack Weinberg on October 1. That catalyst was the anger evoked by picking off and punishing movement organizers, adding deep concerns about due process and basic fairness to the already widespread concern about UC's free speech restrictions. The FSM had a history of acting in solidarity and protesting loudly when such punitive acts were taken against its own. What is more, this time the FSM was better organized and more experienced in mounting protests on campus, including mass civil disobedience. Unlike the September 30 sit-in or the police car blockade, this next Sproul Hall occupation would not be spontaneous. This time the movement had time to plan its demonstration—even to bring in musical accompaniment, provided by folk singer Joan Baez—and also to think beyond the sit-in to a strike by TAs and a student boycott of classes.

Clearly the administration, through its political incompetence, handed the FSM—via those new disciplinary letters—a golden opportunity to bounce back from the nadir it had reached after the failure of the aborted sit-in. In this sense, Savio was right when, in looking back, he credited the administration: "they saved us. . . . We lucked out, time after time."[4] Yet this was more than a matter of luck, for while the FSM was indeed fortunate that the administration had handed it the opportunity for political renewal, Savio and the FSM still needed to demonstrate the political skills necessary to convert this opportunity into a major free speech victory. This meant first duplicating the FSM's earlier, unprecedented success around the police car in mobilizing masses of students for a dramatic act of civil disobedience. On top of this, the FSM also needed to accomplish something it had not managed to achieve during or since that blockade: winning over the faculty. After all, the faculty was the only force on campus with the institutional power to overrule President Kerr and Chancellor Strong. This was the formidable challenge the FSM faced as it responded to the Thanksgiving letters and launched its culminating week-and-a-half of protest in early December 1964.

TO PRESIDENT CLARK KERR

1 DECEMBER 1964

The FSM's strategy was simple. Give President Kerr an ultimatum: withdraw the threat of disciplinary action, move toward the FSM's demand for free speech, or face a new round of mass civil disobedience. Kerr never sent the FSM a response to this letter delivering that ultimatum, which Savio co-wrote with Suzanne Goldberg, a graduate student in philosophy and FSM Steering Committee member—who would later become Savio's first wife. Chancellor Strong's response to the letter was to declare angrily that the administration would not submit to threats.

Savio spoke about the letter at an FSM rally on December 1, explaining that it would be naïve to expect the administration to respond positively to its demands or to think Kerr and Strong would "admit they're wrong." The crucial question was how students would respond to the FSM's call for a new round of mass civil disobedience to reverse the disciplinary offensive and win free speech. "If you don't respond we're dead," Savio told the crowd. "This factory [university] does unjust things, and we'll have to cause the wheels to grind to a halt. . . . If we don't get our rights, we won't let this machine operate."[5]

Dear President Kerr:

Without the use of mass direct action we have been unable to make any substantial gains toward freedom for political activity at the University of California. The Administration has continued to act arbitrarily to repress that activity. We are hereby making a final attempt to restore our political freedom without the use of mass direct action. Nothing short of the following can adequately protect our political rights; we urge that by noon, Wednesday, December 2, (a) points 1, 2, and 4 be adopted and (b) you publically state that you have initiated the adoption of points 3 and 5, as follows:

1. That the Administration withdraw the charges and cease disciplinary action against Mario Savio, Arthur Goldberg, Jackie Goldberg and student organizations cited for their political activity including activity in demonstrations conducted to secure student political rights;

2. That the Administration guarantee that there will be no further disciplinary action taken against students or student organizations for "violations" of University regulations which occur or may have occurred before a final settlement between the Administration and the Free Speech Movement is reached, whether or not such "violations" are incurred by political activity or by participation in demonstrations;

3. That there be no restrictions of on-campus advocacy, and of the on-campus exercise of First Amendment rights generally, other than those already provided by the courts, that the University recognize the courts as the sole regulator of the content of political expression and as the only authority competent to prescribe punishment for abuse of political rights, and that political activity off the campus be declared strictly beyond the jurisdiction of the University;

4. That no regulations governing the form of political expression be permitted which needlessly restrict students or their organizations in the exercise on-campus of political rights;

5. That all regulations governing the form of political expression on the campus shall be determined, interpreted and enforced by a joint committee of faculty members, students and administrators, chosen by their peers, each group having equal power on the committee, the judgments of which committee shall be final.

These five points represent a minimum acceptable position. Points 3, 4 and 5 constitute a distillation of the Free Speech Movement Platform. We urge that these measures be adopted by the University. We await such adoption of points 1, 2 and 4 by tomorrow at noon; we likewise wait until noon for your statement that the adoption of points 3 and 5 has been initiated.

> *Cordially yours,*
> *Mario Savio and*
> *Suzanne Goldberg*
> *for the Steering*
> *Committee of the FSM*[6]
> *cc. Chancellor E.W.*
> *Strong*

Mario Savio archive, copy in editor's possession, published by permission of Lynne Hollander Savio.

MARIO SAVIO REMARKS AT FREE SPEECH MOVEMENT
PRESS CONFERENCE

2 DECEMBER 1964

As part of the mobilization for the mass rally and sit-in at Sproul Hall, the FSM held a press conference in which Savio explained the FSM's demands.

Question: Mario would you, just so I have it on tape, [discuss] the demands you're asking to be met and by when.

Savio: Yes. By noon today that these new charges be withdrawn. That the administration agree—this was in a letter to Clark Kerr, with a copy to Chancellor Strong—that these new charges be withdrawn, that the administration agree until final resolution there will be no disciplinary action against students for political activity or political demonstrations on campus. Three, that there be substantive improvement in regulations governing political activity, in accord with our platform—which means in accord with the following three points: first, that only the courts may regulate the content of political expression, that students, faculty, and administration must jointly make final decisions concerning its form. And that any regulations which do not encourage but needlessly impede the exercise of civil liberties must immediately be repealed.

Q: What is the situation with the eight student organizations that I've heard mentioned?

Savio: Well, they have been cited. . . . Disciplinary action against them has been initiated, . . . which can and—in all probability—will result in their on-campus privileges being rescinded by the administration. Naturally, any such action by the administration will have to be ignored by the student organizations and will be ignored by them. It's clear by this time, of course, that the administration's edicts are totally irrelevant to the exercise of civil liberties on campus. The administration is, at present, simply a hindrance to the university—which is, of course, students and faculty.

Q: The chancellor apparently said that they were being called in just for informational meetings.

Savio: . . . It's one more ploy. We had a meeting on campus in which Vice Chancellor [Alan] Searcy spoke and said all sorts of nice things, the substance of which were lies. Namely, that the policy which had been

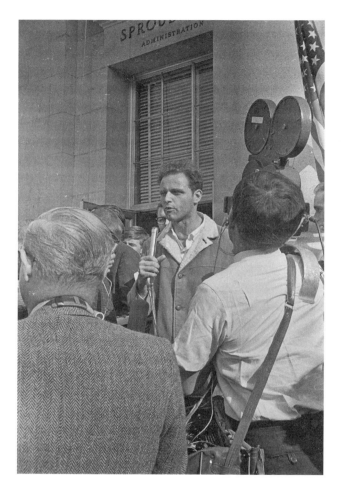

Figure 11. Savio speaking to reporters, December 2, 1964.
Photograph courtesy of Steven Marcus, Bancroft Library
collection.

adopted was substantially the same as one of the faculty proposals. This is
what he said to the group assembled. Whereas, in fact, the chancellor, in
his application of the regents' policy, had adopted *some* of the parts of one
of the faculty proposals and that this application is constantly subject to
revision and this was not part of the regents' policy. So it's come to the
point where, unless we see things in writing, unless they're signed by

someone in authority—which does not mean Chancellor Strong. It's quite clear to all concerned that—and to Chancellor Strong—that Chancellor Strong has no authority on this campus, and that he is simply being controlled by Clark Kerr or by Clark Kerr and the regents. I think this is quite clear at this point.[7]

Q: And so you're going to sit in until you get something on these demands from the president and/or the regents?

Savio: Yeah. We made a mistake—not a mistake. We didn't know, you see. [On] October 2nd we called off a demonstration because we were offered a committee.[8] Now we will only call off demonstrations if there have been, in fact, substantive concessions to our demands. And these must concern certain things definitely. And the ones that I have mentioned. *All* these charges must be dropped. No further charges must be placed against students. And on the substance of civil liberties regulations, there must be changes before any demonstration will be called off. If the administration means to enforce unconstitutional and harassing regulations upon civil liberties, then they will have to do so with police power.

Transcribed from audiotape, Mario Savio archives, copy in editor's possession, published by permission of Lynne Hollander Savio.

"BODIES UPON THE GEARS" SPEECH AT FSM RALLY,
SPROUL HALL STEPS

2 DECEMBER 1964

This is Savio's most widely quoted speech, which he gave just prior to the FSM's culminating act of civil disobedience, the occupation of Sproul Hall, by more than a thousand students. Savio was the final scheduled speaker of the rally leading to the sit-in. The FSM speakers who preceded him, Steering Committee members Martin Roysher and Michael Rossman, had already discussed the new round of disciplinary letters that the administration sent out to FSM leaders and radical student organizations, and they had also covered the issues of free speech and due process at stake in the latest round of the conflict. This freed Savio to sail above these specific grievances and to offer an emotionally and rhetorically powerful appeal to

Figure 12. Savio speaking in front of Sproul Hall. Photograph copyright Howard Harawitz.

resist unjust authority via civil disobedience, as well as a scathing indict-ment of the political compromises and educational failings of the university.

It is not the entire speech, but its most dramatic moments—its fifth and sixth paragraphs—that are famous, widely quoted, and used in clips for movies and on television. It is important, however, to read beyond that famous segment and through to the end of the speech so as to avoid the common mistake of thinking that Savio, in urging the crowd to put their "bodies upon the gears" was proposing martyrdom. In fact, as the final paragraphs of the speech make clear, Savio assumed that mass civil diso-bedience would nonviolently halt "the machine" and yield a sit-in that would be both politically effective and educationally exhilarating (com-plete with Freedom School classes and movies).

When Savio completed this speech, Joan Baez, after urging nonviolence, sang the civil rights movement anthem "We Shall Overcome," as masses of protesters slowly marched in to Sproul Hall.[9]

You know, I just want to say one brief thing about something the previous speaker [Cal ASUC student government president Charlie Powell] said. I didn't want to spend too much time on that, because I don't think it's important enough. But one thing is worth considering. He's the . . . nominal head of an organization supposedly representative of the undergraduates. Whereas, in fact, under the Kerr directives, it derives its authority, its delegated power, from the administration. It's totally unrepresentative of the graduate students and TAs. But he made the following statement, I quote: "I would ask all those who are not definitely committed to the FSM cause to stay away from demonstration." All right, now, listen to this: "For all upper-division students who are interested in alleviating the TA shortage problem, I would encourage you to offer your services to department chairmen and advisers." That has two things: a strikebreaker and a fink!

I'd like to say . . . one other thing about a union problem. Upstairs, you may have noticed already on the second floor of Sproul Hall, Locals 40 and 127 of the Painters' Union are painting the inside of the second floor of Sproul Hall. Now, apparently that action had been planned sometime in the past. I've tried to contact those unions. Unfortunately, and it tears my heart out, they're as bureaucratized as the administration—it's difficult to get through to anyone in authority there. Very sad. We're still . . . making an attempt. Those people up there have no desire to interfere with what we're doing. I would ask that they be considered and that they not be heckled in any way, and I think that . . . there at least need be no . . . excessively hard feelings between the two groups.

Now, there are at least two ways in which sit-ins and civil disobedience and whatever—at least two major ways in which it can occur. One, when a law exists—is promulgated—which is totally unacceptable to people, and they violate it again and again and again until it's rescinded, repealed. All right. But there's another way.

Sometimes the form of the law is such as to render impossible its effective violation as a method to have it repealed. Sometimes the grievances of people are more, extend . . . to more than just the law, extend to a whole mode of arbitrary power, a whole mode of arbitrary exercise of arbitrary power. And that's what we have here.

We have an autocracy which runs this university. It's managed! We were told the following: "If President Kerr actually tried to get something more liberal out of the regents in his telephone conversation, why didn't he make some public statement to that effect?" And the answer we received, from a well-meaning liberal, was the following. He said: "Would you ever imagine the manager of a firm making a statement publicly in opposition to his board of directors?" That's the answer! Now I ask you to consider: if this is a firm, and if the Board of Regents are the board of directors, and if President Kerr in fact is the manager, then I'll tell you something: the faculty are a bunch of employees, and we're the raw materials! But we're a bunch of raw materials that don't mean to . . . have any process upon us, don't mean to be made into any product, don't mean . . . to end up being bought by some clients of the university, be they the government, be they industry, be they organized labor, be they anyone! We're human beings!

And that . . . brings me to the second mode of civil disobedience. There's a time when the operation of the machine becomes so odious, makes you so sick at heart, that you can't take part; you can't even passively take part. And you've got to put your bodies upon the gears and upon the wheels, upon the levers, upon all the apparatus, and you've got to make it stop. And you've got to indicate to the people who run it, to the people who own it, that unless you're free, the machine will be prevented from working at all.

That doesn't mean—and it will be interpreted to mean, unfortunately, by the bigots who run the *[San Francisco] Examiner*, for example—that you have to break anything. One thousand people sitting down someplace, not letting anybody by, not letting anything happen, can stop any machine, including this machine, and it will stop!

We're going to do the following, and the greater the number of people, the safer they'll be, and the more effective it will be. We're going, once again, to march up to the second floor of Sproul Hall. And we're going to conduct our lives for a while in the second floor of Sproul Hall. We'll show movies, for example. We tried to get *Un chant d'amour*.[10] Unfortunately, that's tied up in the courts because of a lot of squeamish moral mothers for a moral America and other people on the outside, the same people who get all their ideas out of the *San Francisco Examiner*. Sad, sad. But Mr. [Saul] Landau . . . has gotten us some other films.[11]

Likewise, we'll do something . . . that hasn't occurred at this university in a good long time. We're going to have real classes up there. There are going

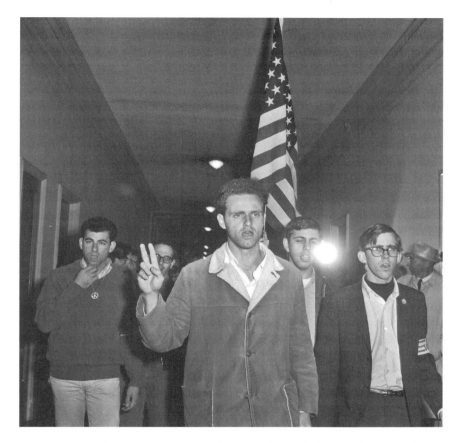

Figure 13. Savio leading demonstrators into Sproul Hall during FSM's culminating sit-in, December 2, 1964. Photograph courtesy of Warren of *SF Call,* Bancroft Library collection.

to be Freedom Schools conducted up there. We're going to have classes on [the] First and Fourteenth Amendments. We're going to spend our time learning about the things this university is afraid that we know. We're going to learn about freedom up there, and we're going to learn by doing.

Now, we've had some good long rallies. We've had some good long rallies, and I think I'm sicker of rallies than anyone else here. It's not going to be long. I'd like to introduce one last person . . . before we enter Sproul Hall. And the person is Joan Baez.

Transcribed from audiotape, Mario Savio archives, copy in editor's posses-
sion, published by permission of Lynne Hollander Savio. Audio also avail-
able online at www.lib.berkeley.edu/MRC/FSM/fsmchronology1.html.

INTERVIEW, SPROUL HALL

2 DECEMBER 1964

This interview with Savio—complete with red-baiting questions from the
press—occurred shortly after the Sproul Hall sit-in began.

Question: Mario, the pamphlet handed to students said, "if the machine of the administration ignores us, we will stop the machine." How do you stop the machine of the University of California?

Savio: Well, Lieutenant Chandler has said that the students will be essentially undisturbed in Sproul Hall until the doors close. "Then" [when the doors close] he said, "there may be trouble." Those were his words. And I presume that means they'll not want us in here after the doors have closed. But unless they accede to our demands, we're not moving from here. And it will be quite difficult for the administration to carry on its business in the administration building, which is where we are, with us here. And we plan to remain. And so I think we will have quite success-fully have stopped the administration of the University of California.

Q: You mean they'll have to carry you out.

Savio: Oh yes, oh yes.

Q: You also announced a few moments ago you were setting up the Free University of California on these three floors. What did you mean by that?

Savio: There are some professors who not only support our aims but likewise support effective means for achieving them. They are in here. They will be conducting classes, various classes—especially classes in First Amendment law and philosophy and likewise in ordinary subjects, Spanish classes, for example. And these will be conducted on these floors.

Q: Why do you think it's necessary to stop the machinery here?

Savio: Well, the university—as is so much else in the society—is totally unresponsive to the needs of individual human beings. It operates in a totally impersonal way. We've tried in countless ways to make clear to the university we consider our constitutional rights to have been abrogated, abridged, trampled upon. But they don't listen. They insist upon making policies by fiat. They don't believe in discussion with those people involved except to explain what the fiat is. This we cannot accept. This is the impersonal operation of a machine. We've not been able to make contact with the human beings supposedly behind it. And, therefore, we're left with only one recourse. We're going to have this machine grind to a halt until we get our rights.

Q: There are twenty-seven thousand students at the University of California. How many of them do you suppose support the Free Speech Movement?

Savio: There are presently in this building more students than ever vote in any student body election at the university.

Q: How many would you say?

Savio: Well, there must be at least 1,500 in here. These are not the only people who support the Free Speech Movement. These are people who not only support it but have had the courage of their convictions to stand in here and be prepared to be arrested for what they believe are their rights.

Q: What is the political spectrum of students who support you, from right to left?

Savio: Well, on the left, socialists of various kinds, on the right, Goldwater supporters. All these kind of people are in here right now.

Q: J. Edgar Hoover says that the W. E. B. Du Bois Club is a Communist front. They have active supporters here in the university. Do you believe it is a Communist front?

Savio: What the . . .

Q: The W. E. B. Du Bois Club, according to Hoover.

Savio: Well, I really don't know enough about the W. E. B. Du Bois Club. I do know enough about J. Edgar Hoover. A very little while ago, Mr. Hoover accused the Nobel Prize winner Martin Luther King of being—I think—"the most notorious liar in the country." I believe that's very close to his words. So I think it's clear that we can hardly trust the kinds of things that Mr. Hoover is likely to say. I'd add furthermore that this movement began because certain people on the outside of the university, William Knowland, for example, were out to crush student participation in the Bay Area civil rights movement. Mr. Hoover has already indicated that he is an unconditional enemy of the civil rights movement in this country.

Q: Mario Savio, it was reported this morning that the first two lines of a statement issued by the Free Speech Movement were essentially the same two lines that started the *Communist Manifesto*. What would be your reaction?

Savio: Oh, in fact, I paraphrased the first—I think it was the first line of the *Communist Manifesto*—precisely because of the bigotry displayed against us by the *San Francisco Examiner* . . . calling us a Communist front. I thought there was only poetic justice in this. The idea was mine. I thought it was kind of clever, as a matter of fact. The first line of the *Manifesto* begins, "A specter is haunting Europe—the specter of Communism." The first line of our leaflet began, "A specter is haunting the University of California—the specter of student resistance to arbitrary administrative power."

Q: And you feel that this was, what, a sarcastic way?

Savio: That's right. I think a very sarcastic way of responding to totally unfounded charges designed to crush what is essentially a student protest to secure our constitutional liberties.

Q: Do you think that most people got the point?

Savio: Well, the people to whom these leaflets were given out, students on the campus, were sufficiently intelligent to have gotten the point. Unfortunately, . . . this is liable to be distorted in the press. . . . We can't expect the people are going to get any straight story from the press. And so we felt our first responsibility was to a little good humor and to our own people on campus.

Q: Are you saying that about all the press. Or are you saying that about radio and television?

Savio: I'm saying it, especially right now, about certain people in the radio, Joe Pine, for example. About the *Tocsin*, a well-known, bigoted, official anti-Communist journal, and about the *San Francisco Examiner*, in so far as Ed Montgomery is representative of the *San Francisco Examiner*.[12]

Q: Mario, we can expect you to stay in until you get arrested, is that right?

Savio: Until our demands are acceded to. If the university chooses to enforce its regulations, it will have to do so with police power.

Transcribed from audiotape, Mario Savio archives, copy in editor's possession, published by permission of Lynne Hollander Savio.

"AN END TO HISTORY" ESSAY, DRAWN FROM SPEECH
INSIDE SPROUL HALL

2 DECEMBER 1964

Though the verbatim text of this speech in Sproul Hall during the FSM's final sit-in seems not to have survived, this essay by Savio, based on those remarks, has been widely quoted and anthologized. It elaborates on key themes in his FSM oratory, including the link between the civil rights movement and the Berkeley student movement, the unresponsiveness of bureaucracies, and the need for students to convert universities from trade schools to centers of dissident thought and egalitarian social change. This essay initially appeared in the December 1964 issue of Humanity, *a Berkeley magazine published by an interfaith editorial board.*

Last summer I went to Mississippi to join the struggle there for civil rights. This fall I am engaged in another phase of the same struggle, this time in Berkeley. The two battlefields may seem quite different to some observers, but this is not the case. The same rights are at stake in both places—the right to participate as citizens in democratic society and the right to due process of law. Further, it is a struggle against the same enemy. In Mississippi an autocratic and powerful minority rules, through organized violence, to suppress the vast, virtually powerless majority. In California, the privileged minority manipulates the university bureaucracy to suppress the students' political expression. That "respectable" bureaucracy masks the financial plutocrats; that impersonal bureaucracy is the efficient enemy in a "brave new world."

In our free speech fight at the University of California, we have come up against what may emerge as the greatest problem of our nation—

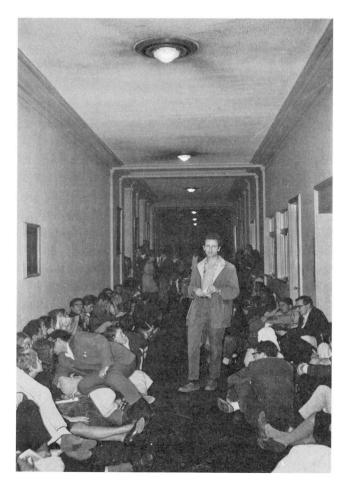

Figure 14. Savio in occupied Sproul Hall, December 2, 1964.
Photograph courtesy of Steven Marcus, Bancroft Library
collection.

depersonalized, unresponsive bureaucracy. We have encountered the
organized status quo in Mississippi, but it is the same in Berkeley. Here we
find it impossible usually to meet with anyone but secretaries. Beyond
that, we find functionaries who cannot make policy but can only hide
behind the rules. We have discovered total lack of response on the part of
the policy makers. To grasp a situation which is truly Kafkaesque, it is

necessary to understand the bureaucratic mentality. And we have learned quite a bit about it this fall, more outside the classroom than in.

As bureaucrat, an administrator believes that nothing new happens. He occupies an ahistorical point of view. In September, to get the attention of this bureaucracy which had issued arbitrary edicts suppressing student political expression and refused to discuss its action, we held a sit-in on the campus. We sat around a police car and kept it immobilized for over thirty-two hours. At last, the administrative bureaucracy agreed to negotiate. But instead, on the following Monday, we discovered that a committee had been appointed, in accordance with usual regulations, to resolve the dispute. Our attempt to convince any of the administrators that an event had occurred, that something new had happened, failed. They saw this simply as something to be handled by normal university procedures.

The same is true of all bureaucracies. They begin as tools, means to certain legitimate goals, and they end up feeding their own existence. The conception that bureaucrats have is that history has in fact come to an end. No events can occur now that the Second World War is over which can change American society substantially. We proceed by standard procedures as we are.

The most crucial problems facing the United States today are the problem of automation and the problem of racial injustice. Most people who will be put out of jobs by machines will not accept an end to events, this historical plateau, as the point beyond which no change occurs. Negroes will not accept an end to history here. All of us must refuse to accept history's final judgment that in America there is no place in society for people whose skins are dark. On campus, students are not about to accept it as fact that the university has ceased evolving and is in its final state of perfection, that students and faculty are respectively raw material and employees, or that the university is to be autocratically run by unresponsive bureaucrats.

Here is the real contradiction: the bureaucrats hold history as ended. As a result, significant parts of the population both on campus and off are dispossessed, and these dispossessed are not about to accept this ahistorical point of view. It is out of this that the conflict has occurred with the university bureaucracy and will continue to occur until that bureaucracy becomes responsive or until it is clear the university cannot function.

The things we are asking for in our civil rights protests have a deceptively quaint ring. We are asking for the due process of law. We are asking for our actions to be judged by committees of our peers. We are asking that regulations ought to be considered as arrived at legitimately only from the consensus of the governed. These phrases are all pretty old, but they are not being taken seriously in America today, nor are they being taken seriously on the Berkeley campus.

I have just come from a meeting with the Dean of Students. She notified us that she was aware of certain violations of university regulations by certain organizations. University Friends of SNCC, which I represent, was one of these. We tried to draw from her some statement on these great principles: consent of the governed, jury of one's peers, due process. The best she could do was to evade or to present the administration party line. It is very hard to make any contact with the human being who is behind these organizations.

The university is the place where people begin seriously to question the conditions of their existence and raise the issue of whether they can be committed to the society they have been born into. After a long period of apathy during the fifties, students have begun not only to question but, having arrived at answers, to act on those answers. This is part of a growing understanding among many people in America that history has not ended, that a better society is possible, and that it is worth dying for.

This free speech fight points up a fascinating aspect of contemporary campus life. Students are permitted to talk all they want so long as their speech has no consequences.

One conception of the university, suggested by a classical Christian formulation, is that it be in the world but not of the world. The conception of Clark Kerr, by contrast, is that the university is part and parcel of this particular stage in the history of American society; it stands to serve the need of American industry, it is a factory that turns out a certain product needed by industry or government. Because speech does often have consequences which might alter this perversion of higher education, the university must put itself in a position of censorship. It can permit two kinds of speech: speech which encourages continuation of the status quo, and speech which advocates changes in it so radical as to be irrelevant in the foreseeable future. Someone may advocate radical change in all aspects of

American society, and this I am sure he can do with impunity. But if some-one advocates sit-ins to bring about changes in discriminatory hiring practices, this cannot be permitted because it goes against the status quo of which the university is a part. And that is how the fight began here. The administration of the Berkeley campus has admitted that external, extra-legal groups have pressured the university not to permit students on cam-pus to organize picket lines, not to permit on campus any speech with consequences. And the bureaucracy went along. Speech with conse-quences, speech in the area of civil rights, speech which some might regard as illegal, must stop.

Many students here at the university, many people in society, are wan-dering aimlessly about. Strangers in their own lives, there is no place for them. They are people who have not learned to compromise, who for example have come to the university to learn to question, to grow, to learn—all the standard things that sound like clichés because no one takes them seriously. And they find at one point or other that for them to become part of society, to become lawyers, ministers, businessmen, people in gov-ernment, that very often they must compromise those principles which were most dear to them. They must suppress the most creative impulses that they have; this is a prior condition for being part of the system. The university is well structured, well tooled, to turn out people with all the sharp edges worn off, the well-rounded person. The university is well equipped to produce that sort of person, and this means that the best among the people who enter must for four years wander aimlessly much of the time questioning why they are on campus at all, doubting whether there is any point in what they are doing, and looking toward a very bleak existence afterward in a game in which all of the rules have been made up, which one cannot really amend.

It is a bleak scene, but it is all a lot of us have to look forward to. Society provides no challenge. American society in the standard conception it has of itself is simply no longer exciting. The most exciting things going on in America today are movements to change America. America is becoming evermore the Utopia of sterilized, automated contentment. The "futures" and "careers" for which American students now prepare are for the most part intellectual and moral wastelands. This chrome-plated consumers' paradise would have us grow up to be well-behaved children. But an important minority of men and women coming to the front today have shown that they will die rather than be standardized, replaceable, and irrelevant.

Published by permission of Lynne Hollander Savio.

TO SAVIO FAMILY FROM SANTA RITA PRISON

4 DECEMBER 1964

This letter, written from jail to his parents, grandmother, and brother the day after he had been arrested at Sproul Hall, was only recently discovered. It is unclear whether Savio actually sent the letter. But it captures Savio's euphoric response to the mass sit-in and arrests, and his conviction that the police invasion of the campus had finally turned around faculty to side with the FSM's free speech demands. Though Savio's reading of the faculty and the campus was perceptive, his upbeat assessment of opinion in California as a whole proved wrong. The California electorate's resounding disapproval of the FSM would be reflected in public opinion polls in 1964 and exploited by Ronald Reagan two years later when he campaigned successfully for the governorship pledging to clean up the "mess" in Berkeley.[13]

Dear Mom and Dad, Noni and Tom,

I won't be in here long, but I thought you might like to receive a letter from the "Birmingham Jail." They arrested about 800 of us students after we seized and held the administration building, Sproul Hall, for about 14 hours. We entered the building between noon and 1 A.M. on Wednesday. Here it's Friday morning already and they have not yet even now completed "booking" us. In a speech on Tuesday noon I gave the administration an ultimatum—24 hours to accede to our demands. When they failed to do so we seized the administration building. Our action has electrified the entire state—as well as many thousands in other states. It was Governor Brown himself—the fink—who ordered our arrest. But the action we took has also lighted a fire under the faculty, who have raised thousands of dollars in bail money, who have demanded we be pardoned, who have demanded that our demands for free speech be met, and who may insist that the Chancellor resign. Furthermore, there is a strike going on right now on campus. The whole campus is shut down—when I urged students to sit in on Wednesday I'd promised that either we would get our rights or we would completely halt the operation of the University! Its operation has been completely halted. So serious is our effort being taken that the Teamsters Union has refused to cross our picket lines. Accordingly, *no* materials which are brought into the University by truck are coming in. That means that *no* food is coming to the cafeterias—none at all. Whereas before the administration held the students in seige *[sic]* in *one building;* now we hold the administration in seige on the entire campus!

Even if the Regents do not now meet all our demands, at least we have brought the faculty over to our side. We have already won substantial victories. I am well and b[u]oyantly happy—if a little grubby. Don't worry, please.

Joan Baez—the world famous folk singer—has taken a key role in the protest. She was with us in Sproul Hall!

With all my love,
Mario

FSM-A Archive, published by permission of Lynne Hollander Savio. Handwritten version available online at www.dailycal.org/2011/11/15/ lost-and-found-mario-savio%E2%80%99s-reflections.

REMARKS AT FSM PRESS CONFERENCE

4 DECEMBER 1964

In the wake of the mass arrests that broke up the Sproul Hall sit-in, Savio discussed the arrests, police brutality, and jail. Savio's FSM press conference remarks were the most extensive he would give on these events.

Now there are a million things to talk to. When I had the preliminary booking down below Sproul Hall, asking if I wanted to make a public statement, you know, I mean a written statement. I said, "well, either the

Figure 15. Savio, unshaven, after spending the night in jail at Santa Rita with hundreds of other FSM arrestees, back on campus and joining the picket line in the student strike, December 4, 1964. Photograph copyright Howard Harawitz.

following one sentence: I hold the total proceedings in complete contempt. Or a book." And here's kind of the preface. The preface concerns police brutality. I'd like to talk to the issues, and I'm going to talk later again to the issue of free speech. But I think we ought to very soberly consider the way justice is administered in Alameda County.

First of all, and especially after the Oakland police, two hundred of them, were turned loose in Sproul Hall, various acts of violence against students were done.[14] Students were thrown down the stairs. There's one person who had his chin bleeding. A couple of people, . . . their heads were allowed to bounce on the floor. People had their arms twisted, their hands bent back. One girl was punched in the neck. There were people who were intentionally roughed up, though they were going along with the police. People were kicked.

At the places where booking was taking place—in my case, it took six hours for the booking procedure to be completed, during which, on two different occasions, it was deemed necessary that I be separated from the rest of the people and put in a special cell. And I'd like to mention one of those instances, which I think was particularly significant. At one point, in a small pen about 160 students were being kept prior to booking. And it was very warm in there. And there was an exhaust fan in one of the windows. And repeatedly the police officers were requested to turn the exhaust fan on. And each time they refused. At one point, one of the students told me that two had passed out.

And so Jack Weinberg and I went to the prison doctor, who was there to complain about the conditions of overcrowding. And to ask that two things be done. One that the exhaust fan be turned on; the other that some of those people be taken out of there be put in another place. And there was plenty of places—room—at Santa Rita. It's the old compound, one of them, where the Nisei Japanese were kept . . . for "safe keeping" during the war. So there was plenty of room.

Well, naturally, they did not heed those requests. But further, for our causing trouble by complaining to the police doctor, Jack and I were put off in a cell by ourselves. I was the first. Well, naturally, we continued to disturb them. We . . . sang songs and so on. We banged on the wall. And so they decided finally that for "safe keeping" that I be put off in this little room. They're very dark, these little rooms, and there are no windows, no place to sit down. And they're called by the inmates "the hole," you see.

They have not had too much experience with people whose spirit cannot be broken. Accordingly, the one person in that room continued to sing quite loudly and bang on the walls at great length.

So then it was considered necessary that I spend the night at the maximum-security section in Greystone barracks.

Now, the point of the whole thing is that it all began because Jack and I complained that there too many people kept in this pen. This points up classically to the total incompetence and brutality with which Santa Rita, their model prison, is run.

Another incident. There are so many. But there are just a few which are really symbolic. Just about when I was being released, I mentioned to one of the guards I'd heard picketing was going on on campus—a rather successful strike had been called and was proceeding, and that some Teamsters were not crossing our picket lines. And he said, "First, I don't know anything about that." Then he said, "I have no opinion on that at all." And after saying those two things, he said, "Nevertheless, if the sheriff would order me right now to shoot you, I would do so." This is the—kind of—the whole Adolf Eichmann syndrome, and it's very sad.

Transcribed from audiotape, Mario Savio archives, copy in editor's posses-sion, published by permission of Lynne Hollander Savio.

PROFESSOR ROBERT SCALAPINO AND MARIO SAVIO
AT THE END OF THE GREEK THEATRE MEETING
7 DECEMBER 1964

A huge outdoor meeting, sponsored by President Kerr and Robert Scalapino of the political science department, who was the head of the newly formed Council of Department Chairmen, was held in Berkeley's outdoor amphi-theater, the Greek Theatre, on December 7, 1964. Kerr had cancelled classes to insure maximum attendance at this meeting, which he hoped would restore the credibility he had lost on campus because of the police invasion of the campus and mass arrests. But the meeting ended disastrously for Kerr. He and Scalapino spoke in defense of law and order and advocated a settlement of the campus crisis, but they did not meet the FSM's free speech demands. Kerr's key blunder was not allowing Savio or any student to speak at this meeting.

Having been refused the right to speak at the meeting, Savio attempted to speak after the last speaker had finished. But as Savio came to the podium, police jumped him—right on stage, in front of thousands of stu-dents and faculty—and dragged him away from the podium. It was one of the most electrifying moments in the FSM crisis. The sight of this public gagging of the Free Speech Movement leader—later dubbed by columnist Ralph Gleason the "Tragedy at the Greek Theatre"—outraged the crowd. Many began chanting, "We want Mario," demanding his release. Students who jumped on the stage to aid Savio—whom police held in a room away from the stage—were tackled by the police. It was pandemonium.

Figure 16. Savio is grabbed by a police officer as he tries to speak at the Greek Theater, December 7, 1964. On the right, a second police officer rushes toward the podium. Photograph courtesy of Ron Riesterer.

Scalapino sought to calm the crowd and defend his leadership of the meeting by explaining why Savio's requests to speak had been denied. What follows is Scalapino's remarks as Savio was in the process of being released and then his exchange with the crowd and Savio, which led to Savio finally being allowed to address the crowd. There then follows Savio's brief remarks to the crowd and reporters.

Professor Robert Scalapino: This meeting was organized by the faculty. The agenda was established by the department chairmen. *[Loud jeers from the crowd.]* Just a moment. I want to make clear what this situation is. The Free Speech Movement, as everyone knows, is having a rally at twelve, in which I assume that we of the departmental chairmen will not move in and try to take over. *[Loud jeers from the crowd. Voices from the*

Figure 17. Moments later, the two police officers drag Savio from the podium and off the stage of the Greek Theatre, in front of a some fifteen thousand shocked and outraged students and faculty. Photograph courtesy of Nat Farbman, Getty Images.

crowd: "But you're welcome to. . . ." "You're invited."] I want to make it clear that our proposal here—this was not an open forum, as far as we were concerned, but a presentation, *[loud jeers]* a presentation.

[Savio emerges, after the police release him, and is asked by reporters if the police had hurt him.]

Savio: Only my clothes here [were ripped and damaged], that's all, you see. I was denied permission to speak here by the police.

Professor Robert Scalapino: We, of course, had no notion that Mr. Savio was going to try to speak at the end of this meeting. *[Jeering. Voices from the crowd: "That is a lie." "Lies." "He requested it." "That is a lie."]* He asked, just a moment. He asked me at the beginning of the meeting whether he would be allowed to speak at this meeting. I said that he would not, because this was a structured meeting, not an open forum, and we had a program which had been approved. *[Jeers.]* We had no notion that he was going to jump up on the stage at the end of this meeting.

Savio: I walked slowly. I'd like to speak here, Mr. Scalapino. May I speak? *[Chants of "We want Mario."]* I'd like to speak, Mr. Scalapino. I'm only going to make a brief announcement. That's all I want do, a brief announcement.

Professor Robert Scalapino: All right. Listen, I am letting Mr. Savio speak, because he has requested it. *[Loud cheers.]*

Savio: I promised Professor [Joseph] Tussman, the chairman of the philosophy department, that I would just make . . . two brief announcements here. I mean to keep *my* word. *[Loud cheers.]* I told him beforehand what they were also, but I didn't ask his permission. They're the following. First, I did, I requested directly of President Kerr, then of the department chairmen, then of Mr. Scalapino, then of the chairmen again, that I be permitted to speak here. Then I asked that I be permitted to make a brief announcement here. Only the announcement that we were having a meeting at twelve. All those requests were denied. Likewise, at that time, Professor [John] Legget [of the sociology department] made that same request, as a faculty member, and was denied. That's the first thing.

Accordingly, we have a meeting scheduled—and this was the announcement I was going to make when I walked up here, the only thing I wanted to say. We have a meeting scheduled for noon on the steps of Sproul Hall. We *invite* these chairmen of departments, who are posing as a faculty, to speak at that meeting, if they have the guts. *[Loud cheers.]* And I am asking you people: all please to come to that meeting now so that we can clear this disastrous scene which has developed here and can get down to discussing the issues.

Transcribed from audiotape, Mario Savio archives, copy in editor's possession, published by permission of Lynne Hollander Savio.

REPORTERS QUESTION SAVIO AFTER HIS REMARKS AT THE GREEK THEATRE

7 DECEMBER 1964

Question: Mario, briefly, what took place on the podium?
Savio: Police seized me at once.

Q: Did you hit them, Mario?

Savio: No, obviously, I didn't hit them.

Q: Were there any blows exchanged?

Savio: No, they just grabbed my arms, pulled me down, my legs, you saw what the scene was.

Q: Where did they take you, Mario?

Savio: They took me into a building adjacent to here and detained me. . . . I demanded to know if I was under arrest. They would not tell me. I tried to leave the building, therefore. They wouldn't let me! A clear abridgement of civil liberties, a disastrous and scandalous situation which obtained here.

Q: Were you hit by any of the police?

Savio: No, I was just grabbed to the ground and my clothes ripped, that's all.

The debacle at the Greek Theatre further eroded the administration's credibility and paved the way for the Academic Senate vote the following day to back the FSM's central free speech demand: that the university cease regulating the content of speech or advocacy. On how Savio's being dragged off the stage ruined Kerr's plans for redemption at the Greek Theatre, Savio would later say, "Kerr was trying, as we saw it, to really snow" the faculty and students. "And it might have worked, except for the little show they put on for the people. The velvet glove got stripped away and the mailed fist was right there and everybody saw. Once that happened, their goose was cooked."[15]

Transcribed from audiotape, Mario Savio archives, copy in editor's possession, published by permission of Lynne Hollander Savio.

NOON RALLY, SPROUL HALL STEPS

7 DECEMBER 1964

Immediately following the Greek Theatre meeting's dramatic ending, students marched down the hill and assembled at Sproul Plaza for what was almost certainly the largest rally of the FSM. Estimates of the crowd, which packed every inch of Sproul Plaza, were as high as ten thousand. Savio's speech at the rally centered on the Academic Senate and the faculty "Committee of Two Hundred," which was planning at the next day's meeting of the senate to introduce a resolution endorsing the FSM's central demand. Savio's call to keep the focus on free speech leaves no doubt that it remained his and the FSM's central goal.

I'd like just to return to as clear and brief a statement of what the free speech issues are, so that when we wait upon the Academic Senate, none of us are going to be floored or fooled or snowed the way that Kerr snowed the governor even—we're not going to have that happen to us. That proposal that Professor [of mathematics Morris] Hirsch read is a damn good proposal. Really is. I really hope . . . unfortunately, I've been told that my endorsement of it weakens its chances. Really is a good proposal, but they're faced with the following kinds of problems, which is why we are so opposed to the setting up of this other committee—department chairmen—because what's going to happen in that meeting. All the prestige of the department chairmen and Clark Kerr all together, descent will have occurred from Mount Olympus, and a *fait accompli* will have been presented to the senate. And then these other members, who are interested not in discussing what committee should resolve the problem but in discussing the problem, discussing the issue, they will have a tremendous obstacle just to overcome, to get where they can start talking. Really essential that we stick with them, that we give them tomorrow one day of real quiet and peace—and hope they can pull it through.

Now, the important points . . . the three that we've maintained all along . . . are the following: the university has no right to regulate the content of speech; that that be entirely up to the properly constituted civil authorities. Content of speech be completely unregulated by any authority except the courts. That's in the proposal—very good. Second, that regulations governing the form of speech not be designed to harass, but rather two things: be designed, one, to encourage free expression; two, to assure that free expression not interfere with the regular academic functions of the university. We've always said that; it's in our platform. We hope they'll be able to get this through. And, third, that some . . . the form we put it in was a tripartite body of students, faculty, and administrators; the form they put it in . . . a committee appointed by the Academic Senate responsible only to the Academic Senate, making final decisions. That this [will] resolve the disputes concerning . . . violations of the form. Believe me, I trust them if they set up such a body and really had those powers. The Heyman Committee is a responsible body. Alright, they're presenting this.

Unfortunately, Clark Kerr and the people he's convinced are presenting a proposal which only in its second point even hints at the issues. The whole thing is about law and order. Only in its second point . . . does it even hint at the issues, and what it says is: we'll go along with the regulations we have until—and possibly after that also, of course—until a proposal of the Academic Freedom Committee of the Academic Senate is made. These other faculty members are *tired* of discussing what committee is going to do it. They want tomorrow to discuss the issues. Let's hope, let's really hope that they can do it. This is the first chance, the first real chance that we have for members of the university community other than those hand-picked by the administration to have a real say in consultation—open deliberation—on what should be the regulations governing political activity on this campus. Let's really hope that they not be bludgeoned by the show you saw put on today. Let's really hope that all this business about law and order not clog up the proceedings interminably, but rather that they discuss the issues. I hope . . . this particular meeting doesn't . . . concern [itself] with police brutality. Later, later. Right now, free speech, that's what we want!

Just two things: one, after this meeting, picket lines are going on. We have to protest what occurred in there. Picket lines are going on, but they end midnight tonight. And I would urge people here to take part in that protest. Secondly, as soon after this meeting as is physically possible, Jack [Weinberg] and I are going to see the governor. So long!

Transcribed from audiotape, Mario Savio archives, copy in editor's possession, published by permission of Lynne Hollander Savio.

SPEECH AT FSM RALLY, SPROUL PLAZA

9 DECEMBER 1964

On December 8 the Berkeley faculty, assembled in the most well-attended Academic Senate meeting in its history, ended the campus free speech crisis by voting overwhelmingly, 824–115, to adopt a set of historic resolutions, which came to be known as simply "The December 8 Resolutions." The first of these resolutions vacated the disciplinary process that Chancellor Strong had initiated against Savio, three fellow FSM organizers, and the student political groups by declaring "that there shall be no university discipli- nary measures . . . connected with the current controversy over political speech and activity." The crucial third resolution overruled Kerr and Strong on the free speech issue, adopting the FSM position "that the content of speech or advocacy shall not be restricted by the University. Off-campus student political activities shall not be subject to University regulation." For Savio, the free speech principles adopted in the December 8 resolutions represented "a kind of Magna Carta or Constitution for the campus."[16]

When the Academic Senate adopted these resolutions, the proceedings were broadcast to a large crowd of students assembled outside the building. The students reacted joyously, and when the senate meeting ended, many— some with tears of joy in their eyes—greeted the faculty leaving the build- ing with cheers and applause. The FSM rally the following day was an extension of this celebration. Savio's brief speech at that victory rally was his most joyous and hopeful of the semester.

It's been said that we've been revolutionaries and all this sort of thing. In a way, that's true. We've gone back to a traditional view of the university. The traditional view of the university is a community of scholars, of fac- ulty and students who get together, who, with complete honesty, . . . bring the hard light of free inquiry to bear upon important matters in the sci- ences but also in the social sciences—the question of . . . what ought to be, not just what is. Now that traditional view of the university, that's the one that had been attacked by the revolutionaries, by those who would make it into a kind of adjunct to industry, to the government, and so forth. Clearly the people, *us*, you know, who fought this fight are maybe the most conservative people on the campus.

We're asking that there be *no*, no restrictions on the content of speech, save those provided by the courts. And that's an enormous amount of free- dom. And people can say things within that area of freedom which are not responsible. Now . . . we've finally gotten into a position where we have to consider being responsible, because now we have the freedom within which to be responsible. And I'd like to say at this time I'm confident, I'm confident that the students and the faculty of the University of California *will* exercise their freedom with the same responsibility they've shown in winning their freedom.

Transcription from audiotape, Mario Savio archives, copy in editor's possession, published by permission of Lynne Hollander Savio. Videotape is available online at https://diva.sfsu.edu/collections/sfbatv/bundles /209401.

"THE BERKELEY KNOWLEDGE FACTORY," SPEECH AT QUEENS COLLEGE, QUEENS, NEW YORK

11 DECEMBER 1964

Savio's Queens College speech was part of a triumphant campus tour that he and other FSM leaders—Suzanne Goldberg, Bettina Aptheker, and Steve Weissman—made to spread the word of the Berkeley revolt to other campuses and to raise funds for the legal defense of protesters who had been arrested. The trip was paid for by Les Crane's television talk show, which had invited these FSMers to appear on the show to discuss the Berkeley revolt.

At the time of the Queens College speech, Savio did not know yet whether the FSM's free speech victory would prove enduring or whether UC's Board of Regents would, in its mid-December meeting, overrule the faculty resolution and enforce the campus regulations restricting the content of political speech on campus. Savio alludes to this concern in his speech, a reminder that the battle for free speech seemed by no means over. A week after his Queens speech, the Board of Regents, though expressing support for President Kerr and affirming existing campus regulations, also pledged for the first time that UC rules on speech would not violate the First and Fourteenth Amendments. The board was, in its own grudging way, conceding that it would not dare to explicitly overrule the faculty and turn back the clock on free speech. The FSM's free speech victory would stand.

Unknown to Savio at that time, the FBI monitored him and the other FSM leaders on this East Coast tour and planted hostile, red-baiting ques-

Figure 18. Savio speaks at Columbia University during the FSM leaders' East Coast tour, mid-December 1964. Photograph courtesy of Art Gatti.

tions in the press, which generated negative media coverage of the tour. In fact, at the news conference Savio held at JFK airport, FBI special agents attended, posing as newspaper reporters.[17] This was only the start of years of FBI work against Savio, which included placing him on a list of national security threats, making pretext calls to his family members, and scouring the country for "any information relating to SAVIO which might connect him with any subversive groups. . . ."[18]

The 1964 campus tour took Savio and fellow FSM leaders to Harvard, Columbia, Brandeis, the University of Michigan, and Queens College, and it proved very successful. As Bettina Aptheker recalled, "everywhere we went we were greeted as heroes, with standing-room-only crowds of thousands of students (and some faculty). It was a jubilant time. As a result of

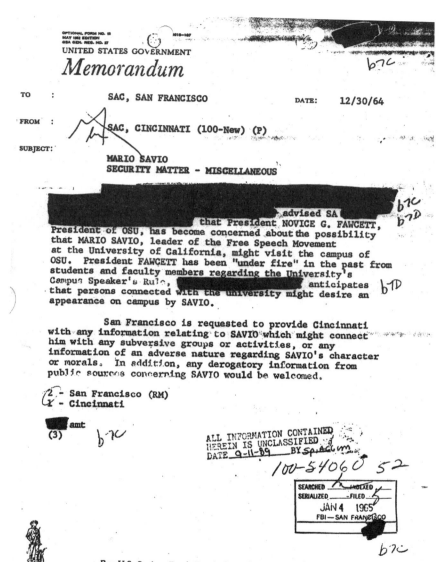

OPTIONAL FORM NO. 10
MAY 1962 EDITION
GSA GEN. REG. NO. 27

UNITED STATES GOVERNMENT

Memorandum

TO   :   SAC, SAN FRANCISCO   DATE: 12/30/64

FROM   :   SAC, CINCINNATI (100-New) (P)

SUBJECT:
                 MARIO SAVIO
                 SECURITY MATTER - MISCELLANEOUS

                                         advised SA
                            that President NOVICE G. FAWCETT,
President of OSU, has become concerned about the possibility
that MARIO SAVIO, leader of the Free Speech Movement
at the University of California, might visit the campus of
OSU. President FAWCETT has been "under fire" in the past from
students and faculty members regarding the University's
Campus Speaker's Rule,   anticipates
that persons connected with the university might desire an
appearance on campus by SAVIO.

                 San Francisco is requested to provide Cincinnati
with any information relating to SAVIO which might connect
him with any subversive groups or activities, or any
information of an adverse nature regarding SAVIO's character
or morals. In addition, any derogatory information from
public sources concerning SAVIO would be welcomed.

2 - San Francisco (RM)
1 - Cincinnati

   amt
(3)

ALL INFORMATION CONTAINED
HEREIN IS UNCLASSIFIED
DATE 9-11-89 BY Sp.accum

100-54060 52

SEARCHED____ INDEXED____
SERIALIZED____ FILED____
JAN 4 1965
FBI—SAN FRANCISCO

Buy U.S. Savings Bonds Regularly on the Payroll Savings Plan

Figure 19. The FBI searches for derogatory information on Savio to prevent him from
inspiring free speech protests at Ohio State University, December 30, 1964. Savio
FBI file.

the FSM . . . schools across the country changed their regulations concerning freedom of speech, and I think all of us believed at the time that the reception we received on our tour had something to do with this."[19]

Savio's speech at Queens extended his critique of Clark Kerr's vision for higher education and, in an account laced with humor, offers the most detailed narrative he would ever present of the Greek Theatre meeting's dramatic ending.

Just one little note of explanation. When I was here [as a student at Queens College], I was Bob Savio. My parents had always called me Bob. And when I had to register for the draft, I had a hell of a time proving who I was [because his birth certificate named him Mario Robert Savio], and I found out then that I had to go by the name I was given originally, my first name [Mario], and I have come to like it very much.

I've chosen the title "The Berkeley Knowledge Factory" because I thought it would strike some responsive chords among people going to Queens College. President Kerr is kind of an ideologist for a new view of the university, which we hope can stop before it gets started. In a book that I recommend to everyone here, *Uses of the University*, President Kerr describes what he calls the "multiversity" and, using the following metaphor—the following very frightening metaphor—he called it a "knowledge factory." He said that it has a president, a president of the university. There's a board of directors, a Board of Regents. It has employees, the faculty members—I'm sure faculty members here don't like that; they don't like it there [at Berkeley] either. And it has raw materials, the students, especially the undergraduates, and these are molded into finished products—two batches every year. The kind of talent necessary to run it are managerial skills, skills of labor-management mediation and arbitration.

And President Kerr is well suited for this kind of thing. He was professor of industrial relations. He's had a wealth of experience in labor-management negotiations, and, as I say, he is very skilled in the kind of management that he describes in *Uses of the University* and in a book that he collaborated on—and I mean collaborated—*Industrialism and Industrial Man*.[20]

We have counterposed to this a more traditional view of the university. It turns out that we're the traditionalists and he's the revolutionist. Our view of the university is a community of scholars and students completely free to inquire and to profess—that's what the word *professor* means—to inquire and profess all points of view, intellectual points of view, political points of view, and that the university best serves the community when it has the freedom [for such inquiry and expression].

In President Kerr's view, the university serves society in a somewhat different way. And he describes the warm and intimate relationship which exists between the knowledge factory and what he calls, and has been called now by many, the "industrial-military complex." That the university has its defense contracts and is mostly concerned with the graduate schools (that's a problem you don't have here the way they have it there [at Berkeley]). That has two products. It has the students, especially the undergraduates, who are turned out as finished products at the end of four years. And then the graduate students turn out a product which is sold at a higher rate: knowledge.

President Kerr says it now has the largest percentage of the gross national product; knowledge is the largest percentage of the gross national product. That's what he maintains, and that, therefore, he is a great industrial leader. A captain of bureaucracy—I didn't invent the phrase, I give credit to Hal Draper; it's a very apt description. Our traditionalist view would liken the university to a classical Christian concept of men in the world but not of the world. That it [the university] exists. That it has safeguards built right about it. So that it's protected, it receives financial assistance from the state, but it's not dictated to in the matter of what is to be discussed, how it's to be discussed, what is to be taught. And that those people who are to run the university are faculty, in consultation with, and giving responsible voice to, students. That the administration is to take an ancillary role, assistance the administration should be to the university proper, maintaining sidewalks clean, seeing that there are good buildings. If the society at large insists upon grading—which is often degrading—then the university can arrange for how many credits courses are supposed to be. But the important matters of educational policy and the regulation of speech and to its form, these are matters for the university community and not for the administration.

The view that Kerr presents reminds me of nothing so much as a Brave New World—that only those ideas and only that mode of presentation which is safe can be permitted. But the First Amendment exists to protect consequential ideas, exists to protect speech with consequences. So on the Berkeley campus, the aura of a free university could have been maintained if students wanted to speak on two kinds of matters. If they wanted to advocate the status quo—Republican or Democrat—or if they wanted to advocate changes in the social structure so radical as to not be about to come off. Civil rights people advocating real things like picket lines and sit-ins and changes in discriminatory hiring policies, and those things that we can bring off this week and next week, and we've been bringing them off for quite a few weeks now. This the university, because it maintains an intimate connection with the financial community, can't tolerate—it would rock the boat. The university then is possibly in the position of having its appropriations reduced or not having quite so many defense contracts. The state government, the Democratic Party of California, these people they can't take too much of this boat rocking. They can't take too much of the pressure from people like Senator [William] Knowland and Assemblyman [Don] Mulford. They can't take too much pressure from the Republican Party in California, which tends to be pretty conservative.

And so the university reserves to itself the right, under certain circumstances, to regulate the content of speech. And I'll try to explain the circumstances, the whole question of freedom of advocacy. We hold that only the courts are justified in regulating the content of speech. And that the form [of speech] should be decided upon by faculty and students. And that the form should be decided upon in such a way as (1) to encourage political expression; (2) to see to it that the normal educational functions of the university be not interfered with. But on the question of the content of speech only the courts [can rule].

The university, by contrast—I should say the administration—the administration maintains that students may not on the campus advocate actions off campus which are themselves unlawful or have actions flowing out of them which are unlawful. I wonder what they are talking about. Civil rights activity in the Bay Area would be crippled if students could not advocate sit-ins—where people are often arrested (I know I was, at the Sheraton Palace [sit-in]). They would really be crippled if they couldn't advocate picket lines, and very often illegal actions occur on picket lines. There already are laws governing speech. Speech under certain circumstances is illegal. And when it is illegal, the courts provide proper punishment. It is not the business of the university to be doing their job. It is not the business of the university to be deciding that the legislature has not already set sufficiently strict barriers about speech. It is not the business of the university to be interpreting the powers of the court, to be providing punishment for transcending those barriers about speech. The university wants to do both. Neither the faculty nor the Berkeley students are about to let them do either.

I'd like to now go through a little bit deeper description of the manner in which President Kerr and the other university managers had a plot to manage the university. . . . In his book, he divides the university community into the managed and the managers. The managers are the administration and the managed is everybody else. And one of the methods President Kerr has used, and this he describes at great length, is the following. One of his peculiar skills, the mediator, he talks to the governor, to the legislature, the Board of Regents, the faculty, and the students. There's only one person who talks to all of them. That's President Kerr. So there's only one source from which they're all getting information. It ends up that he develops a kind of monopoly on the information they get.

I was speaking with [California] Governor Brown over the phone, and I pointed out, wouldn't it be a good idea if he [the governor] heard from the other side in the dispute? And he said no; at that time, it would not be appropriate. The next day—it was a bit later than that—I spoke with his executive secretary (apparently it was no longer appropriate for me to speak with Governor Brown), and his executive secretary said that it was the opinion of the governor's office that it was a controversy without parties, and he had already spoken to President Kerr and was fully confident President Kerr was handling the matter. That the council of department chairmen had been set up to handle the matter by President Kerr, that the governor was fully confident that President Kerr was doing a good job. He'd let the president handle the case. I pointed out that the president's been a party to the dispute. That was a scandal, [to imply bias on the part of] the president of the University of California.

Their problem has been that when complaints occur—this is what a bureaucrat does—when complaints occur, they don't ask, "What are you complaining about?" But [instead they ask] how they can stop you from complaining. "What can I do [to stop the complaining]?" See? It ends up that President Kerr has succeeded in devising a technique designed to stop the students from complaining. If you keep them from complaining, it's not too important, what they're complaining about.

President Kerr, in addition to all his connections with all these famous people, all these official types, has had control over the press. See? And so there appeared, among other things, a series of articles in the *San Francisco Examiner*. One of them named a particular person who was bringing us orders from Cuba. Somebody told me about the article. I was in Southern California when the article was printed. It was the person who was named who told me about it. I was walking down Telegraph Avenue in Berkeley, and someone came up to me, a fellow I'd never met before, a Cuban student at the university. And he said, "look at this article"; I looked at it. And he said, "well, that's me. I didn't get any money!" Well, it's one thing when they exaggerate, but when they start making up stories! We're going to sue them for libel.

Then they have another technique. And they've used this very well until we shafted them, which I'll describe. The president has to be able to maintain the image that he consulted faculty, [since] it's a university. It turns out that [there is] one group of quasi-faculty members over whom he has considerable control, because their interests coincide more with his than with the faculty's, namely the department chairmen. So I mention in particular, single out for special note, Professor Scalapino, chairman of the department of political science. I've got to explain something about his title first, because that really points up what the problem is. He's the chairman of political science. First, political science [and what it] means. In America, there is no political philosophy associated with political science. That's the first problem [with] political science. In America political ideas of all kind, the idea of political ideas, this hasn't been popular at all. So there isn't much politics in political science. And then chairman of political science. The problem with chairmen is that they're administrators. They're more closely plugged in to the administration than to the faculty. And the result, Professor Scalapino became chairman of the council of chairmen.

On Monday last, a meeting was called at the Greek Theatre on the Berkeley campus. And Ralph Gleason described it as appropriate for the

Greek Theatre, because it was a genuine tragedy.[21] Before the meeting, I asked President Kerr if I could make a response at the meeting. And he may have more style, but we have quite a bit; we have a kind of monopoly on drama on the campus. . . . President Kerr said, "Well, this meeting isn't being called by me but by the council of department chairmen"—which was true in only the most formal sense. Well, I said "oh"; you know, it's hard to argue with him. I pointed out that it wasn't completely honest [arranging a meeting in which he was] excluding one of the parties in the dispute [from the right to speak]. He said, "you'll have to speak to the department chairmen." So I went to where they were meeting, and there were a couple of them who had assembled. This is some time before the [Greek Theatre] meeting. I presented the case to them. They said, "Well, we can't help you. You'll have to see the man in charge, Professor Scalapino," the chairman of the chairmen.

I saw Professor Scalapino. Professor Scalapino said, "Well, no, you see." These were his words: "This will be a structured meeting, not an open forum." All right. We argued with him in some way. He said, "Well, you see, it is a faculty meeting. You're a student. It's really not appropriate for you to speak at that meeting." Well, just then to my left was Professor John Leggett of the sociology department. And he said to Scalapino, "I'm a faculty member, and I'd like to speak at the meeting. Can I speak at that meeting?" And Professor Scalapino said, "It's a structured meeting, not an open forum. It would really be inappropriate. The meeting was not an open forum." We were clear on that by then. We fought it out for a while. And behind the Greek Theatre stage, it was getting quite messy. There were other department chairmen there. Some of them had just been totally snowed by Scalapino.

So I waited down in the audience near the stage. And I made it clear to Scalapino when I talked to him, when he said I couldn't make a response. "Well, I just want to make an announcement," I told him. I pointed out that we're having a meeting at the end of this meeting, lower down on campus, so that people could come and hear our side of it. I made it clear I only wanted to make an announcement. And that too was not appropriate. So I sat down near the stage, and then I realized it was going to be necessary to get that microphone. At first I thought in terms of rushing it. And I spoke to a friend, Tom Miller, a member of campus CORE who had experience with rushing a microphone. And I said, "Well, you can run interference with the department chairmen while I get [the microphone].

Then Bettina Aptheker had an excellent idea. She said, "Why don't you just walk up there [to the stage] very slowly? I'm sure that all the students out there [in the Greek Theatre audience] will want you to speak." And so that's what we did. I walked by the stage. I waited until President Kerr had concluded his remarks, kind of half-and-half, fabrication and platitude. Then Professor Scalapino, who had spoken previously on law and order, he got up to adjourn the meeting. So the meeting was adjourned, and I walked up to the microphone. And I didn't even say a word. I think the *Times* article had said I was catching my breath, [getting ready] to speak. And then there were these three policemen, and there was one with his arm around my throat. They could have done lots of things if they really wanted [to halt this use of police violence]. President Kerr could have gotten up and said, "Okay, Mario, you can speak." And that wouldn't have worked nearly so well [for the FSM] as what they did do. They detain you without arrest. And I insisted, "either let me go or arrest me." That kind of thing. And our lawyer pointed out they were abridging civil liberties. And there were people banging on the door [of the room off the stage in which the police had dragged him] to get me out. So [the police released me] I went up and made the announcement.

Professor [Joseph] Tussman, chairman of the philosophy department, was one of those most concerned that I speak. And he said, "Well, Scalapino didn't tell me anything about that. I didn't know you'd been denied the right to speak here. And I know that if I and other department chairmen who feel as I do had known that you had wanted to speak, we would never have denied you the right." And then they started to realize what was going on. And they held an emergency meeting of the council of department chairmen with gasps and tremendous splits at that meeting. They really turned out. And that was the beginning of the demise of the Scalapino-Kerr axis.

Early the next day—it was the date of the Academic Senate meeting [of December 8, 1964]—I saw Professor Tussman, and he was jubilant. I'd never seen him so happy. The man had finally been freed. He'd been able to do what he'd wanted to do all along: support the full free speech demands that we'd been making. He'd been so convinced prior to that [that] if you don't settle the thing this [Kerr's] way, then there are going to be further riots on the campus, and they'd cut off the money from Sacramento and so on. The man had finally been freed.

He hadn't wanted to go along with the Scalapino and Kerr plan. You know this is what they said at that meeting at the Greek Theatre. They presented their five points. Their plans always seemed to have five points. And only one of them, number two, even hinted at the issue. And it said, "we're going to wait for a meeting, for a report from the Academic Senate's Academic Freedom Committee." We [the students] had been debating the issues, waxing eloquent for three months on the issue of free speech. This plan was going to cut off all dialogue now, put the thing to rest. It was a way of stopping them [the students] from complaining without finding out what they were complaining about. That's what they [the UC administrators] were going to do. And the next day [after the Greek Theatre meeting], they were going to present the plan to the Academic Senate, which met the very next day, Tuesday, for ratification. Rubber-stamp congress. It was going to be a *fait accompli*. They were going to present it to the Academic Senate for approval, a plan which was being backed by President Kerr and the unanimous declaration of the department chairmen. You know, that's called "democratic centralism."

So they were going to go to the Academic Senate for the plan to be ratified. And Professor Tussman, he was so relieved. He was so happy and I was so happy, because there were many really, really good men among the council of department chairmen who didn't have the political slickness of Scalapino, weren't as clever as Kerr, who really thought that this plan was necessary in order to insure peace on the campus. Really, what was really necessary was listening to the free speech demands of the students. That was the shafting at the Greek Theatre.

Now we have the problem with the Board of Regents. On the next day, the Academic Senate, in the most heavily attended meeting [of the Berkeley faculty] ever recorded, voted 824–115 to support the Free Speech Movement demands. It was magnificent. Now the faculty and students are really united on the issue that only the courts, not the university— under no circumstances can the university regulate the content of speech. The faculty and students powerfully united. The matter is coming up before the Board of Regents on December 18th. And technically, they have the power to repudiate the faculty position. And some of their members, [Regents] Hearst, Chandler, Rafferty, these are people who don't like our having this free speech, because of the civil rights movement and the fact that we advocate that sort of thing.[22] But to me, it would be unthinkable for them to repudiate that mandate of the faculty. And yet before we can be too optimistic, we should think back upon the [Loyalty] Oath fight [the purging, during the McCarthy era, of faculty who refused to sign an anti-Communist loyalty oath], . . . where the faculty were decimated. The administration had no concern that they were destroying the university. They lost some of their best faculty members. And we're hoping that they're not going to try something like that again.

I'd like before closing to deal with just one more matter: the motivation of the students. Jack Weinberg, a key starter of this movement, a brilliant tactician, the fellow who was in that [police] car for thirty-two hours [during the October 1–2 sit-in around the police car that had helped launch the FSM]. He was working late one night after the October demonstrations with a student who just joined the movement. And the student said to him, "You know, Jack, I don't give a damn about free speech." Jack was really surprised.

The student didn't mean that he didn't want free speech, although that [the free speech issue] wasn't what had brought him into it [the FSM]. Jack was quite surprised and asked him what was it [that had brought him into the movement]. And the student said, "I am sick and tired of being shat upon." That is the issue. For instance, a totally unresponsive bureaucracy, a managerial conception of the university which results in a student body terribly alienated from the administration and, until recently, from the faculty. No one really gives a damn about undergraduate education—not really—because the product coming out of the graduate school brings a higher price.

I think the clearest description of the depths of this alienation would be a description of the last [November 1964] regents meeting, in which the regents adopted this policy that we're protesting. We turned in all kinds of petitions; we'd been working with passion for two months to get our free speech. And five spaces had been reserved for us in the press gallery. We'd made [and been denied] a request to appear before the regents and present our case. We're sitting there, and there was this long oval table around about which were seated the members of the Board of Regents. This thick pile rug. All the sounds were muffled in the room. And above the table long fluorescent fixtures covered in one of those translucent plastic shades so that even the lights were confusing.

There was one member of the board speaking in monotonous low tones, citing off a list of numbers. At first I couldn't understand what he was saying, and I tried to. He explained how it was that the university was coming along. He was describing the progress of the investments of the University of California. He was describing how its endowments were increasing, how its alumni were supporting it in this way, and was reciting these figures as evidence of how well the university was doing.

Then it was President Kerr's turn and he stood up. And he had his secretary there. And he had her pass out to the members of the board thick packets, folders containing all of the petitions, letters, recommendations, and plans for free speech. . . . Then he says "gentlemen, the issues are complex and subtle, and you may want time to study them in some detail after this meeting. That's why I've prepared for you packets. But for now I just have two recommendations." And he presented the first, which was to stiffen the recommendations an Academic Senate committee on student conduct had made concerning eight suspended students [this was the Heyman report of the Academic Senate, which Kerr viewed as too lenient in its punishment of FSM leaders]. The Board of Regents, without discussion—with no discussion—voted unanimously to accept that recommendation. Then he had a recommendation concerning free speech. He said, "well, these are complicated matters, where the microphones go and things like that. That doesn't interest you. This is one main question, the constitutional question," with the general counsel cutting in with what he had prepared more than a month in advance. This recommendation had two parts.

The first was an endorsement of existing university regulations. And then a policy of advocacy: that in certain circumstances, the university could indeed regulate the content of speech. And then the first discussion. One of the members of the board asked that the question be divided to hold these discussions. On the first part, the vote was unanimous. On the second part, there were two dissenters, who thought the policy [of the university on political advocacy] too liberal. And that was it. He concluded in ten minutes, upsetting what we'd been working on for more than two months. And then he just sat down.

You try to picture how—I mean, it seemed Kafkaesque. A frightening thing. We'd made use of every official channel open to us. We followed the channels through to the very end. We'd opened up some new channels, the Committee on Campus Political Activity and the Heyman Committee— that's that Academic Senate Committee on Student Conduct, those came out of the agreement we'd signed [with Kerr, ending the police car sit-in] on October 2nd. We followed those channels through to their conclusion. All these channels proved fruitless, totally fruitless. All doors were closed to us. Those least inclined to civil disobedience, the Goldwater supporters, they [along with hundreds of other FSM activists] sat in at Sproul Hall and were arrested. All channels were closed to us. Jack has described it not so much as a political revolt but rather as an existential one. We wanted to be heard, someone should listen to us. So we went into Sproul Hall [and sat in on December 2, 1964, sparking the largest mass arrest of students ever seen at a university in the United States].

Here is a quotation from the ninth chapter of *Moby Dick*. It's a very serious book. There is a quotation from the ninth chapter of *Moby Dick* which I think is very appropriate—kind of our motto: "Woe unto him who would pour oil on the waters when God had brewed them into a gale."

Transcript of Art Gatti's audiotape recording. Initially published in New Politics. *Reprinted with permission of Lynne Hollander Savio.*

SPEECH AT THE CALIFORNIA FEDERATION OF TEACHERS CONVENTION, FRESNO

29 DECEMBER 1964

Throughout the semester, the FSM's community support came primarily from civil rights and civil liberties groups and from labor unions. The California Federation of Teachers had been one of the earliest and most supportive unions. So Savio knew he was among friends when he gave his last speech in 1964, and he laced his account of the FSM struggle with humor—even singing a chorus from one of the FSM's sarcastic Christmas Carols. The speech would make headlines because of the clever way Savio sought to turn the tables on the California politicians who had had called for investigations of the FSM to track down the subversives and outside agitators they blamed for the Berkeley rebellion. Savio responded defiantly, calling for an investigation of UC's undemocratic Board of Regents, an appropriate way to end a tumultuous semester of challenging the rules, structure, and governance of the University of California.[23]

I'd like to comment on some questions and answers in an interview which occurred last night, which Stanley Crockett for San Diego NBC made with our great speaker of the [California State] Assembly [Jesse Unruh]. The questions dealt with the response that the Academic Senate made on December 8 to the Free Speech Movement. And Mr. Unruh said, among other things, that the Academic Senate was overly responsive to its constituency. And then Mr. Crockett asked what would be forthcoming from Mr. Unruh, first of all, if we could expect the Board of Regents to give additional powers to the Academic Senate, the faculty. And Mr. Unruh said he would strenuously oppose the regents giving additional powers to the Academic Senate, though he did not think the regents would do so. Nor do I. . . .

[A recent newspaper report] begins the following way: "Assembly Speaker Unruh urged yesterday that the legislature investigate who really is agitating these students and promoting this activity." That's from the *San Francisco Chronicle.* And I'm reminded of how the administration, the Democratic Party establishment agitation began with President Kerr indicating that—or it was reported this way anyway—that 49 percent of the [FSM's] hard core are "Castro-Maoist-Communists." Well, I've yet to determine whether I am, in fact, one of the hard core. But fortunately or unfortunately—I think perhaps unfortunately—we have become progressively more responsible. The newest charge, this time from our chancellor, is that it's not from Peking nor from Havana that we are getting our money and instructions but from Moscow—we've become more responsible. If we become too responsible, we will lose, I'm afraid.

I'd like to give some idea—kind of an unorthodox way to have a speech— some idea of the spirit of things on the Berkeley campus, if I may, by singing a song. This is one of the satirical songs that was made up in one of our blackest moments on the campus, when we were really as desperate as we could be. And it's sung to the tune of the closing chorus of Beethoven's Ninth Symphony.

> From the tip of San Diego
> To the top of Berkeley's hills
> We have built a mighty factory
> to impart our social skills
> Social engineering triumphed,
> Managers of every kind
> Let us all with drills and homework
> Manufacture human minds
> Make the students safe for knowledge,
> Keep them loyal,
> Keep them clean,
> That is why we have a college,
> Hail to IBM machine!

Well, the history of the movement, very briefly, began on September 14th, when a letter came down from Dean Towle, which said that certain rights, certain political rights, that students had been enjoying for years at the Bancroft-Telegraph entrance to the university would no longer be enjoyed. These included soliciting funds, membership sign-ups for various partisan causes, trying to get people to come down to do precinct work, in general, the advocacy of off-campus political and social action. And we protested it. And after a vigil and picket lines and all sorts of things, on October 2, under pressure of about six hundred policemen on campus, we signed an agreement, very prejudicial against us. We signed it, and we instituted a self-imposed moratorium on our exercise of our rights. You know you can't take rights away, but people can choose not to exercise them for a while, and that's what we did. And there were set up two committees, the Committee on Campus Political Activity and the Heyman Committee. The Heyman Committee was made a group of five faculty members [and was] set up to try the cases of eight students suspended indefinitely—a species of suspension invented for the purpose by the administration—suspended indefinitely for political activity on the campus.

The CCPA deadlocked after five weeks. We'd been doing nothing for five weeks. The "No on 14" campaign was running into the ground.[24] And we were just waiting around this committee, and . . . it deadlocked on the issue of advocacy—our position being that only the courts have the right to regulate the content of speech. We lifted the moratorium [on campus protests]. We still wanted to meet with the committee [CCPA] to see if we could hammer out with the faculty some reasonable regulations regarding the *form* of political expression. But the chancellor decided that, seeing as we'd left the committee and it could no longer be used for the purpose of stalling, that committee would be dissolved.

So November 20 came along and the Board of Regents met, . . . and they repudiated the Heyman Committee report because it was too liberal, ... [The Heyman report] criticized the administration more than the students. And so that report was repudiated by the Board of Regents. And the Board of Regents adopted [the] position that the administration adopted, adopted a worse position, embodying the worst of the administration position in the Committee on Campus Political Activity, plus some other things. And it was unacceptable to us. A lot of people had been surprised: "Why didn't you accept these great liberalizations which have been made?" Well, there were none. The rule which we had been protesting had not been enforced prior to September 14. And so while the regents at least nominally liberalized that rule, they finalized restrictions greater than those which had been placed upon us up to and including September 14. So there had been no liberalizations.

Well, that brings us to December. And we were unfortunately bound to be content with a de facto situation on campus which was not good. And the chancellor decided to discipline four students for things they'd allegedly done two months before [and] likewise discipline [their student] organizations. And that we could not accept. You know, it is as though your [union's] chairmen and your officers were taken out by some administrator in some school that you're in, beaten up for something, and then what would become of the union? The union would act, I presume. I would hope. Well, we're not part of the establishment. We did act.

We gave the university administration twenty-four hours. That was a pretty gutsy thing to do, I must say, and I wasn't sure at the time [if it] was going to be bought by the students. They were with us. They realized what had happened. One hallmark of the movement: loyalty—loyalty of the people to themselves, to one another—concern, fraternalism, and fraternity. Our demands were that discipline dropped, that no further discipline be instituted, and that we'd get our free speech. Those demands we gave them twenty-four hours to do the first and begin on the second—we realized that the regents had to act. And what would count as a beginning? A statement by Clark Kerr saying, . . . "Yes, the university has no right to regulate the content of speech."

Well, of course, our demands were not met. And we sat in. What kinds of things did we do? Well, we conducted classes. We set up the first session of the Free University of California. We sang songs. A couple of people climbed into double sleeping bags. We had Chanukah services inside Sproul Hall, which may well have compromised the university in article 9, section 9, bringing down the sectarian influence upon it. And then the police came.

And, you know, we have many great problems, and a lot of them may be found in Oakland, in the ghetto. And so you need the police. You need certain kind of police to take care of those problems. And I am not being facetious. They are needed, you see, because the problem exists. It's the problem we should get rid of. As long as the problem exists, you need the police. And those police, trained to sadism, were brought on the campus. And first it was the Berkeley police in charge. And in many ways they are a model force. And so students were taken one at a time. Brought down the elevator. And then things were taking too long. We planned this thing quite well, I think. So they turned loose the Oakland police. And they were in a hurry. So they started throwing us down the stairs. People were kicked, without provocation, punched, men and women. We're not going to be able to get rid of that situation till we get rid of the Oakland situation. But we should know about it and start working on getting rid of it.

Well, most of the leadership was in jail. But leadership has a way of just springing up when you need it. And so a strike committee, most of which was out of jail, called a strike. And the papers reported that only two thousand were out of classes, and so on. And the thing was closer to about 70 percent effective. Anyone on campus was very much aware of, well of, the anarchy. No one was in class. Few were in class. Both professors and students were hardly able to conduct their activities normally. I'm rather happy and proud about the strike. I suppose I can say it at this meeting. I can't say it in other places.

So then this brings us to the Greek Theatre. Clark Kerr, from October 2nd on, had maintained himself aloof. And then Clark descends, in this case he descends from Mount Olympus, went to the fray. . . . But he has to do so in a way which lends an air of respectability, that which we shun, to what they were doing. There is only one way you can do that on a university campus. You have got to involve the faculty. And so you must choose your faculty carefully. You must be sure that they look like faculty members, while being appropriately plugged in to the administration. I'm sure you had your name for them; in Mississippi they were called Uncle Toms. Anyway, three groups of people who fit this bill. Certain department chairmen, they're mostly administrators. Now this is not a blanket condemnation of department chairmen. We have good department chairs. We have the naïve ones. I mean politically naïve. Then we have those, maybe the largest group—and it is very sad—people who were so crushed by the Loyalty Oath fight, they just haven't recovered. Then we have those who are just weak. And there's a lot of overlap between the second and third group. Then we have a small group, and those are the ones Kerr is counting on. They're the sharpies, you see—they're the ones who spend their time in Academic Senate politics. People like Arthur Ross, for example, . . . a good friend of Clark Kerr, skilled in the techniques of labor management, very appropriate on the kind of campus we have.[25]

Accordingly, a council of department chairmen was set up. And the chairman of the chairmen was Professor Scalapino, chairman of political science. And they had a meeting; they convened a meeting in the Greek Theatre. During the time this was going on, another group of faculty members—the radicals, the young Turks, two hundred members strong—[was] meeting and drew up a set of proposals, very good proposals, and they embodied our essential demand.[26] But Kerr and Scalapino were determined to outflank these people by holding a meeting in the Greek Theatre where the faculty—that is the department chairmen—would present their peace proposal. And the next day, when the Academic Senate met, Tuesday, they would present these to the senate for ratification, a rubber-stamp procedure, and the prestige of senate would be right on each proposal.

Well, the proposals included nothing. I mean, there were the usual platitudes about "we're in favor of law and order. And we're against disorder and violence." Things that I'm against and in favor of. And there was only one place that they even hinted at free speech. They said, "we'll wait until the Academic Senate Academic Freedom Committee meets and gives its report." Well, we'd been waxing sometimes quite eloquent for four months—three months—on the free speech demand and on the free speech issue. But they needed another committee. So these peace proposals from the department chairmen had nothing. Well, you know what happened, of course. I am not wearing that tie, the one [referring to the one he was wearing at the at the Greek Theater, which the police grabbed as they physically removed him from the stage], Mr. [Hal] Draper gave me a union tie here.[27] You know what happened—no speaking.

But after the meeting, there was an emergency meeting of the council of department chairmen. And there was a split in it. Whereas they had reported it out unanimously before—which . . . is called "democratic centralism"—this time there was a split, and after all, they couldn't quite go along with Professor Scalapino and these smooth types.

And so the next day the Academic Senate had that magnificent vote of 824–115 to support the free speech demands of the Free Speech Movement. Then the Board of Regents met and made it clear [that] it would do what Mr. Unruh said he hoped they would do, namely, not give additional power to the faculty. One of the things the faculty had demanded was that *they* be responsible solely for disciplining students for violating reasonable regulations on the content of their speech. And the Board of Regents said, "Oh no, not that, [we] can't control them."

What, after all, have been the issues in this? Gives you a kind of feeling for the history of this. What have been the issues? The issues have been speech with consequences. That's why we have a First Amendment. Not for speech, just plain speech doesn't need any protection. But speech with consequences. That means not people advocating the status quo. Nor people advocating changes so comprehensive as to be impossible to pull off in the near future. The people advocating picket lines and sit-ins. . . . People advocating civil rights demonstrations are advocating things [and] have speech that has consequences. And it is for speech with consequences, for this that the restrictions exist, and for this that the suppression exists, and for this that the regents are so up in arms again. And why? It is because regents are the same people that you picket when you have civil rights demonstrations. . . . Our businesses, our newspapers, our universities, and to a large extent our political parties are all owned by the same people. That's very serious. Very big problem. A lot of those people sit on the board [of regents].

What were we demanding that they could not accept? That the content of speech—that the university have no right to regulate the content of speech. And they were taking the following position. That under certain circumstances, namely, when a student on campus advocates so-called unlawful off-campus acts that then the university has the right to regulate the content of his speech, to punish him, and to punish his sponsoring organization. Well, what counts as unlawful campus acts? Well, sit-ins do, you see. Well, I was arrested at the Sheraton Palace. I was acquitted. For doing precisely the same thing, other people were convicted. . . . Someone advocated going to the Sheraton Palace to picket. And that picket suddenly became a sit-in. Were the people on campus [urging people to picket the Sheraton], would they have been [deemed guilty by the UC administration of] advocating unlawful off-campus activity [even though they had advocated only a lawful picket, and even though the sit-in's unlawfulness was unclear, since some who sat in were tried and acquitted, while others sitting in were convicted]? Well, under the purview of the regents' policy, yes, because the regents claim the authority to discipline you if it can be shown at *their* hearings that you are a willful link in a causal chain which resulted in some unlawful off-campus act. They don't even specify in that policy, as they had previously in the Committee on Campus Political Activity, . . . that the unlawful act has to be unlawful by some criteria related to California or federal law.

In other words, you can even be disciplined under the purview of the regents' policy for advocating people go up to Mississippi and break *their* laws. But let's not say that they will do that. Let's just say, at the very minimum, that if Don Mulford gets mad again because somebody sat in at some drug store in Oakland, that would be enough.[28] That would be enough. Those on campus who did the advocacy, their organizations, those would be disciplined.

And how would it be determined that you were a causal link, a willful link in a causal chain resulting in the unlawful act? How? By an administrative hearing. Well, an administrative hearing. It's *worse* than double jeopardy. Administrative hearings have only two defects: they usurp the powers of the courts, and they usurp the powers of the legislature. If they just usurped the powers of the courts that would be double jeopardy. But no, the powers of the legislature as well, because they bring charges on matters which could never become indictments in a court—you know, culpability, that is, this business about becoming a willful link, this business. That doesn't hold up in any court. There are only two laws in California against illegal speech: conspiracy and solicitation to crime—it's almost never used. Just as the rabbis build very strong walls around Torahs, there are very strong walls built by the Supreme Court around the First Amendment. It's very difficult to convict someone of conspiracy. The only cases that were brought to the Supreme Court have been thrown out. Very difficult to convict someone of solicitation of a crime. The latter [solicitation] makes it a misdemeanor to advocate committing a crime; conspiracy makes it a felony, under certain circumstances, to commit a crime, even if the crime is a misdemeanor.

What the administration wants to do is, on far weaker charges, hold a hearing, decide that you are culpable, and punish you. Well, we just can't do it. That cuts off all sorts of advocacy of effective civil rights action. And why do they want this power? They made it very clear. In the Committee on Campus Political Activity, they gave one and only one reason. They need the power in order to be able to effectively respond to external, extralegal pressures on the university. That's what they said, and I'm content to quote. Some have said it's pandering. I say it's cynicism—whatever, we can't permit it. If anything is forbidden by the First Amendment, it's that a public institution protect itself from external pressures by restricting the rights of people over whom it has power. One thing you cannot do. The First Amendment does not place restriction on speech, but on restrictions on the restriction on speech, and this is one of the clear ones.

All these things that have happened raise a bigger question. In some ways the newspapers have been right: who runs the University? That is the question. And it's right that we are challenging university governance. Correct. About time. In the traditional view, the university is autonomous. The university can only serve the state if the state does not control it. The state should give the money. The state shouldn't decide what gets taught or how it's taught. The state shouldn't decide who hires and fires teachers. Only your colleagues are competent to decide if you're competent. Very important.

The traditional Christian concept of man, namely, that he is in the world but not of the world, should apply to the university. To serve as a kind of gadfly. That doesn't mean that the university shouldn't be there to, say, fulfill defense contracts—well, I take that back—shouldn't be there to fulfill certain kinds of contracts. But that is not its primary function. . . . And to fulfill its primary, the primary demand upon it, its primary call, it must be autonomous.

And so we come to what has been thrown at us: article 9, section 9 of the state constitution. It says the university should be free from sectarian influence. Well, I maintain that the Board of Regents have violated article 9, section 9. Accordingly, to outdo Jesse Unruh and to outdo Mr. [Hugh] Burns [who called for an investigation of the Free Speech Movement], I call for a legislative investigation—of the Board of Regents.[29] There are certain very serious things wrong with them. They do not represent the people of California. . . . Apparently there is a good deal of overlap between the interests they do represent and the places the university ends up investing in, for example.

And so what kind of an institution do we have in contraposition with this autonomous institution, in the world but not of the world? Well, I'd like to close on that note, the kind that we have, namely, the knowledge factory. And I'd like to expand on that as the final thing. President Kerr, in a wonderful book, which I hope everyone will read, *The Uses of the University*, describes the knowledge factory. These are his metaphors. They've got to be quite picturesque. It has a board of directors, the Board of Regents, the president of the firm, that's Clark. It has employees, those are the professors—you know about that. And it has raw material. That's me. Some of the raw material is more intractable than they'd hoped. The concept that Kerr presents of the university is that there are managers and there are the managed—those who command and those who obey. And the thing is stood on its head. Kind of what Marx said he did to Hegel, Kerr has done to the traditional concept of the university. Just turned it upside down. Those who should be giving orders have to obey orders. Those [administrators] who should serve in an ancillary capacity as assistants to the professors and students—they tell the professors and students what to do.

And so we have on the university campus a perfect model, a social model. And the lines are not nearly so clear in macrocosm, but in the university microcosm, we have a social model for—if I may be allowed this—class conflict. And so there is extreme alienation on the campus [among] the professors and, more clearly, the students and, most clearly, the undergraduates—because nobody cares about them. The university, with its knowledge factory, has two kinds of classes. The graduate school—it responds to defense contracts and so on; it turns out one kind of product: knowledge. And President Kerr says that's one of the largest parts of the gross national product: knowledge. And that's the most remunerative of their products: knowledge. But on the other side, the undergraduate school—it has its products, two batches a year. And these—they don't come nearly at so high a price. People with the bachelor's degrees are pretty easy to come by. And so everything conspires to make undergraduate education worse and worse and worse until finally there is an explosion. Jack Weinberg, one of the people most responsible for the Free Speech Movement, was working one day—after October 2nd, after the incident with the car—was working with someone who had just joined the movement. And this fellow turned to Jack, and he said, "No, I don't give a damn for free speech." Weinberg was very confused. The student didn't mean that he didn't want free speech, but that—of and by itself—would never have explained his involvement in the Free Speech Movement. What he said was, "I'm just sick and tired of being shat upon."

The issue is this, people. This principle, this business, about some people who give orders and some who take them. And some who are sick and tired, sick at heart that they're just numbers on punch cards. It's the same thing when you're in front of a TV set. It's not important who you are but that you are part of an audience of thirty million. So when that commercial comes on, there will be enough people buying products. The same thing at the university. It's not important who you are, just important that on the bell curve, there are so many here and so many here and here. That the process goes on in an orderly fashion. That's what's important.

It's really like something out of Franz Kafka or Camus. The thing that I keep remembering is that scene just after Meuersault in *The Stranger,* just after he has been on trial. He's considering with himself, his subjective reaction, most of what he considers in the whole book, his subjective reaction is at the trial. Here is the prosecutor at one side and his counsel supposedly at the other, and they were shadow boxing back and forth. They were deciding that he was guilty of murder because he didn't cry at his mother's funeral. And then he, he wanted to say something; he said to himself that it is important who this accused person is—that's a significant thing. I should be able to speak up on my own behalf at my own trial. I should be able to take a part, in other words, in deciding what rules are put upon me, whether they're justified, how they're enforced. I should have a hand in all those things. I should have a hand in this pleading of guilty. I should have a hand in deciding just how come I came to be guilty because I must be guilty. Just that thing. That's the thing that goes on daily in our society, in every single aspect of it.

That's what goes on on the university campus—that the accused, those of us who are guilty, every one of us, don't have any say, have no hand at all in deciding how we came to be guilty, don't know who's accusing us even.

That's the kind of thing which is important on a university campus— the question of incredible alienation. At a certain point, you get so torn up inside—at some point, you can't bear it any longer. You've tried *all* the channels, you've gone though to the end of all the channels, you've made some new ones, you've gone though to the end of those. *Total futility.* You can't get anywhere with these channels. There's got to be an explosion somewhere. And I'd like to take this kind of as maybe the motto for the Free Speech Movement, something [from] a very serious book, Herman Melville's *Moby Dick,* chapter 9, says: "Woe to him who seeks to pour oil upon the waters when God has brewed them into a gale." Thanks.

Transcribed from audiotape, Mario Savio archives, copy in editor's possession, published by permission of Lynne Hollander Savio. Audio also available online (but incorrectly dated January 3, 1965) at www.lib.berkeley. edu/MRC/FSM/fsmchronology1.html.

Coda

After the Free Speech Movement, Savio was active in the movement against the Vietnam War, but pulled back from political leadership. Though sidetracked from both politics and education by his problems with depression in the late 1960s and 1970s, Savio returned to the academic world in late 1970s, and in the early 1980s he earned a BS and MS in physics and began teaching at the college level. He also returned to the political stage, first as an activist in the Left-liberal environmentalist Citizens Party and then as a critic of Ronald Reagan's counter-revolutionary proxy wars in Central America and as a voice on behalf of the antiapartheid divestment movement. In the final decade of his life, Savio would organize a statewide campus coalition in California in defense of affirmative action and immigrant rights. He died in 1996 amid a battle against fee hikes at Sonoma State University (where he was teaching mathematics, logic, and interdisciplinary courses in science and literature), struggling to keep higher education affordable for low-income students.[1] Savio is survived by fellow FSM veteran Lynne Hollander Savio, to whom he had been married since 1980, their son, Daniel, and by his first wife, Suzanne Goldberg, and their sons, Stefan and Nadav.

Figure 20. Savio speaks at an antiwar protest, Berkeley Student Union, November 30, 1966. When the UC administration allowed the U.S. Navy ROTC to set up a recruitment table but barred antiwar protesters from setting up a counter-recruitment table, there was a sit-in, in which Savio was arrested. Photograph courtesy of Bettmann/Corbis.

For more than a quarter century after the Free Speech Movement, Savio and the FSM remained too controversial on the Berkeley campus for UC's administration to acknowledge their role in expanding free speech there. In 1989 more than one hundred Berkeley faculty, headed by the distinguished art historian Peter Selz, founded the Berkeley Art Project to fund and oversee a competition for a permanent, site-specific work on Sproul Plaza "to commemorate the 25th anniversary of the Free Speech Movement and the political activities that ensued, including . . . Civil Rights and Anti-War" protests.[2] But UC Berkeley chancellor I. Michael Heyman rejected the idea of so honoring the Free Speech Movement. Heyman argued that

> The free speech movement . . . was not in 1964, or in the campus community today, a universally shared value. For many, perhaps most, 1964 was a

time of agony.... Describing the events of 1964 as "the free speech movement" was in itself a political act, a particular point of view sought to package its position, as it were, in a widely shared value the way post–Civil War politicians used to wave the bloody shirt.... To view it heroically now is part of politics, but is also a rhetorical device that seems to me arguably inconsistent with the University's mission of the dispassionate search for truth.[3]

Heyman cited faculty critics of the FSM, such as journalism professor David Littlejohn, who suggested that "the events of 1964" had bequeathed to Berkeley a student Left that was intolerant of "dissident points of view," and the chancellor even suggested that "the rowdiness displayed at my inaugural" in 1980 was part of the FSM's legacy.[4]

The Art Project was thus forced to abandon its goal of explicitly honoring the Free Speech Movement and instead shifted to finding an artwork that evoked the spirit of free speech without mentioning the FSM. In June 1990 Chancellor Heyman accepted the winning sculpture "Column of Earth and Air" by Mark A. Brest Van Kempen for installation on Sproul Plaza, praising it as "a symbolic memorial to the universally shared value of freedom of speech." But Heyman reiterated that he "would have rejected ... the sculpture" had it mentioned or memorialized the FSM.[5] Savio was so outraged that a free speech art competition had, in effect, been censored—barred by the chancellor from mentioning the FSM either in the memorial chosen or the publicity surrounding it—that he refused to attend the dedication ceremony.[6] Former FSM Steering Committee member Michael Rossman was even more scathing, terming "the sculpture, sunk in the center of Sproul Plaza, a monument not to the FSM but to the university's cowardice and shame."[7]

Not until Heyman's tenure as chancellor ended would the UC administration warm up to Savio and the FSM. In 1994, on the occasion of a noon rally on Sproul Plaza celebrating the FSM's thirtieth anniversary, Heyman's successor, Chang-Lin Tien, sent a representative who read a statement acknowledging the importance of the FSM. Two years later, Genaro Padilla, UC Berkeley's vice chancellor for undergraduate affairs, spoke at the Berkeley memorial ceremony for Savio, praising his activism and the FSM's impact on the university.[8]

The first successful move to memorialize Savio more formally came from the Berkeley student body and was initiated in spring 1997 by ASUC president Grant Harris and the ASUC Senate. They proposed—and Chancellor Tien approved—the honoring of Savio for his role in leading the Free Speech Movement by naming the steps of Sproul Hall—from which he gave his most famous speeches—the Mario Savio steps. They were so dedicated in December 1997.[9] In 1997, the university also agreed to publicize, though it did not fund, an annual Mario Savio Memorial Lectureship—an idea initiated by Suzanne Goldberg at the suggestion of consumer advocate Ralph Nader. Lynne Hollander Savio established the Mario Savio Young Activist Award, presented each year at the Savio lecture.[10]

Three years later, the university further honored Savio and the student movement by opening the Free Speech Movement Café next to the undergraduate library, along with an archive on the movement. These were part of a major gift to the university library, endowed through a $3.5 million donation by FSM-era Cal alumnus Stephen M. Silberstein, the founder of Innovative Interfaces, which developed the software used by most major libraries. In announcing this endowment, UC chancellor Robert M. Berdahl, a noted historian, remarked that from the moment

> Mario Savio removed his shoes and mounted the top of a police car to defend the right of free speech . . . life has never been the same . . . on the Berkeley campus or any other major university in the United States. . . . The Free Speech Movement had a significant role in placing the American university center stage in the free flow of political ideas, no matter how controversial. . . . As a result of those events, universities everywhere have been more open to student political activism and engagement with issues facing society.[11]

Regarding his gift to the university and why he chose to donate it in the name of Savio and the Free Speech Movement, Silberstein explained, "We owe no small debt to Mario Savio and the individuals who made up the Free Speech Movement. Despite great personal and family sacrifice, they spoke up for the ideals upon which our society is based, and in which we all believe: a more just world, civil rights, and the removal of limitations on the free discussion and advocacy of ideas."[12] Silberstein, who worked in

UC's libraries for a decade, also saw his financial support of "one of the world's truly great libraries" as "something . . . Mario would appreciate."[13] Silberstein's creation of the Mario Savio/Free Speech Movement Endowment, which supplements the state funds for the university's collection in the humanities, is not merely a tribute to Savio and the FSM, but a new kind of challenge to the movement's detractors, who have argued that the legacy of Savio, the FSM, and New Left was damaging to the university. Here is a case where the FSM's legacy was literally to enrich the university intellectually and materially.

How then do we make sense of the decades of UC administration resistance to honoring Savio and the FSM? There are political reasons why Mario Savio and the FSM tradition of student protest made campus administrators like Heyman nervous long after the 1960s. Here the key issue was not free speech but civil disobedience and student power. Savio and the FSM revealed that civil disobedience and nonviolent sit-ins, including building occupations, can empower students and, through their disruptive force, can compel university administrators to listen to them and even, at times, heed their advice or demands. Heyman had himself been on the losing end of such disruptive protests from Berkeley's antiapartheid movement, which in April 1985 used the largest campus sit-in, mass arrest, and TA/student strike since the 1960s to push UC to divest its holdings in companies that did business with South Africa's racist regime. Savio himself came back to campus to speak at the divestment movement's rally after the arrest of 158 Berkeley protesters at Sproul Hall, declaring that UC administrators "are trying to make examples of the people they have arrested. Turn those examples around. Build the movement on their stupidity."[14] The movement was not only built, but the following summer it would triumph—overcoming the opposition of Heyman and UC president David Gardner. California governor Deukmejian, who was up for reelection, dropped his resistance, enabling the UC Board of Regents to divest the university of its $3.1 billion worth of stock in companies connected to South Africa.[15] It is little wonder, then, that with regard to Savio and the FSM, a fearful Heyman seemed haunted by William Faulkner's maxim: "The *past* is *never* dead. It's not even *past*."

THE DAILY CALIFORNIAN

SERVING THE CAMPUS COMMUNITY SINCE 1871

VOLUME XVII, NO. 68   WEDNESDAY, APRIL 17, 1985   BERKELEY, CALIFORNIA

UC COPS ARREST 158; STUDENTS CALL FOR CLASS BOYCOTT TODAY

Staff, faculty, students urged to stay home

UC Berkeley's Graduate Assembly Tuesday called for a campuswide boycott of classes and work by UC Berkeley students, faculty and staff today after UC police arrested 158 people at campus demonstrations.

The boycott was also endorsed by the Association of Graduate Student Employees and the American Federation of Teachers — the only faculty union on campus — at a meeting Tuesday night.

In addition to the called-for boycott, a teach-in and study-in are planned as well as a noon rally on Sproul Plaza, a march on University Hall, and pickets at campus entrances.

American Federation of State, Municipal, and County Employees (AFSCME) has asked its members to support the student boycott in whatever way "their conscience dictates" rather than calling for any official labor action.

AFSCME members fill clerical, service, and patient care jobs on the Berkeley campus.

The action taken by the GA calls for a rally today at noon on the steps of "Stephen Biko" Hall. Singer Holly Near will play at the rally and UC

See page 9 for text of AGSE boycott statement

Berkeley faculty as well as representatives of local anti-apartheid groups will speak.

The GA's resolution also calls for a march to University Hall — the UC systemwide administrative offices in downtown Berkeley — immediately following the noon rally.

A "teach-in" will be held either on
SEE PAGE 17

Top: A crowd of over 2000 gathered on 'Stephen Biko' Plaza in an anti-apartheid rally Tuesday. Left: FSM leader Mario Savio urged students during the noon rally to hold fast in their demands for UC divestment in South Africa. Right: One of 141 arrested at a pre-dawn raid Tuesday.

Sproul cleared in dawn raid; sit-in resumes

University police arrested 158 anti-apartheid demonstrators and cleared the steps of Sproul Hall Tuesday, but by evening the week-old protest had resumed — with 350 protesters camping on the steps.

Demonstrators began re-occupying Sproul steps immediately following a noon rally, at which a crowd of 3500 gathered to hear speeches by Free Speech Movement leader Mario Savio and local politicians.

UC Berkeley Chancellor I. Michael Heyman ordered the UC police to remove protesters who had been camping on the steps of Sproul Hall since last Wednesday.

In another roundup, 16 ASUC senators and officers and one non-student were arrested at University Hall, the administration building for the entire UC system, located one block west of campus.

Most of the 158 arrested were released Tuesday night and immediately returned and resumed their occupation of the steps.

University spokesperson Ray Colvig said university officials would monitor the renewed protest, attempt to talk with the protesters and then decide whether further arrests were necessary.

Tuesday night, newly elected ASUC President Pedro Noguera met with student regent Fred Gaines, Vice Chancellor Roderic Park and John Cummins, executive assistant to Heyman. The administration has been presenting Noguera with proposals they hope the demonstrators will accept, demonstrators have said.

Heyman has scheduled a forum on apartheid on April 24 at which the university community can discuss its views of apartheid and the university's
SEE PAGE 10

'UC 38' supporters unhappy with judge

By JACK ROBINSON
STAFF WRITER

As Alameda County deputy sheriffs hauled scores of anti-apartheid demonstrators off to Santa Rita Jail Tuesday, supporters of those arrested in a similar protest four months ago made heated charges against a municipal court judge who has declared herself strongly sympathetic to their cause.

"If I didn't have to work today," Berkeley Municipal Court Judge Julie Conger said in an interview Tuesday morning, "I'd probably be down there showing my support" for the students and community members protesting the university's ties to companies do-

ing business with South Africa.

But lawyers for the "UC 38" arrested Dec. 7 outside University Hall angrily denounced Conger, saying she rescinded an earlier decision in an effort to please Assistant District Attorneys Jeff Horner and Greg Bailey. Neither Horner nor Bailey would return phone calls Tuesday.

Critics also blame Conger for plea bargains which resulted in three-day jail terms for 17 of the defendants, and are unhappy with her decision to disqualify herself from the case and any future cases against anti-apartheid protesters.

Supporters of this week's campus sleep-in, which resulted in 158 arrests early Tuesday, fear the disqualification will mean a rough ride judicially for the latest crop of protesters.

In a letter April 1 to prosecutors and defense attorneys, Conger said that her experience with the Civil Rights Movement in the 1960s and her "deep-rooted repugnance for racism in all forms" would prevent her "from giving the district attorney a fair hear-

ing in these cases."

By disqualifying herself, Conger outraged many Berkeley progressives.

"If we cannot elect judges at the local level that are reflective of local concerns and the local conscience, then why have a municipal court at all?" asked Anna De Leon, one of the defense attorneys.

Berkeley Vice Mayor Veronika Fukson said Tuesday that the disqualification move was "tragic."

"One of the reasons we vote for people who are principled is so they will take positions of power," Fukson said.

A bias against racism "is something we'd expect of anyone," Fukson said.

"Julie got elected on the basis of being a progressive person," said a city staff member familiar with the court, who asked for anonymity.

"What people tried to do was to get a progressive judge in place. And now, she's saying 'Because I have these political perspectives, I'm disqualifying
SEE PAGE 9

EDITORIAL

Strike!

Don't go to class today. Show the university administration you won't support their investments in South Africa. Show the university we will not allow our friends to be herded off to jail when they stand up for moral and ethical behavior.

The administration treats students like children. When protests threaten to bring about real changes in public opinion, the administration suddenly declares them illegal. They want "student input" only when it's non-controversial.

The university belongs to the students. If the regents are going to create policies that are morally repugnant — like investing in South Africa — then they'll do it without our support. We're not going to attend.

The student strike is backed by several local unions, AGSE, faculty members and almost the entire spectrum of campus organizations. We urge you to boycott your classes and attend the teach-ins.

Figure 21. Savio returns to the Berkeley campus to speak at antiapartheid rally, following the mass arrest of divestment protesters, April 16, 1985. Courtesy *Daily Californian.*

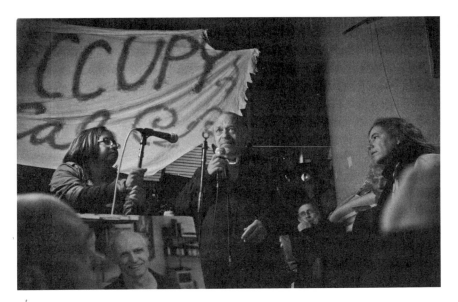

Figure 22. Savio Memorial Lecture by Robert Reich, UC Berkeley professor and former U.S. secretary of labor, as part of the Occupy Cal day of protest, November 15, 2011. Savio's photo is on the podium. Photo courtesy of Stephen Lam, Reuters/Corbis.

Surely Faulkner's words do apply to Berkeley, Savio, and the FSM. Over the half century since the FSM, Berkeley has remained a center of protest, not only on apartheid, but also on immigrant rights, campus racial diversity, US imperialism, justice for Palestinians, and tuition hikes. Savio's name has been invoked as students demonstrated and engaged in civil disobedience on behalf of all these causes. This ongoing dissident tradition, sustained by activist-oriented students drawn to Berkeley because the FSM made Berkeley's very name synonymous with campus protest, is a living monument to Savio and the FSM.

As recently as 2011 this dissident Berkeley tradition was making headlines. Masses of students protested tuition hikes—a campus counterpart to the Occupy Wall Street movement. They defied campus rules by encamping in tents on Sproul Plaza—in the spirit of Occupy's Zuccotti Park—and were forcibly evicted by the police. Students, faculty, and FSM veterans defended the protests as a form of free speech true to the ideals that the FSM and Savio championed in 1964.[16] The Savio memorial lecture that year became a part of this new student movement, when it was— at the request of the protesters—held out on Sproul Plaza and made a key event in that movement's Open University Strike and Day of Action. The lecture was by Berkeley public policy professor Robert Reich, former U.S. secretary of labor, on "class warfare" in America. Thousands came to hear it.[17]

Neither Savio nor the FSM believed that disruptive tactics should be used rashly, and they employed them on campus only as a last resort, when negotiations had failed. The Academic Senate's December 8 resolutions, which ended the FSM crisis and established a free speech framework for the Berkeley campus—and which Savio cherished as the university's "Magna Carta"—were not a license for anarchy. They provided that speech be "subject to reasonable regulation" regarding its time, place, and manner so as to "prevent interference with the normal functions of the university." In other words, the FSM—and the December 8 resolutions that it won—established freedom of speech for the university in ways that were entirely compatible with its educational mission.

At times, however, those on both sides of campus political battles have focused on the FSM's sit-in tactics rather than the free speech principles embodied in the December 8 resolutions. With that shift, Savio and the FSM can be (and have been) loathed or loved as emblems of disruptive, even anarchic student protest. Conflicting memories of the polarized Berkeley political scene of the late 1960s—especially the violence that marred the Third World Strike and People's Park struggles— have added an emotional edge to the debate about the FSM's legacy. The debate may never entirely end as to whether Savio and the FSM ought to be denounced for their disruptiveness, as they were in 1990 by Chancellor Heyman, or praised and memorialized as avatars of free speech and political engagement, as they were by Chancellor Berdahl in 2000. But the establishment of the FSM Café, the Savio steps, and the library endowment suggests that—at least on the Berkeley campus—the legacy of Savio and the FSM is now far more admired than feared, even by the administration.

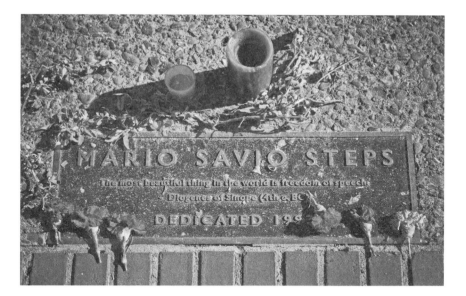

Figure 23. Mario Savio Steps plaque, with flowers laid on it by Occupy Cal activists, November 15, 2011. Photograph courtesy of Andy Scott Chang/Corbis.

Historical monuments and memorials to political causes, however, risk making the cause itself so abstract that we lose sight of the people who made this history and the way they experienced it. What did it feel like to participate in 1960s America's first mass student rebellion on a college campus and the first to use mass civil disobedience to change a university? To cross America's racial divide and bring the black freedom movement's democratic ethos to a predominantly white campus run undemocratically and bureaucratically? To look back on that moment in 1964 when the FSM (much like the lunch-counter sit-in movement of 1960) prevailed, winning a surprising victory for freedom that inspired others, helping to produce the luminous rainbow of protest movements that defined the 1960s as an era of egalitarian change? Savio addressed these questions in 1984 when a coalition of FSM veterans, together with Berkeley students and faculty, organized a weeklong commemoration of the FSM on its twentieth anniversary. In a letter written in support of that commemoration, Savio, reflecting on the Free Speech Movement's personal meaning to him and his fellow movement veterans, noted:

> It affected my own life very deeply. Through two decades of some joy, but marked with much sadness and personal tragedy, it has remained for me a brilliant moment when . . . we were both moral and successful. . . . This sense of the specialness, the beauty, the personal and collective power of those days has been equally constant in the lives of those movement activists with whom I have remained in touch.[18]

The legacy of progressive thought and action that Mario Savio embodied can be supported though donations (which are tax deductible) to the Mario Savio Young Activist Award (www. savio.org; P.O. Box 152, Guerneville, CA, 95446) and to the Mario Savio Memorial Lecture Endowment Fund. Donate online at givetocal.berkeley.edu/savio. To give by check, make the check payable to "Mario Savio Memorial Lecture and Supporting Fund," and mail it to:
Mario Savio Fund Gifts
College of Letters & Science
101 Durant Hall, MC 2930
University of California, Berkeley
Berkeley, CA 94720-2930

Afterword

Mario Savio's speeches and writings did change America. They reverberated across the land, turning what had started as a controversy at one university over whether and where students could recruit members to their various clubs and organizations, including those dedicated to civil rights, into a national movement for free speech and human dignity.

We must be careful, however, not to lionize this eloquent young man too much, lest we fail to understand the deeper origins of that movement. One of the ways American society often minimizes its capacity for social change is to personalize it—making it about some individual rather than about the cumulative experiences and collective ideals that propel it. Mario Savio had a gift for putting into words what many young people felt, and he was at the right place at the right time. He gave reasoned and indignant voice to a generation determined to achieve a more just society. He embodied the Free Speech Movement, but he was not the movement.

The Free Speech Movement grew out the civil rights movement, which had revealed to the entire nation the great gulf that existed between America's animating ideals and the daily reality experienced by a large portion of its population. That dissonance had summoned hundreds of students to Mississippi in the summer of 1964 to register black voters.

Mario Savio had been part of Freedom Summer and, like many other volunteers, had met with the violence by Mississippi whites, often encouraged by local police. He noted in one of his letters that despite the beatings and death threats, "none of us have backed out, even after the disappearance of those three volunteers in Neshoba County."

The animating ideal of the civil rights movement was a democracy that guaranteed every citizen not only the right to vote but also the right to fully participate in deliberations over issues that affect their lives. In the minds of those who risked their lives for civil rights, voting and deliberating were inextricably related. Absent public debate and discussion, votes were mere tallies of preferences. Self-government required full and active political engagement.

One objective of those who participated in Freedom Summer was to strengthen the Mississippi Freedom Democratic Party—which had been organized to counter the regular Mississippi Democratic Party, from which blacks had been effectively excluded. Writing that "the regular Democratic Party is not a democratic party," Savio sought the help of California governor Edmund G. Brown in seating the Freedom Democratic Party's interracial delegation at the upcoming Democratic National Convention. It was not to be.

The Berkeley students who returned the campus from Mississippi that September had had a powerful and direct education in the fight for democracy. Other Berkeley students had heard about Freedom Summer on the news and were sensitized to the issues of arbitrary power and repression of dissent.

The University of California's ban on political advocacy on the strip of sidewalk adjoining the campus's south entrance, which the university owned, was small potatoes relative to Mississippi's denial of democratic rights to its black citizens, but to Savio and other Berkeley students, it was close enough to justify similar indignation. The university was not just preventing civil rights organizers from recruiting students to the cause; it was preventing students from exercising their essential right to democratic deliberation. "The people must participate in making decisions that affect their lives," Savio wrote—encapsulating the central motivating idea of the era.

Berkeley's administrators and campus police offers were a far cry from Mississippi's lawmakers and sheriffs, but their response to student demands seemed analogous. They refused to budge on banning any recruitment for political action or political causes, or the solicitation of funds for them. Students held meetings with administrators to no avail. After students picketed the administration building and engaged in an all-night vigil outside, the administration cracked down, arresting a free speech activist on Sproul Plaza in the middle of a crowded day—dramatizing their intransigence.

The Berkeley students' means of achieving their objectives—their inclusive methods of deciding democratically what actions to take, their commitment to peaceful civil disobedience, their pickets and vigils, and, eventually, sit-ins—were also analogous to the means used by civil rights organizers. And the movement that emerged from this conflict—known as the Free Speech Movement—was fueled by the same energies and indignation that fueled the movement for civil rights. In the minds of many, including Savio, the Free Speech Movement was part of civil rights movement.

Mario Savio was not only a brilliant orator but also an insightful strategist. He was one of many young men and women who gave force and effect to a new demand for democracy in America. They succeeded in some respects. Nationally, a Civil Rights Act and Voting Rights Act advanced and protected the rights of blacks to equal participation in America. At campuses such as Berkeley, administrators relented and finally welcomed free speech. But in other ways, the ideal articulated by Martin Luther King Jr., Mario Savio, Cesar Chavez, and many others remains more of an ideal than a reality, a half century later.

Robert B. Reich
Chancellor's Professor of Public Policy
University of California, Berkeley

Epilogue

It is September 30, 1964. I have just been released from my last-period class and am walking across the campus toward the Sather Gate and home. It is my final semester at Cal; in January I will graduate with a BA in English. That is, if I complete all my courses! I am already behind, with a paper due and a few hundred pages to read before I can even start writing. As I pass in front of Sproul Hall, I see people on the balconies of the building, yelling "join us, join us." I know what they're doing there—a dean has called some students to his office for violating the new university regulations banning most political activities. Others have gone with them, in solidarity. "Join us, join us," a voice calls again from the balcony, and I recognize Mario Savio, head of University Friends of SNCC. I debate with myself for a few seconds—thinking of the homework, thinking of the deaths of three civil rights workers in Mississippi that summer—and I walk into Sproul Hall.

It was a fateful decision, determining career choices, friendships, and eventually, some years later, my marriage—to the man on the balcony.

. . . . .

In the fall semester of 1964, the FSM brought the discipline of nonviolence and the tactic of the sit-in practiced by the civil rights movement to new ground. African American students in the South had pioneered the use of civil disobedience in their daring, nonviolent lunch-counter sit-ins against Jim Crow, beginning at the Woolworth's in Greensboro, North Carolina, in February 1960. Now, for the first time, students from the "majority" population were making the national headlines by engaging in mass political protest on campus.

Our example aroused students all over the country, upset about racial discrimination in America, anxious and angry about the war, or moved by other concerns, into direct action on and off their campuses (though not always as nonviolently as the FSM). The struggle at Berkeley advanced the principle that students do not lose their First Amendment rights when they pass through campus or schoolhouse gates, a principle affirmed by the U.S. Supreme Court in Tinker v. Des Moines (1969).

The first impact on the Berkeley campus of the FSM victory was the space it created for the massive anti–Vietnam War movement that emerged in the Bay Area only a few months later. Many other protests— some more successful than others—have followed on Sproul Plaza over the years, including the *very* successful antiapartheid campaign (an important part of the national campaign). More recently, Berkeley students organized Occupy Cal, a campus counterpart to Occupy Wall Street, aiming to free UC from major tuition hikes. This movement also became a free speech struggle after club-wielding police evicted protesters encamped—Zuccotti Park–style—on Sproul Plaza.

But perhaps the deepest legacy of the FSM has been its impact upon its participants, whether they were protest leaders or rank-and-file members. We began lifelong relationships with other students and with faculty members that changed us and enriched our lives. Love affairs and marriages were initiated (for example, both Mario's first wife and I are FSM vets). Friendships were established. Thanks to the FSM, on the huge, impersonal Berkeley campus, we became acquainted with hundreds of people by name or by sight or by hearsay, as we shared an experience that was intense—physically, emotionally, intellectually, and morally. At the time, this created a sense of camaraderie and community, and this community has persisted, to a surprising extent, up to this day.[1]

The FSM altered our lives and our thinking in political ways too. Students who participated in the FSM often went on to become lifelong activists and supporters of social justice, organizing and marching against the Vietnam War, building the women's movement, founding the Peace and Freedom Party, organizing farm workers' and hospital workers' and other labor unions, opposing U.S. intervention in Central America and the Middle East, working for improved prison conditions and in antipoverty and legal aid programs (when they existed), taking jobs in education, health, social work (sometimes having to fight to get credentialed or licensed, because their arrest during the FSM was held against them), defending poor people and political protestors, and trying to stop the destruction of the planet.

·   ·   ·   ·   ·

Mario, on the other hand, except for participating in a couple of important campus-based protests in the years directly following FSM, withdrew from almost all active political participation for over a decade. He was tired, disliked being a celebrity, and was uncomfortable with the rhetoric of the Left during the late 1960s and the 1970s. Perhaps more critically, he was beset by health problems and family difficulties and had to struggle to make a living.

But a permanent withdrawal from political engagement proved impossible. America's drift to the right was too upsetting. By the time Ronald Reagan ran for reelection, we had married, Mario had returned to school, and we had spent a few months helping to build the new Citizens Party in San Francisco, before becoming disillusioned by its incompetent and undemocratic national leadership. As the twentieth anniversary of the FSM approached, a big reunion and rally on campus was being planned by FSM vets working with current activist students. I was eager for us both to participate and urged Mario to agree.

At this distance, it's hard to recall whether my motives had anything political in them. I knew that Mario's absence would put a damper on the celebration that had been planned, and I looked forward to our reconnecting with old comrades. But Mario was reluctant to attend the reunion. We had both been troubled by the U.S. opposition to liberation movements in

El Salvador and Nicaragua, and Mario feared that even this one speaking engagement would entrap him in full-time antiwar organizing, derailing his academic career much as the FSM had. If he were once again a public figure, he would be unable to turn down requests to speak. He would feel too compelled by the moral imperative of his Catholic youth: resist evil! But he finally agreed, mainly to please me, and made his first speech on Sproul Plaza in decades at the FSM's twentieth anniversary.

Mario gave an eloquent, moving speech that drew thousands of current students, along with many FSM vets, and made the front page of the San Francisco newspapers. His speech called upon students of the 1980s to ally themselves with the Central American liberation struggle just as we had supported the struggle for civil rights in Mississippi.[2] It turned out that he had been right; speaking drew him back into activism. He took a leave from his graduate studies to do so, until winding up in the hospital with a heart infection.

Mario eventually finished his master's degree studies in physics, and over the last decade of his life, although absorbed by his work teaching at Sonoma State University and our family life, he would occasionally respond to requests to speak, supporting students at UC in their antiapartheid campaign, and giving talks at several schools and colleges about the struggles of the 1960s and their relevance to the present. In his last few years, he grew increasingly active in local and statewide campus organizing. He had been told by his middle son, Nadav, that he "must do something else" if he followed his inclination and didn't vote in the 1994 election. "That sort of challenge . . . really gets the testosterone flowing," Mario reported later. He turned to old FSM comrades then teaching in California universities and community colleges to help organize students, staffs, and teachers to fight against California's right-wing assault on immigrant rights and affirmative action, which he denounced as "a rising tide of barbarism." At the time of his death, he was helping students at SSU oppose a fee increase and protesting manipulation of the election by the administration.

· · · · ·

"I am well and boyantly [sic] happy—if a little grubby," Mario wrote to his parents as he sat in Santa Rita jail, waiting to be booked for refusing to leave Sproul Hall on December 2. Those words described how many of us, perhaps most of us, felt throughout that fall semester, though it was mixed with our anger and occasional despair. The number of requests for counseling and psychotherapy at the student health center went down substantially from previous semesters. We were having a great time! The sheer fun of it, the excitement, the exhilaration of that semester brightened our college days, while it gave us a political and civic education that has stayed with us perhaps more permanently—and more influentially—than what we learned in many of our courses.

We developed a lifelong skepticism about authority and the veracity of its pronouncements and a similar distrust of the media—its accuracy as well as its integrity. We became acutely sensitive to encroachments upon the rights that are guaranteed to Americans under the Bill of Rights, especially, but not only, the First Amendment.

We learned some important principles of organizing quickly, some of it from the more experienced activists among us, the rest just as we went along—the need to educate, to communicate, and to build alliances and involve large numbers if we wanted to have an impact, as well as the need to negotiate when possible and make civil disobedience a last resort rather than a first strike. We learned to let all voices be heard, to listen, to strive for consensus, to abide by majority vote when consensus cannot be reached, but—and this came through bitter experience—to reconsider and reflect more deeply when there is significant disagreement between people who are on the same side.

We never questioned the principle that to sustain a political struggle, leadership is necessary, but we believed strongly in collective democratic leadership. Mario exercised great influence in the FSM Steering Committee and its parent body, the Executive Committee, perhaps a disproportionate influence, but others did too. Most of us needed to go to classes, so we were content to have a representative government structure—but day after day in Sproul Plaza, from 12 to 1 P.M. (and later, on special occasions), in constant dialogue, we engaged in participatory democracy, voting with our voices and our bodies.

Our core principle was solidarity—with other struggles, particularly those for civil rights, and with each other. We knew, instinctively, that we had to protect and defend each other. "All of us or none" was a motto widely understood and accepted unquestioningly. When it appeared that most students had settled for a partial victory and would no longer follow the leadership into direct action, it was the disciplinary proceedings brought against Mario and three other FSM activists over Thanksgiving break that galvanized most of the campus, provoking the successful December sit-in, student strike, and, ultimately, victory.

Growing up in a time of widespread prosperity and self-satisfaction, we were a generation that deeply believed in American ideals and American democracy, and we had been shocked and appalled when we began to see its cracks and contradictions. The struggle of African Americans against segregation in the South and discrimination in the Bay Area had inspired us. It was an antidote to alienation, our generation's equivalent of "the Good War," a fight against evil, a story of great risk-taking and sacrifice. We were not going to let the university administration impede its success.

Awed by the courage of the students in the South who were facing far greater dangers than we ever would, we came to believe very deeply that sometimes you just had to stand up for your principles, for what you had been taught and knew in your conscience was right and just, whatever the cost. Mario, with his acute sensitivity to the moral dimensions of every situation and his ability to elucidate them with crystal clear logic and passionate eloquence, roused the moral philosopher in us all. FSMers would typically describe his aptitude for leadership as the "ability to express what we were all feeling," and that realization made us feel good about ourselves and what we were doing.

Speaking to a reporter inside Sproul Hall in December 1964, Mario, referring to students in America, noted "a growing understanding . . . that a better society is possible, and that it is worth dying for." Thirty-one years later, speaking to students in a class at UC Santa Cruz, he defined their issues as fundamentally the same as those of our generation: those of "hierarchy—in race, gender, class, the environment, and empire (i.e., one nation *über alles*)," as Cornel West had delineated them. He expressed again his faith in people and the possibility of creating a better world, this time in almost religious terms: "I believe people have . . . a deep hunger for doing right by one's brothers and sisters." Acknowledging that as a statement of faith, he also observed that it would ultimately be verifiable—"if we win."

Now, fifty years later, could any of us still honestly sing, as we did marching into Sproul Hall on December 2, "deep in my heart, I do believe we shall overcome someday"? Despite so much contrary evidence over these years, our victory at Berkeley appears to have created a foundation of incurable optimism. There are few cynics among us. Our experience in the Free Speech Movement and the struggle for civil rights, from which it drew so much of its intensity, taught us that if people join together, if they are willing to submerge their differences and struggle together, they can begin to overcome more powerful forces and achieve some control over the decisions that affect their lives. They can even make history.

Lynne Hollander Savio

Notes

FOREWORD

1. Seth Rosenfeld, *Subversives: The FBI's War on Student Radicals and Reagan's Rise to Power* (New York: Farrar, Straus and Giroux, 2012), 187–89.

2. Ibid., 508–9. The first revelations concerning FBI misconduct in relation to Savio and the FSM came out in 1982, as a result of the *Daily Californian*'s Freedom of Information Act requests. Drawing on these FBI documents, Rosenfeld published a series of *Daily Californian* articles exposing the FBI's spying and its illicit and covert campaign to discredit first Savio and the FSM and then the Berkeley antiwar movement.

3. *San Francisco Chronicle*, June 9, 2002.

4. Rosenfeld, *Subversives*, 237–41.

5. Robert Cohen, *Freedom's Orator: Mario Savio and the Radical Legacy of the 1960s* (New York: Oxford University Press, 2009), 317.

6. Gary Nash, *The Unknown American Revolution* (New York: Viking, 2005), 425.

7. Cohen, *Freedom's Orator*, 6.

8. Ibid., 371.

9. Ibid., 373.

10. Ibid., 375.

INTRODUCTION

1. *Daily Californian*, October 2, 1964. Lt. Merrill F. Chandler, Police Department, University of California, Berkeley, Supplementary Report, File 25397, October 1, 1964—11:45 A.M., Chancellor's Papers, University Archives, Bancroft Library, UC Berkeley. These events were audio recorded as part of KPFA's radio coverage of the Berkeley revolt and can be heard by accessing the UC Berkeley Media Center's online audio recordings of the Free Speech Movement at www. lib.berkeley.edu/MRC/FSM/fsmchronology1.html. The published account of the arrest and start of the police car blockade that makes the most extensive use of these tapes is Max Heirich, *The Beginning: Berkeley, 1964* (New York: Columbia University Press, 1968), 98–119. For accounts of these events and the rally that make the most extensive use of oral histories with the protesters, see David Goines, *The Free Speech Movement: Coming of Age in the 1960s* (Berkeley: Ten Speed Press, 1993), 161–236; Robert Cohen, *Freedom's Orator: Mario Savio and the Radical Legacy of the 1960s* (New York: Oxford University Press, 2009), 98–120. There is a brief video clip of the arrest of Jack Weinberg in the documentary film *Berkeley in the Sixties*, produced by Mark Kitchell (1990).

2. The car-top rally tapes, parts 1–12, can be found at the Free Speech Movement, UC Berkeley—Online Audio Recordings, www.lib.berkeley.edu/MRC/FSM/fsmchronology1.html; Cohen, *Freedom's Orator*, 99–104, 108–9. The nonviolence of the blockade and the FSM itself was almost—but not entirely—perfect (as one might expect, given the training and discipline one needed to maintain nonviolence in the face of threats and violence). On the rare FSM exceptions to the rule regarding nonviolence, see chap. 3, n. 42.

3. Goines, *The Free Speech Movement*, 230–32; for the signed copy of the Pact of October 2, see Jo Freeman, *At Berkeley in the Sixties: The Education of An Activist, 1961–1965* (Bloomington: Indiana University Press, 2004), 167.

4. Heirich. *The Beginning*, 178–86; Hal Draper, *Berkeley: The New Student Revolt* (Alameda, Center for Socialist History, reprint of 1965 edition) 99–102; Cohen, *Freedom's Orator*, 164–65, 178–207. Savio's speeches before and after the regents meeting of November 20 are in chapter 3 of this volume and his "Bodies upon the Gears" speech is in chapter 4. The most famous segment of the "Bodies upon the Gears" speech can be viewed online at www.youtube.com/watch?v = fYSY2ohHFnQ. In Henry David Thoreau's most famous writing on civil disobedience, "Resistance to Civil Government" (1849, posthumously renamed "On Civil Disobedience" [1866]), he had urged defiance of oppressive laws: "Let your life be a counter friction to stop the machine." On the similarities as well as the differences in the imagery of Savio's "Bodies upon the Gears" speech and Thoreau's essay on civil disobedience, see Cohen, *Freedom's Orator*, 459, n. 17.

5. On the confused and inconsistent police and administration statements concerning the number of arrests made in breaking up the Sproul Hall sit-in, see

California Monthly, "Chronology of Events: Three Months of Crisis," in Seymour Martin Lipset and Sheldon S. Wolin, eds., *The Berkeley Student Revolt: Facts and Interpretations* (Garden City, NY: Doubleday, 1965), 175; Summary Report By Chief A. H. Fording, December 22, 1964, www.oac.cdlib.org/view?docId=kt3 199p5tk;NAAN=13030&doc.view=frames&chunk.id=div00002&toc. depth=1&toc.id=&brand=oac4; and Goines, *The Free Speech Movement,* 449; Freeman, *At Berkeley in the Sixties,* 215.

6. Bettina Aptheker, *Intimate Politics: How I Grew Up Red, Fought for Free Speech, and Became a Feminist Rebel* (Emeryville, CA: Seal Press, 2006), 140–49. Goines, *The Free Speech Movement* 361–415.

7. Excerpts from the key speeches at the Greek Theatre meeting by President Clark Kerr and Professor Robert Scalapino and dramatic news footage of the police seizure of Savio and the outraged student response to it are included in the film *Berkeley in the Sixties.*

8. Reginald E. Zelnik, "On the Side of the Angels: The Berkeley Faculty and the FSM," in Robert Cohen and Reginald E. Zelnik, eds., *The Free Speech Movement: Reflections on Berkeley in the 1960s* (Berkeley: University of California Press, 2002), 312–24

9. Mario Savio remarks at FSM Press Conference, January 5, 1965.

10. *Report of the President's Commission on Campus Unrest* (Washington, DC: US Government Printing Office), 22–23.

11. Henry May, *Ideas, Faith, and Feelings: Essays on American Intellectual and Religious History, 1952–1982* (New York: Oxford University Press, 1983), 90.

12. Seth Rosenfeld, *Subversives: The FBI's War on Student Radicals and Reagan's Rise to Power* (New York: Farrar, Straus and Giroux, 2012), 202–15, 225–33.

13. Clark Kerr, letter to the editor, *Daily Californian,* December 1, 1964, reprinted in Heirich, *The Beginning: Berkeley, 1964,* 196–97. For a fuller discussion of Kerr's red-baiting of the FSM, see Cohen and Zelnik, *The Free Speech Movement,* 40–42.

14. Summary of Edward W. Strong telephone call from Clark Kerr, November 10, 1964, 9:50 P.M., Chancellor's Papers.

15. Robert Cohen, "'This Was *Their* Fight and *They* Had to Fight It': The FSM's Non-Radical Rank-and-File," in Cohen and Zelnik, *The Free Speech Movement,* 227–63.

16. Tom Hayden, *The Port Huron Statement: The Visionary Call of the 1960s Revolution* (New York: Thunder's Mouth Press, 2005); Tom Hayden, *Inspiring Participatory Democracy: Student Movements From Port Huron to Today* (Boulder: Paradigm, 2012).

17. Draper, *Berkeley: The New Student Revolt,* 71–72.

18. John W. Johnson, *The Struggle for Student Rights: Tinker v. Des Moines and the 1960s* (Lawrence: University Press of Kansas, 1997).

19. Rick Perlstein, *Before the Storm: Barry Goldwater and the Unmaking of the American Consensus* (New York: Nation Books, 2009), 449.

20. There was, however, some African American student involvement in the FSM. See https://oregondigital.org/cdm4/item_viewer.php?CISOROOT=/cultural&CISOPTR = 1904; Jean Golson Mule telephone interview with Allyson McGinty and Robert Cohen, December, 2, 2013.

21. Taylor Branch, *Parting the Waters: America in the King Years, 1955-1963* (New York: Simon and Schuster, 1989); Taylor Branch, *Pillar of Fire: America in the King Years, 1963-1965* (New York: Simon and Schuster, 1998). Savio's comparison of these FSM events to Birmingham and the March on Washington is from his November 20, 1964 speech before the Regents meeting which appears in chapter 3 and his reference to a "letter from the 'Birmingham Jail'" is from his December 4, 1964, letter to his family, in chapter 4 of this volume.

22. Mario Savio, "Beyond the Cold War: An Education in Politics," unpublished book proposal, 20-22; Mario Savio interview with Bret Eynon, San Francisco, March 5, 1985, 23, 27-28; Jack Weinberg interview with the editor, May 19, 2005, 24; Aptheker, *Intimate Politics*, 124-26.

23. The sit-in movement, most famously at Greensboro in February 1960, and then across the South, launched by African American students, pioneered the use of civil disobedience by college students in 1960s America. But the sit-in movement and the Black-led student organization, SNCC, that grew out of that movement targeted *off-campus* institutions: downtown lunch counters and other businesses that discriminated against blacks. These black student activists in the early 1960s South were too engaged in the massive struggle against white racists off campus to even consider using civil disobedience as a tool to reform their own historically black colleges and universities (HBCUs). There were problems with free speech and administration paternalism at the HBCUs, but these were not seen as urgent or as oppressive as the systemic discrimination inflicted on the black community by racist white businesses and government officials. And whatever the flaws in HBCU administrative leadership, HBCU students knew that their black elders who administered those campuses, in the words of one black student leader from the Atlanta movement, "did not hate us" as the white segregationists did. So those black college administrators and the HBCUs did not become targets of the black student movement in the early 1960s. It was the Free Speech Movement that first took the black freedom movement's tactic of mass civil disobedience—sit-ins—which had been so effective off campus, and used it as a tool for change on campus. See Robert Cohen and David. J. Snyder, eds., *Rebellion in Black and White: Southern Student Activism in the 1960s* (Baltimore: Johns Hopkins University Press, 2013), 34, n. 36; Betty Stevens Walker telephone interview with the editor, March 29, 2013.

24. Savio, "Beyond the Cold War: An Education in Politics," 18-20.

25. Cohen, *Freedom's Orator*, 76-77.

NOTES TO PAGES 8-12

26. Draper, *Berkeley: The New Student Revolt,* 46; Jack Weinberg interview with editor, 50–51.

27. Heirich. *The Beginning,* 109.

28. Jack Weinberg interview with editor, 10–11; Jo Freeman, "From Freedom Now! to Free Speech: The FSM's Roots in the Bay Area Civil Rights Movement," in Cohen and Zelnik, *The Free Speech Movement,* 82.

29. Cohen, *Freedom's Orator,* 347. See Waldo Martin, "'Holding One Another': Mario Savio and the Freedom Struggle in Mississippi and Berkeley," in Cohen and Zelnik, *The Free Speech Movement,* 83–102.

30. James T. Patterson, *Grand Expectations: The United States, 1945–1974* (New York: Oxford University Press, 1996) 480.

31. Freeman, *At Berkeley in the Sixties,* 84–116; Aptheker, *Intimate Politics,* 112–13.

32. Cohen, *Freedom's Orator,* 41–42.

33. Freeman, *At Berkeley in the Sixties,* 113.

34. In his Davis speech, Kerr tried to have it both ways—looking liberal by saying that the university would not discipline those arrested in off-campus civil rights protests, because they were acting as citizens, not students, but at the same time, acting conservatively by insisting that no such protests could be organized from the campus. On the origin of the ban on political advocacy on the Bancroft strip and its relation to Kerr's speech at UC Davis, see Cohen, *Freedom's Orator,* 77–82; Heirich, *The Beginning,* 52.

35. Katherine A. Towle, "Statement Concerning the Application of University Policies and Berkeley Campus Regulations at the Bancroft-Telegraph Entrance, October 9, 1964," in Clark Kerr, ed., *Documentary Supplements to "The Gold and the Blue"* (Berkeley: Berkeley Public Policy Press, Institute of Governmental Studies, 2003), 87.

36. Heirich, *The Beginning,* 50–51; Notes on Meeting of Strong, Kerr, and Cunningham, November 10, 1964, 2 P.M. Chancellor's papers, University Archives, Bancroft Library.

37. On the student movement of the 1930s, see Robert Cohen, *When the Old Left Was Young: Student Radicalism and America's First Mass Student Movement, 1929–1941* (New York: Oxford University Press, 1993), passim. That book covers Berkeley student activism in the 1930s on 93, 97, 100–102, 122–23, 198, 203–4, 211–12, 307. Also see Max Heirich and Sam Kaplan, "Yesterday's Discord," in Seymour Martin Lipset and Sheldon S. Wolin, eds., *The Berkeley Student Revolt: Facts and Interpretations* (Garden City, NY: Anchor Books, 1965), 11–17.

38. For the most complete account of the origins of UC's restrictions on political advocacy, see C. Michael Otten, *University Authority and the Student* (Berkeley: University of California Press, 1970), 108–28. The Sproul administration's antiradicalism yielded not only these free speech restrictions but also collusion with local law enforcement officials in assembling a political

intelligence network monitoring the off-campus political activities of Berkeley student radicals. See Cohen, *When the Old Left Was Young*, 100–102. On President Kerr's perpetuation of the rules Sproul created restricting political advocacy on campus, see Clark Kerr, "Fall of 1964 at Berkeley: Confrontation Yields to Reconciliation," in Cohen and Zelink, *The Free Speech Movement*, 365–66.

39. David Horowitz, *Student* (New York: Ballantine Books, 1962), 29.

40. Ibid., 18–41; Michael Rossman, *The Wedding within the War* (Garden City, NY: Anchor Books, 1971), 30–71. Also see "SLATE: Interviews with Mike Miller and Brad Cleveland"; Robin Room, "Slate and the Spirit of a Generation"; and Robby Cohen, "Pre-FSM Activism," all in Robby Cohen, *The FSM and Beyond: Berkeley Student Protest and Social Change in the 1960s* (privately printed, 1994), 3–17.

41. On the impact of "Operation Abolition" in eliciting attention and support at Harvard for Berkeley's anti-HUAC protester, see Frank Bardacke's comments on this in the documentary film *Berkeley in the Sixties*. On a similar impact at the University of South Carolina, see Dan T. Carter, "Deep South Campus Memories and the World the Sixties Made," in Cohen and Snyder, *Rebellion in Black and White*, x. On the anti-HUAC protests and the FBI's attempts to discredit the protesters by circulating an inaccurate, red-baiting report about them, see Rosenfeld, *Subversives*, 77–111.

42. Savio, "Beyond the Cold War: An Education in Politics," 17–18.

43. Ibid.; Savio interview with Eynon, 10.

44. Cohen, *Freedom's Orator*, 28–30, 369.

45. Ibid., 37–42.

46. Ibid., 76–78.

47. Ibid., 39–48.

48. Ibid., 49–72.

49. Ibid.; Doug McAdam, *Freedom Summer* (New York: Oxford University Press, 1988), 72.

50. Cohen, *Freedom's Orator*, 53–71. On this question of violence, see Akinyele Omowale Umoja, *We Will Shoot Back: Armed Resistance in the Mississippi Freedom Movement* (New York: New York University Press, 2013), 50–260.

51. Cohen, *Freedom's Orator*, 42–43, 49–50; Freeman, *At Berkeley in the Sixties*, 86.

52. An example of this press hostility to the FSM can be seen in the December 2, 1964, press conference with Savio—which appears below, in chapter 4—in the midst of the sit-in, as reporters, eager to discredit the movement, asked repeatedly about the influence of the Communist Party and the Communist Manifesto on the FSM. Some of the press red-baiting of the FSM was covertly initiated by the FBI. See Rosenfeld, *Subversives*, 212–15, 226.

53. "Students: When and Where to Speak," *Time Magazine* (December 18, 1964), 68.

54. *San Francisco News-Call Bulletin,* December 3, 1964. This tendency to refer to the FSM protests as "riots" was so widespread that on the nationally televised talk show, *The Les Crane Show,* where Savio and other FSM leaders appeared after the December 8 victory, the host used the term in his introduction. Savio promptly corrected him, noting the FSM's commitment to nonviolence (audio tape of the Les Crane show, December 10, 1964).

55. "Remembering Mario Savio," essays by Mark Schechner et al., in *Tikkun* January 1997), 27–30, 75–76; Cohen and Zelnik, *The Free Speech Movement,* 551–70.

56. Reginald E. Zelnik, "Mario Savio: Avatar of Free Speech," in Cohen and Zelnik, *The Free Speech Movement,* 569.

57. Greil Marcus, "On Mario Savio," in Cohen and Zelnik, *The Free Speech Movement,* 567.

58. Robert Scheer, "The Man Who Stopped the Machine," *Los Angeles Times,* November 12, 1996.

59. Cohen, *Freedom's Orator,* 179.

60. Ibid., 458, n. 15.

61. David Stein e-mail to the editor, November 10, 2013; SA, Berkeley, report on Mario Savio Vietnam Day Speech, May 22, 1965, FBI Files SF 100–54559, June 2, 1965.

62. Reginald Zelink remarks from Savio memorial service, UC Berkeley, December 1996, and at Organization of American Historians session on Savio, San Francisco, April 1997, excerpted in Cohen, *Freedom's Orator,* 118.

63. Cohen, *Freedom's Orator,* 65–66.

64. Wendy Lesser, "Elegy for Mario Savio," in Cohen and Zelnik, *The Free Speech Movement,* 564; Kate Coleman telephone interview with Maryanne Greenaway and Robert Cohen, November 25, 2013.

65. Cohen, *Freedom's Orator,* 127.

66. Sara Davidson, *Loose Change: Three Women of the Sixties* (Berkeley: University of California Press, 1997), 78.

67. Cohen, *Freedom's Orator,* 435 n. 83; For the full Savio quote on the Free Speech Movement as a pun, see www.fsm-a.org/stacks/mario/savio_gilles.htm. Note that though the quote is accurate, it is misdated (the Giles interview with Savio was in 1994, not 1964).

68. Cohen, *Freedom's Orator,* 76–77.

69. See www.fsm-a.org/stacks/mario/savio_gilles.htm.

70. Cohen, *Freedom's Orator,* 2.

71. Ibid., 180.

72. Ibid., 127.

73. On Savio's planning for the "Bodies upon the Gears" speech, see Bettina Aptheker's memories of this speech in Cohen, *Freedom's Orator,* 183.

74. See Savio's October 5, 1964, speech in chapter 3 below and Savio's December 29, 1964, speech to the California Federation of Teachers in chapter 4.

75. See Savio's Queens College speech, December 11, 1964, for his fullest critique of Kerr's vision of the multiversity, in chapter 4 below.

76. Ibid.; Savio's December 29, 1964, speech to the California Federation of Teachers in chapter 4. Also see Doug Rossinow, "Mario Savio and the Politics of Authenticity," in Cohen and Zelnik, *The Free Speech Movement*, 533–51.

77. See Savio's victory speech, December 9, 1964, and his Queens College speech, December 11, 1964, both in chapter 4.

78. Ibid.

79. *Daily Californian*, April 20 and 30 and May 31, 2007.

80. David Kirp, *Shakespeare, Einstein, and the Bottom Line: The Marketing of Higher Education* (Cambridge, MA: Harvard University Press, 2003) 219; Sheila Slaughter and Gary Rhoades, *Academic Capitalism and the New Economy: Markets, State, and Higher Education* (Baltimore: Johns Hopkins University Press, 2004).

81. Rosenfeld, *Subversives*. 7–8, 64, 73, 97, 203–4, 229–31, 237, 250, 259, 283, 285, 287–88, 291, 304, 362, 368–78.

82. W. J. Rorabaugh, "The FSM, Berkeley Politics, and Ronald Reagan," in Cohen and Zelink, *The Free Speech Movement*, 515; Rosenfeld, *Subversives*, 300; Gerard J. De Groot, "Ronald Reagan and Student Unrest in California, 1966–1970," *Pacific Historical Review* (1996): 107–13; Michelle Reeves, "'Obey the Rules or Get Out': Ronald Reagan's 1966 Gubernatorial Campaign and the 'Trouble in Berkeley,'" *Southern California Quarterly* (Fall 2010): 275–300.

83. Thomas Casstevens, *Politics, Housing, and Race Relations: California's Rumford Act and Proposition 14* (Berkeley: Institute of Government Studies, 1967), 68.

84. Robert Cohen, "The Many Meanings of the FSM," in Cohen and Zelink, *The Free Speech Movement*, 40–42.

85. Scott Saul, "A Body on the Gears," *Nation* (March 11, 2010), www.thenation.com/article/body-gears#.

86. On this decline and the historical context for it, see Christopher Newfield, *Unmaking the Public University: The Forty Year Assault on the Middle Class* (Cambridge, MA: Harvard University Press, 2011); Colleen Lye and James Vernon, "The Humanities and the Crisis of the Public University." The Townsend Center for the Humanities (February 2011), http://townsendcenter.berkeley.edu/publications/humanities-and-crisis-public-university.

87. Cohen, *Freedom's Orator*, 319–20.

88. Ibid., 20–25, 450, n. 79.

89. In his August 12, 1964, letter to Cheryl Stevenson (which appears in chapter 2), Savio himself notes that a rare day of inactivity had left him feeling depressed, but that for most of the summer, his civil rights organizing in Mississippi had kept him so busy that he had no time to reflect on his psychological problems: "I'm reasonably safe from myself so long as I keep busy."

90. Cohen, *Freedom's Orator*, passim.

91. Cheryl Stevenson telephone interviews with the editor, December 19, 2005, and December 20, 2013.

92. Suzanne Goldberg telephone interview with the editor, January 22, 2014; Suzanne Goldberg e-mail to the editor, January 22, 2014.

93. Suzanne Goldberg telephone interview with the editor, January 22, 2014.

94. For Savio's discussion linking knowledge with action, see his November 20, 1964, speech before the regents meeting, in chapter 3 below, and on "learning by doing" see his "Bodies upon the Gears" speech in chapter 4.

95. On Savio's ideas concerning "consequential speech" see his December 29, 1964, speech to the California Federation of Teachers; Cohen, *Freedom's Orator*, 78–79.

96. The University of Mississippi was desegregated by James Meredith in 1962. It took until 1995 for students there to organize on behalf of a campus civil rights monument, endorsed by the administration there in 1996. The monument honoring Meredith was dedicated on the Mississippi campus in 2002. Autherine Lucy attempted to desegregate the University of Alabama in 1956 and attended only a few days before she was driven off by a racist mob and expelled by university officials. It was not until 1992 that Alabama honored her by endowing a scholarship in her name and unveiling a portrait of her on campus. In 2010 the University of Alabama named a campus plaza for Vivian Malone and James Hood, the African American students who desegregated that campus in 1963, and also dedicated a clock tower to Autherine Lucy Foster. In 1985 the University of Georgia endowed an annual lecture series in honor of its first two African American students, Charlayne Hunter and Hamilton Holmes, who desegregated that campus in 1961—and in 2001 named a campus building after them. See Charles W. Eagles, *The Price of Defiance: James Meredith and the Integration of the University Ole Miss* (Chapel Hill: University of North Carolina Press, 2009), 436–43; E. Culpepper Clark, *The Schoolhouse Door: Segregation's Last Stand at the University of Alabama* (Tuscaloosa: University of Alabama Press, 2007), 260; "Dedication of Malone-Hood Plaza and Autherine Lucy Clock Tower," University of Alabama, www.ua.edu/features/foster.html; "Celebrating Courage: 50th Anniversary of Desegregation at UGA," University of Georgia, http://desegregation.uga.edu/history; and Robert Cohen, "Race, History, and the Holmes-Hunter Lectures," UGA *Columns* (October 30, 1995), 4.

CHAPTER 1. THE MAKING OF A BERKELEY CIVIL
RIGHTS ACTIVIST

1. Mario Savio, "Beyond the Cold War: The Education of an American Radical" (unpublished book proposal), 4, copy in editor's possession.

2. Ibid.

3. Ibid.

4. Ibid., 4–5; Mario Savio, "Thirty Years Later: Reflections on the FSM," in Cohen and Zelnik, *The Free Speech Movement*, 61.

5. Savio interview with Eynon, 13.

6. Savio, "Beyond the Cold War: The Education of an American Radical," 5.

7. Savio interview with Eynon, 18.

8. Ibid.

9. Freeman, "From Freedom Now! to Free Speech," Aptheker, *Intimate Politics*, 112–13, 121–23.

10. Aptheker, *Intimate Politics*, 112–13, 121–23; Freeman, *At Berkeley in the Sixties*, 86–90; Bettina Aptheker telephone interview with editor, December 1, 2013.

11. Freeman, "From Freedom Now! to Free Speech," 74.

12. Savio, "Beyond the Cold War: The Education of an American Radical," 5. Mario Savio interview with Max Heirich, June 8, 1965, 34–35.

13. Goines, *The Free Speech Movement*, 93; Savio interview with Heirich, 29–30.

14. Savio interview with Heirich, 37.

15. Ibid., 35.

16. Ibid., 36.

17. Ibid., 46–49; Savio, "Thirty Years Later," 63–34; Goines, *The Free Speech Movement*, 94; Cheryl Stevenson telephone interview with editor, December 19, 2005, 1–3.

18. Mario Savio, "Beyond the Cold War: An Education in Politics" (unpublished book proposal), 18, copy in editor's possession.

19. *Berkeley in the Sixties* film prospectus, 4; Savio interview with Heirich, 52.

20. Savio, "Beyond the Cold War: The Education of an American Radical" (unpublished book proposal, version 2), 5, copy in editor's possession.

21. Savio interview with Heirich, 47, 49, 52.

22. Ibid., 45.

23. Tracy Sims (whose surname Savio misspelled as "Simms"), a young African American civil rights activist, was a leader of the Sheraton Palace Hotel protests.

24. Though Savio's letter did not lead the dean to allow him to drop his chemistry course, it did convince him that "unforeseen circumstances" left Savio unable to complete the course. So he granted Savio "deferred completion of that course without loss of grade points." See George S. Murphy, assistant dean of students, to Dean [William] Fretter, May 29, 1964, Mario Savio disciplinary file, Chancellor's papers, University Archives, Bancroft Library, UC Berkeley.

25. Savio interview with Eynon. 25.

26. In recommending Savio for Freedom Summer work, Mississippi Project's staff praised him: "Experienced in civil rights work in the SF Bay area. Proper attitude and hard working. Willing to do any type of work. Highly recommended." Savio's interviewer, Malcolm Zaretsky, however, was initially ambivalent about Savio's potential as a political activist and leader—reflecting both Savio's limited leadership experience at the time and Zaretsky's underestimation of Savio's political potential and talent. Zaretsky reported:

Mario Savio—Univ. California—I worked with him earlier this year in Friends of SNCC; he then got diverted into an abortive tutorial project which folded six weeks after it had begun. Generally what I have to say about him is this: not a very creative guy although he accepts responsibility and carries it through if you explain to him exactly what needs to be done; not exceedingly perceptive on the movement, what's involved, etc.; not very good at formulating notions with which one moves into the Negro community (this in relation to the planning sessions we had on the collapsed tutorial program . . . was more interested in "getting the thing into operation" than in discovering purposes for which that kind of a program be established . . . in the end the program was formulated (altho[ugh] not only because of his thinking cause he did not really play that much of a leadership role) in terms of helping the poor kids in the ghetto get through school easier . . . hardly my idea of why to establish tutorials and related programs. On the other hand I think that he's a grad student (tho[ugh] can't remember) and probably would be of good use in the freedom schools depending upon what subject he's in (math? . . . can't remember, again). Can't decide if I were picking people if I would choose him . . . probably he would be one of those "average" people who I'd want to see the results of the interview, reference forms, etc. and his performance at Berea before making a judgment.

When Savio read Zaretsky's assessment years later, the only part he took issue with was its criticism of the inner-city tutoring program he had worked in, and Zaretsky's suggestion that working on such a program reflected some lack of political vision. Savio continued to view the tutoring project as a good initiative, teaching math to students who had been so poorly served by the public schools. (Mario Savio interview with Ronald Schatz, August 13, 1996, 29–30).

27. Tom Savio, Mario's younger brother.

28. Savio is referring to being accepted by SNCC to work in its Mississippi Freedom Summer campaign.

29. The anti-Rumford initiative was a movement to repeal California's fair-housing law.

30. Noni was Mario's grandmother.

31. Savio's joining the Socialist Party was a symbolic expression of his disillusionment with the two-party system and did not represent a deep commitment to the Socialist Party, whose meetings Savio did not attend.

32. Senator Alan Cranston (D) from California.

CHAPTER 2. GOING SOUTH

1. Savio, "Beyond the Cold War: The Education of an American Radical," 5.
2. Savio, "Beyond the Cold War: An Education in Politics," 20.
3. Ibid.
4. Savio, "Beyond the Cold War: The Education of an American Radical," 6.
5. Savio, "Thirty Years Later," in Cohen and Zelnik, *The Free Speech Movement*, 64.
6. Savio, "Beyond the Cold War: An Education in Politics," 20.
7. Savio, "Thirty Years Later," 64–65.
8. Savio, "Beyond the Cold War: An Education in Politics," 21.
9. Savio interview with Eynon. 28.
10. Ibid.
11. Ibid., 51.
12. Savio, "Thirty Years Later," 64.
13. Savio interview with Eynon, 27.
14. Ibid., 28.
15. Ibid., 45.
16. Ibid., 44.
17. Savio, "Beyond the Cold War: An Education in Politics," 21–22.
18. Mario Savio interview with Robert Cohen and David Pickell, Berkeley, September 29, 1984.
19. Cheryl Stevenson telephone interview with editor, December 20, 2013.
20. Oxford, Ohio, on the campus of what is now Miami University, is where the Freedom Summer project staged its orientation sessions for the new volunteers in its civil rights work.
21. The Fillmore, the black community in San Francisco where Savio and Stevenson had done political canvassing against the San Francisco Redevelopment Agency's "urban renewal" project that by 1964 had displaced thousands of African American residents.
22. KPFA is the Berkeley-based listener-sponsored Pacifica radio station, which was a key institution of the Bay Area Left; it covered the civil rights movement extensively and sympathetically.
23. Donna Richard Moses, a SNCC organizer, who in 1964 was the wife of Freedom Summer leader Bob Moses of SNCC.
24. Civil rights workers James Earl Chaney, Michael Schwerner, and Andrew Goodman went missing on June 21, 1964, in Neshoba County, Mississippi, after investigating the firebombing that destroyed Mt. Zion Baptist Church, the black church at which Schwerner had recently spoken. The three were murdered by the Ku Klux Klan, in collusion with local police. Their bodies were discovered on August 4, 1964, below an earthen dam in Philadelphia, Mississippi.

25. A reference to the fact that neighboring black farmers nearby the Freedom House were armed for self-defense in case of attacks by the KKK.

26. Carol Matthews was a SNCC staff member for Holmes County. Steve Bingham was a Freedom Summer volunteer.

27. The white Citizens' Council, sometimes referred to as the "uptown Klan" was a white supremacist organization, founded in 1954, as part of the segregationist backlash against the *Brown* decision. The Citizens' Council had chapters across Mississippi and used economic intimidation against African Americans who demanded voting rights or racial integration.

28. A legacy of the New Deal's Farm Security Administration's land redistribution work was that an unusual number of African American farmers in Holmes County had been able to purchase—and in 1964 still owned—their own farms.

29. The Council of Federated Organizations (COFO) was the coordinating group for the Freedom Summer Project that Moses and SNCC initiated, which involved other civil rights organizations, including CORE, SCLC, and the NAACP.

30. Robert David Osman statement to the FBI, Jackson, Mississippi, July 23, 1964, FBI file 44–2300, July 30, 1964, Special Agents Joseph B. McAleer and Harold F. Good.

31. FBI hostility toward the Freedom Summer project is evidenced by the fact before the summer project had even begun, the bureau—as of airtel instructions of June 12, 1964—began investigating Savio and his fellow Freedom Summer volunteers for "pertinent information of a criminal or subversive nature"—treating students who had risked their lives in the freedom movement as if they were criminal suspects or disloyal Americans. See Supervisor [name deleted by FBI censors] to SAC, Los Angeles, "Mario Savio, Racial Matter," August 21, 1964, FBI file 157–984 291790. This document is reproduced in this volume, see figure 4.

32. Cohen, *Freedom's Orator*, 59–60, 433, n. 53.

33. Osman's deposition for the U.S. District Court confirms Savio's account of police misconduct and adds one other point: that in the station, one of the police officers referred to the assault as "a fight." Osman said, "[it was a way] to make us appear to be also at fault and to challange [sic] our position of non-violence." (Robert David Osman Deposition, July 18, 1964, witnesses, Daniel D. Paulman and Mario R. Savio, United States District Court for Southern District of Mississippi, Jackson Division Council of Federated Organizations, et al. Plaintiffs v. L. A. Rainey, et al. Defendants Civil Action No. 3599 (J) (M), Mississippi Department of Archives and History).

34. Governor Brown did not respond to Savio's appeal on behalf of the MFDP. Brown's assistant for human rights did, however, write Savio a sympathetic letter expressing his and the governor's support for the voting rights work that he and

the movement were doing in Mississippi. (William L. Becker to Mario Savio, August 13, 1964). In Atlantic City, Brown would side not with the MFDP delegation but with President Johnson in the battle over that delegation's seating at the convention.

35. Savio, "Thirty Years Later," 65.

36. McComb is in Pike County, just east of Amite County, and in 1964 it was also one of the most Klan-infested and violent parts of the state.

37. Jesse Harris was a SNCC staff member for southwest Mississippi (Natchez, Amite, and McComb).

38. The Democratic Party's national convention.

39. This refers to the agreement Republican presidential nominee Barry Goldwater and President Johnson made in July, in the wake of the East Coast ghetto rebellions, not to inflame racial passions during the presidential race.

40. Savio is alluding to his problems with depression, rooted in a difficult childhood, which included the trauma of child abuse.

41. "In White America," a play by historian Martin Duberman, explores the history of American racism from slavery through the mid-twentieth century.

42. The Democratic Party's national convention in Atlantic City.

43. Savio is referring to his plan to consult a psychiatrist to get help with his problems with depression.

44. Cohen, *Freedom's Orator*, 62.

45. Branch, *Pillar of Fire*, 474.

46. The San Francisco Redevelopment Agency, whose "urban renewal" project Savio, Stevenson, and other Bay Area civil rights activists organized against because it displaced black residents.

47. The anti-Rumford initiative, which appeared on the California ballot in 1964 as Proposition 14, repealed the Rumford Act (California's fair-housing act of 1963), a demoralizing defeat for the civil rights movement.

48. Savio would change his major to philosophy and, years later, would earn bachelor's and master's degrees in physics.

49. Jimmy Travis, who had been a Freedom Rider, was a key SNCC staff member and movement hero. He survived an assassination attempt in 1963 in which he was shot in the neck while traveling in a car with Bob Moses.

50. On appeal, in October 1964, the sentence for the assault was reduced to a $50 fine.

CHAPTER 3. LEADING THE FREE SPEECH
MOVEMENT

1. Savio, "Beyond the Cold War: The Education of An American Radical," 6; Mario Savio to Friends, August 24, 1984.

2. Savio, "Beyond the Cold War: An Education in Politics," 22.

3. Savio interview with Eynon, 47.

4. Savio, "Beyond the Cold War: An Education in Politics," 23.

5. Ibid.

6. Ibid., 24.

7. Savio, "Beyond the Cold War: An Education in Politics," 24.

8. *Report of the President's Commission on Campus Unrest* (Washington, DC: US Government Printing Office, 1970), 22–23.

9. Savio, "Beyond the Cold War: The Education of An American Radical," 7.

10. Ibid., 6; Savio, "Beyond the Cold War: The Education of An American Radical," version 2, 6

11. Savio, "Beyond the Cold War: The Education of An American Radical," 7.

12. Savio, "Beyond the Cold War: An Education in Politics," 24.

13. Savio, "Thirty Years Later," in Cohen and Zelnik, *The Free Speech Movement*, 68.

14. Mario Savio interview excerpt in Mark Kitchell, *Berkeley in the Sixties* typescript.

15. Savio, "Thirty Years Later," 68.

16. *The Beginning: Berkeley, 1964*, 59–63; Editors of *California Monthly:* "Three Months of Crisis," in Lipset and Wolin, *The Berkeley Student Revolt*, 100–103; Goines, *The Free Speech Movement*, 113–19.

17. Heirich, *The Beginning*, 63–70; Lipset and Wolin, *The Berkeley Student Revolt* 102–5.

18. Savio, "Thirty Years Later," 66; Savio interview with Eynon, 48.

19. Heirich, *The Beginning: Berkeley, 1964*, 64–65, 69–70.

20. Draper, *The New Student Revolt*, 36–38.

21. Cohen, *Freedom's Orator*, 86.

22. Ibid., 84.

23. Ibid., 84–85.

24. This refers to the spontaneous act of solidarity these free speech activists displayed in their initial conflict with the deans on Sproul Plaza. When the dean cited one student for staffing a political advocacy table in violation of the ban, that student would leave the table and another student would take her or his place.

25. So many students defied the ban on Sproul Plaza that the deans could not cite them all, and, in fact, as the deans retreated from the plaza, after issuing only a handful of citations, Savio urged them to stay and take hundreds more names, since many other students were there to defy the ban.

26. Savio added an appendix to this reply to the Williams memo that made two important additional points. (1) Williams's memo offered only a truncated account of the free speech conflict and told the story in such a way as to make Savio and his fellow protesters sound as if they had rashly broken university

rules. The dean left out of his account that Savio and his fellow activists had met with Dean Towle several times, seeking to get the ban lifted. Mass protest and defiance of UC regulations, in other words, occurred only *after* the administration refused to reconsider this ban, which had, in Savio's words, "crippled . . . the campus political life of the students." (2) The administration's autocratic behavior had led to the protests because UC had "no procedure for" consulting "with the students and faculty" on new regulations "prior to their going into effect." Savio said, "[it is] vile that those who are to be governed by certain laws [i.e., campus regulations regarding political advocacy] should have no voice in framing those laws." (Mario Savio, "Supplementary material in my case pending before the *Ad Hoc* Committee on Student Conduct of the Academic Senate," Savio disciplinary file, Chancellor's papers).

27. Savio interview with Heirich, 70.

28. Goines, *The Free Speech Movement*, 153.

29. Clark Kerr, *The Uses of the University* (1963). Kerr used the term "knowledge industry." The term "knowledge factory" came from Hal Draper, Berkeley's leading veteran of the socialist movement of the 1930s, whose critical lecture on Kerr influenced Savio. That lecture would be published as a pamphlet, "The Mind of Clark Kerr," which is reprinted in Draper, *Berkeley: The New Student Revolt*, 229–48.

30. In this speech from the first sit-in, Savio was already using the "machine" metaphor for the university, which would occupy so central a place in his most famous speech, "Bodies upon the Gears," before the FSM's culminating sit-in on December 2, 1964.

31. Barry Goldwater was the 1964 Republican presidential nominee and William E. Miller, a New York congressman, was his running mate. Savio is referring to the Tonkin Gulf incident, which President Johnson used to get a blank check from Congress to use force in Vietnam.

32. Carter, a wealthy retailing executive, was the chairman of UC's Board of Regents.

33. *Daily Californian*, October 1, 1964.

34. KCM, Notes on Meeting with Kerr, Strong, Sherriffs, Williams, Towle, Malloy, Alumni House—6–7 P.M. September 30, 1964, Chancellor's papers.

35. Police Department, University of California, Berkeley, by Lt. Merrill F. Chandler, File 25397, Supplementary Report, October 1, 1964, 11:45 A.M., Chancellor's papers.

36. Ibid.

37. Mario Savio interview with Mark Kitchell, tape 1, 5–6.

38. Note that here and after all of the demands Savio made in this first car-top speech the crowd reacted with cheers and applause.

39. Heirich, *The Beginning: Berkeley, 1964*, 118.

40. Minutes of Meeting with the Chancellor at the Request of Charles Powell, ASUC President, with self-stated leader of protest groups, Mario Savio, October 1,

1964, [also] present: Alex Sherriffs, Lincoln Constance, Prof. Thomas Barnes, Daily Cal reporter, ASUC Vice President Goldstein, Saxton Pope, Chancellor's papers.

41. Savio interview with Heirich, 94–95; Savio interview with Eynon, 59.

42. *Berkeley in the Sixties* (Rossman quoted in the film's FSM segment).

43. Savio interview with Heirich, 97. There were, however, a few brief points, when the free speech activists' commitment to nonviolence gave way under pressure from the police and hecklers. This occurred first during the "pack-in" at Sproul Hall, which occurred when several hundred demonstrators left the blockaded police car to demand action from the administration in the wake of Strong's stonewalling. When protesters tried to block the police from sealing the building, police began stepping on them, and the students responded by pushing back and trying to remove the shoes of the officers. In this melee, Savio—irritated "at having his head trampled by policemen's heels"—ended up biting a police officer on the leg, an act for which he would apologize and over which he felt embarrassed, since it violated his commitment to nonviolence. (Draper, *Berkeley: The New Student Revolt*, 109; Cohen, *Freedom's Orator*, 106). Similarly, the discipline of nonviolence could not always be maintained completely when threats came from hecklers. It is true that when belligerent hecklers from the fraternities came and threatened violence late into the first night of the police car blockade, most of the free speech activists remained nonviolent, at the urging of Savio and other movement leaders. But out of sight of the demonstration's leadership, Brian Turner, an FSMer, faced with these threatening fraternity boys, "dropped one with a punch to the solar plexus." And had the hecklers actually opted to move from verbal to physical violence and "attempted to charge in," some of the movement's monitors, who had their backs to the hecklers," might (according to one monitor's recollections) "have fought to defend [themselves]." (Jack Radey, email to the editor, March 9, 2014).

44. Cohen, *Freedom's Orator*, 113.

45. The Pact of October 2.

46. This muddled sentence almost certainly missed part of Savio's meaning. Savio frequently mentioned UC's seventy-two-hour rule—the requirement that nonstudents get permission from the UC administration and wait seventy-two hours before they can speak on campus—as inhibiting free speech, since it denied students timely access to outside speakers. And so, as this account indicates, Savio would often say that such arbitrary rules discriminated against the free expression of nonstudents and served no function other than harassment. But Savio would not have characterized the new Communist speaker rule, which finally allowed Communists to speak on campus, as a form of harassment. Savio did, in some of his FSM oratory, dismiss Kerr's allowing of Communists to speak on campus as being an act of little consequence, since unpopular revolutionaries calling for radical change that was unlikely to ever occur posed little threat to the status quo. Savio claimed that what Kerr and his fellow administrators really

feared—and so barred from campus—was civil rights activists issuing calls for specific acts of protest that could, via pickets and sit-ins, threaten the status quo immediately (which Savio termed "consequential speech"). This point, however, got lost in this account for Bolton, which conflated it with Savio's denunciation of the seventy-two-hour rule.

47. After FSM objections to its name and undemocratic constitution, the Study Committee would be renamed the Campus Committee on Political Activity, and FSM and the Academic Senate would be given greater representation on it. But until such changes were made, the FSM was threatening to boycott the proceedings, which is why Savio suggested in this speech that the FSM might not join the Study Committee.

48. Savio is referring to the fact that the UC Berkeley student government (the Associate Students of the University of California, or ASUC) was, according to the Kerr Directives, subordinated to the UC administration—barred from taking positions on off-campus issues, and had constitutional or financial decisions subject to veto by the chancellor. The National Student Association (NSA) was the national organization of U.S. college and university student governments, whose politics were generally liberal—though later revelations found CIA funding of the NSA so as to generate student support of the Cold War.

49. The Katz case provoked faculty criticism of the UC Berkeley administration, which grew heated in this same mid-October period when Savio gave this speech. In Berkeley's Academic Senate, critics accused Chancellor Strong of violating the academic freedom of Eli Katz, an acting assistant professor of German. Strong had questioned Katz—improperly, in the view of many of his colleagues—about his past associations with the Communist Party, as a "precondition for the regularization" of his faculty appointment. Katz would be fired after refusing to justify to Strong his "unwillingness" to answer questions before HUAC." See Reginald E. Zelnik, "'On the Side of the Angels': The Berkeley Faculty and the FSM," in Cohen and Zelnik, *The Free Speech Movement*, 278; and Leon Wofsy, "When the FSM Disturbed the Faculty Peace," in Cohen and Zelnik, *The Free Speech Movement*, 350.

50. Savio is referring to the Academic Senate here and suggesting that this faculty body was treated by the UC administration in the same dismissive way as the campus's powerless student government.

51. Minutes of October 12 meeting between FSM Steering Committee and Strong, Sherriffs, Docterman, Landon, Elberg, Ross, Chancellor's papers, University Archives, Bancroft Library.

52. Roysher was a member of the FSM Steering Committee. Paley was a professor of English.

53. Knowland, the right-wing publisher of the *Oakland Tribune*, was a frequent critic and nemesis of the student movement. He had been rumored to be responsible for pressuring the UC administration to ban advocacy on the Bancroft strip.

54. Searle, a professor of philosophy, had been Savio's teacher and was a leading faculty free speech activist. Later in the 1960s he became a vocal critic of the New Left.

55. *San Francisco Chronicle*, November 21, 1964.

56. Savio was charging bad faith here on the part of the administration—that while claiming to be negotiating with students and faculty about liberalizing UC's speech regulations, Kerr had already decided on and was moving to implement regulations that continued to bar on campus advocacy of demonstrations that led to unlawful acts (i.e., civil disobedience). This was based on the "purloined letter" affair, in which a student worker in Kerr's office leaked an unsigned Kerr letter that seemed to support this charge of bad faith—though Kerr denied that the letter represented his views at that time.

57. This refers to the procedures the faculty delegation on the CCPA proposed, which would have left it to the courts to determine whether such acts were unlawful.

58. Savio's point is that this sit-in was not aimed at stopping the conduct of business in Sproul Hall. The protesters were not going to block the halls but just sit along the corridor walls as an act of moral witness.

59. History professors Reginald Zelnik and Lawrence Levine were key faculty supporters of the FSM's free speech demands.

CHAPTER 4. "NO RESTRICTIONS ON THE CONTENT
OF SPEECH"

1. Heirich, *The Beginning, 194.*

2. Mark Kitchell, *Berkeley in the Sixties* (film summary), 6.

3. Reginald E. Zelnik, "'On the Side of the Angels': The Berkeley Faculty and the FSM," in Cohen and Zelnik, *The Free Speech Movement*, 289.

4. Savio, "Thirty Years Later."

5. Cohen, *Freedom's Orator, 176.*

6. Perhaps reflecting the haste with which the letter was written, it left out (in demand one) the name of one of the four students targeted in these Thanksgiving disciplinary letters, Brian Turner.

7. Chancellor Strong had, in fact, been repeatedly overruled by Kerr during the FSM crisis, which damaged their working relationship and contributed to Strong's ouster from the Berkeley chancellorship.

8. Savio is referring to the Pact of October 2, which ended the police car blockade.

9. Reflecting the prefeminist movement politics of the time, Baez was the only woman to speak at this crucial FSM rally, making a brief plea for nonviolence before singing freedom songs.

10. *Un chant d'amour* (1950), a short, experimental silent film is considered a classic in gay cinema and is the only film by Jean Genet, who wrote and directed it.

11. Saul Landau, an award-winning radical filmmaker, produced more than forty films and was also an accomplished journalist.

12. Montgomery wrote a wildly red-baiting series on the FSM for the *San Francisco Examiner*, which was planted by the FBI. See Rosenfeld, *Subversives*, 212–14.

13. W.J. Rorabaugh, "The FSM, Berkeley Politics, and Ronald Reagan," 515.

14. For Savio's linkage of Oakland police brutality with its role in the ghetto community, see his speech to the California Federation of Teachers, the final speech in this volume.

15. Savio quoted in Kitchell, *Berkeley in the Sixties* (film summary), 6.

16. Savio remarks at FSM press conference, January 4, 1965.

17. Rosenfeld, *Subversives*, 226.

18. SAC, Cincinnati to SAC, San Francisco, subject: "Mario Savio Security Matter." December 30, 1964, FBI file 100–54060–52; Rosenfeld, *Subversives*, 225, 254–55, 407–11, 413–15.

19. Bettina Aptheker e-mail to the editor, March 7, 2005.

20. John T. Dunlop, Frederick H. Harbison. Charles A. Myers, and Clark Kerr, *Industrialism and Industrial Man: The Problems of Labor and Management in Economic Growth* (New York: Heinemann, 1962).

21. Gleason was a great jazz critic and one of the few Bay Area newspaper columnists friendly to the FSM. He later was a founding editor of *Rolling Stone* magazine.

22. Regent Catherine Hearst was the wife of Randolph A. Hearst, heir of the national newspaper chain; regent Dorothy Chandler was the wife of Norman Chandler, publisher of the *Los Angeles Times;* regent Max Rafferty was California's voluble right-wing state superintendent of public instruction.

23. *Fresno Bee*, December 29, 1964.

24. "No on 14" was the campaign to stop the repeal of California's Rumford Act (the fair housing act).

25. Professor Arthur Ross was the director of UC's Institute of Industrial Relations.

26. Savio was referring here to the Committee of Two Hundred, the pro-FSM faculty, many of whom (though not all) were young, whose organizing led to the Academic Senate's passage of the December 8 resolutions.

27. As a light-hearted gesture and birthday gift, Hal Draper—at the FSM victory rally—presented Savio with a clip-on tie, so that the next time the police tried to drag him off by the tie, as they had at the Greek Theatre, the tie would come off when they grabbed it.

28. Don Mulford (R), a California Assemblyman from 1957 to 1970, was an outspoken foe of the student movement and had called for the UC administration to punish students who participated in the Sheraton Palace sit-in.

29. Hugh Burns, California State Senator (D) from Fresno headed the Senate's Fact-Finding Subcommittee on Un-American Activities.

CODA

1. Cohen, *Freedom's Orator*, 231–322, 333–417.

2. Berkeley Art Project, "Freedom of Speech, Call for Entries" (1989); Peter Selz to I. Michael Heyman, February 7, 1990, Chancellor's papers, University Archives, Bancroft Library.

3. Ira Michael Heyman to Peter Selz, Galen Cranz, and Charles Schwartz, January 18, 1990, Chancellor's papers, University Archives.

4. Ibid. On Littlejohn's opposition to an artwork honoring the FSM and similar arguments by philosophy professor John Searle, see their op-ed articles in *Daily Californian*, February 20, 1990.

5. Ira Michael Heyman to the Berkeley Art Project, June 19, 1990, copy in editor's possession. This would not be Heyman's last act of censorship. After he left the Berkeley chancellorship and became the secretary of the Smithsonian Institution, Heyman ordered the cancellation of the Enola Gay exhibit at the National Air and Space Museum because its critical depiction of the U.S. atomic bombing of Hiroshima and Nagasaki during World War II had led veterans' groups to denounce it. Heyman's decision led to the resignation of museum director Martin Harwit. See *Baltimore Sun*, January 31, 1995, and September 4, 1996; *Chicago Tribune*, May 3, 1995.

6. Lynne Hollander Savio e-mail to the editor, December 30, 2013.

7. Michael Rossman, "Savio steps dedication," December 2, 1997, http://h-net. msu.edu/cgi-bin/logbrowse.pl?trx=vx&list=h-public&month=9712&week=&ms g=y62tQ2btxLIm2rDuWGVFOA&user = &pw=.

8. Ibid. Chancellor Tien also sent a condolence note to Lynne Hollander Savio, praising Savio's contribution to the university and to the struggle for freedom of speech. See Cohen, *Freedom's Orator*, 317. Note that the first attempts to honor the Free Speech Movement came from Berkeley students. Long before the UC administration embraced the FSM, Berkeley's graduate student government (the Graduate Assembly), in the aftermath the FSM's twentieth anniversary commemoration, initiated a successful bill, cosponsored by California Assemblyman Tom Bates, to honor the FSM by declaring October 1 Free Speech Day in California. See *Daily Californian*, October 1, 1985.

9. Cohen, *Freedom's Orator*, 317; *Daily Californian*, April 25, 1997.

10. Lynne Hollander Savio e-mail to the editor, December 30, 2013. The Savio lectureship in 2014 will be transferred to UC Berkeley's Division of Social Science, which has established an endowment fund for it.

11. Chancellor Robert M. Berdahl, press conference statement announcing library gift, April 29, 1998; Chancellor Robert M. Berdahl and university librarian Gerald R. Lowell, Memo re: The Free Speech Movement Café Opening, January 31, 2000, Chancellor's papers, University Archives.

12. The Free Speech Movement Digital Archive, at http://bancroft.berkeley.edu/FSM/about.html.

13. Ibid.

14. *Los Angeles Times*, April 17, 1985.

15. *New York Times*, July 21, 1986.

16. Berkeley's Academic Senate passed four resolutions criticizing the campus administration for its use of police force against the Occupy Cal demonstrators on Sproul Plaza. See *Daily Californian*, November 28, 2011. The attack of baton-wielding police on the nonviolent protesters encamped on Sproul Plaza was caught on video and lampooned on the *Colbert Report* (www.colbertnation.com/the-colbert-report-videos/402024/november-10-2011/occupy-u-c--berkeley).

17. *Daily Californian*, November 13 and 14, 2011; *Huffington Post*, November 11, 2011.

18. Mario Savio to friends, August 29, 1984, copy in editor's possession.

EPILOGUE

1. This community was nurtured by the late Michael Rossman, the guiding spirit behind the creation of the Free Speech Movement Archives, aided by the fact that a fairly large number of participants stayed in the Bay Area. In more recent years, it has been maintained and expanded through the dedicated work of Barbara T. Stack and the magic of e-mail.

2. For the text of Savio's FSM-20 speech, see Cohen, *Freedom's Orator*, 346–49.

Select Bibliography

BAY AREA CIVIL RIGHTS MOVEMENT AND THE
CALIFORNIA CONTEXT

Barlow, William, and Peter Shapiro. *An End to Silence: The San Francisco State College Student Movement in the '60s* New York: Pegasus, 1971.

Boyarsky, Bill. *Big Daddy: Jesse Unruh and the Art of Power Politics.* Berkeley: University of California Press, 2007.

Brilliant, Mark. *The Color of America Has Changed: How Racial Diversity Shaped Civil Rights Reform in California, 1941–1978.* New York: Oxford University Press, 2010.

Brown, Willie L. *Basic Brown: My Life and Our Times.* New York: Simon and Schuster, 2008.

Cannon, Lou. *Governor Reagan: His Rise to Power.* New York: Public Affairs Press, 2003.

Casstevens, Thomas W. *Politics, Housing, and Race Relations: California's Rumford Act and Proposition 14.* Berkeley: Institute of Governmental Studies, 1967.

Dallek, Matthew. *The Right Moment: Ronald Reagan's First Victory and the Decisive Turning Point in American Politics.* New York: Free Press, 2000.

Freeman, Jo. "From Freedom Now! to Free Speech: The FSM's Roots in the Bay Area Civil Rights Movement." In *The Free Speech Movement: Reflections on*

Berkeley in the 1960s, edited by Robert Cohen and Reginald E. Zelnik, 73–82. Berkeley: University of California Press, 2002.

HoSang, Daniel Martinez. *Racial Propositions: Ballot Initiatives and the Making of Postwar California*. Berkeley: University of California Press, 2010.

Miller, Paul T. *The Postwar Struggle for Civil Rights: African Americans in San Francisco*. New York: Routledge, 2010.

Moore, Shirley. *To Place Our Deeds: The African American Community in Richmond, California, 1910–1963*. Berkeley: University of California Press, 2000

Rarick, Ethan. *California Rising: The Life and Times of Pat Brown*. Berkeley: University of California Press, 2005.

Self, Robert O. *American Babylon: Race and the Struggle for Postwar Oakland*. Princeton, NJ: Princeton University Press, 2003.

THE MISSISSIPPI FREEDOM MOVEMENT
AND FREEDOM SUMMER

Branch, Taylor. *Pillar of Fire: America in the King Years, 1963–1965*. New York: Simon and Schuster, 1998.

Brooks, Maegan P., and Davis W. Houck, eds. *The Speeches of Fannie Lou Hamer*. Jackson: University of Mississippi Press, 2010.

Carson, Clayborne. *In Struggle: SNCC and the Black Awakening of the 1960s*. Cambridge, MA: Harvard University Press, 1995.

Crosby, Emilye. *A Little Taste of Freedom: The Black Freedom Struggle in Claiborne County Mississippi*. Chapel Hill: University of North Carolina Press, 2005.

Dittmer, John. *Local People: The Struggle for Civil Rights in Mississippi*. Urbana: University of Illinois Press, 1995.

Hogan, Wesley. *Many Minds, One Heart: SNCC's Dream for a New America*. Chapel Hill: University of North Carolina Press, 2007.

King, Mary. *Freedom Song: A Personal Story of the 1960s Civil Rights Movement*. New York: William Morrow, 1987.

Lewis, John, and Michael D. Orso. *Walking with the Wind: A Memoir of the Movement*. New York: Mariner, 1998.

Martin, Waldo. "'Holding One Another': Mario Savio and the Freedom Struggle in Mississippi and Berkeley." In *The Free Speech Movement: Reflections on Berkeley in the 1960s*, edited by Robert Cohen and Reginald E. Zelnik, 83–102. Berkeley: University of California Press, 2002.

Martinez, Elizabeth, ed. *Letters Home from Mississippi: Reports from Civil Rights Volunteers and Poetry of the 1964 Freedom Summer*. Brookline, MA: Zephyr Press, 2007.

McAdam, Doug. *Freedom Summer.* New York: Oxford University Press, 1988.
Moses, Robert P., and Charles E. Cobb, Jr. *Radical Equations: Civil Rights from Mississippi to the Algebra Project.* Boston: Beacon Press, 2002.
Moye, J. Todd. *Let the People Decide: Black Freedom and White Resistance in Sunflower County, Mississippi, 1945–1986.* Chapel Hill: University of North Carolina Press, 2004.
Payne, Charles. *I've Got the Light of Freedom: The Organizing Tradition and the Mississippi Freedom Struggle.* Berkeley: University of California Press, 2007.
Sojourner, Sue, and Cheryl Reitan, *Thunder of Freedom: Black Leadership and the Transformation of 1960s Mississippi.*
Umoja, Akinyele O. *We Will Shoot Back: Armed Resistance in the Mississippi Freedom Movement.* New York: New York University Press, 2013.

THE FREE SPEECH MOVEMENT

Adler, Margot. *Heretic's Heart: A Journey through Spirit and Revolution.* Boston: Beacon Press, 1997.
Aptheker, Bettina. *Intimate Politics: How I Grew Up Red, Fought for Free Speech, and Became a Feminist Rebel.* Emeryville, CA: Seal Press, 2006.
Cohen, Robert. *Freedom's Orator: Mario Savio and the Radical Legacy of the 1960s.* New York: Oxford University Press, 2009.
Cohen, Robert, and Reginald E. Zelnik, eds. *The Free Speech Movement: Reflections on Berkeley in the 1960s.* Berkeley: University of California Press, 2002.
Colvig, Ray. *Turning Points and Ironies: Issue and Events—Berkeley, 1959–1967.* Berkeley: Berkeley Public Policy Press, 2004.
Draper, Hal. *Berkeley: The New Student Revolt.* New York: Grove Press, 1965.
Eynon, Brett. "Community in Motion: The Free Speech Movement, Civil Rights, and the Roots of the New Left." *Oral History Review* (Spring 1989): 39–69.
Freeman, Jo. *At Berkeley in the Sixties: The Education of An Activist, 1961–1965.* Bloomington: Indiana University Press, 2004.
Glazer, Nathan. *Remembering the Answers: Essays on the American Student Revolt.* New York: Basic Books, 1970.
Goines, David Lance. *The Free Speech Movement: Coming of Age in the 1960s.* Berkeley: Ten Speed Press. 1993.
Heirich, Max. *The Beginning: Berkeley, 1964.* New York: Columbia University Press, 1968.
Kerr, Clark. *The Gold and the Blue: A Personal Memoir of the University of California, 1949–1967,* vol. 2, *Political Turmoil.* Berkeley: University of California Press, 2003.

———. *Documentary Supplements to "The Gold and the Blue."* Berkeley: Berkeley Public Policy Press, 2003.

Lipset, Seymour Martin, and Sheldon S. Wolin, eds. *The Berkeley Student Revolt: Facts and Interpretations.* Garden City, NY: Anchor Books, 1965.

Miller, Michael, and Susan Gilmore. *Revolution at Berkeley: The Crisis in American Education.* New York: Dell, 1965.

Otten, C. Michael. *University Authority and the Student.* Berkeley: University of California Press, 1970.

Rorabaugh, W.J. *Berkeley at War.* New York: Oxford University Press, 1989.

Rosenfeld, Seth. *Subversives: The FBI's War on Student Radicals and Reagan's Rise to Power.* New York: Farrar, Straus and Giroux, 2012.

Rossman, Michael. *The Wedding within the War.* Garden City, NY: Doubleday, 1971.

Searle, John. *The Campus War: A Sympathetic Look at the University in Agony.* New York: World Publishing, 1971.

Stadtman, Verne. *The University of California, 1868–1968.* New York: McGraw-Hill. 1970.

Van Houten, Peter S., and Edward L. Barrett, Jr. *Berkeley and Its Students: Days of Conflict and Change, 1945–1970.* Berkeley: Berkeley Public Policy Press, 2003.

Wolin, Sheldon S., and Jack Scharr. *The Berkeley Rebellion and Beyond.* New York: Random House, 1970.

THE NEW LEFT AND THE 1960S

Anderson, Terry. *The Movement and the Sixties.* New York: Oxford University Press, 1996.

Aronowitz, Stanley, *The Death and Rebirth of American Radicalism.* New York: Routledge, 1996.

Breines, Wini. *Community and Organization in the New Left.* New Brunswick, NJ: Rutgers University Press, 1981.

Buhle, Paul, and John McMillian, eds. *The New Left Revisited.* Philadelphia: Temple University Press, 2002.

Cohen, Robert, and David S. Snyder. *Rebellion in Black and White: Southern Student Activism in the 1960s.* Baltimore: Johns Hopkins University Press, 2013.

Evans, Sara. *Personal Politics: The Roots of Women's Liberation in the Civil Rights Movement and the New Left.* New York: Vintage, 1980.

Farber, David. *The Age of Great Dreams: America in the 1960s.* New York: Hill and Wang, 1994.

Farber, David, and Beth Bailey. *The Columbia Guide to the 1960s.* New York: Columbia University Press, 2003.

Foner, Eric. *The Story of American Freedom.* New York: Norton, 1999.

Gitlin, Todd. *The Sixties: Years of Hope, Days of Rage.* New York: Bantam, 2013.

Gosse, Van. *The World the Sixties Made: Politics and Culture in Recent America.* Philadelphia: Temple University Press, 2003.

——. *Rethinking the New Left: An Interpretative History.* New York: Palgrave Macmillian.

Hayden, Tom. *The Long 60s: From 1960 to Obama.* Boulder, CO: Paradigm, 2011.

Isserman, Maurice. *If I Had a Hammer: The Death of the Old Left and Birth of the New Left.* Urbana: University of Illinois Press, 1993.

Isserman, Maurice, and Michael Kazin. *America Divided: The Civil War of the 1960s.* New York: Oxford University Press, 2011.

Kelley, Robin D. G. *Freedom Dreams: The Black Radical Imagination.* Boston: Beacon Press, 2003.

Klatch, Rebecca, E. *A Generation Divided: The New Left, the New Right, and the 1960s.* Berkeley: University of California Press, 1999.

Lyons, Paul. *New Left, New Right, and the Legacy of the 1960s.* Philadelphia: Temple University Press, 1996

Marwick, Arthur, *The Sixties: Cultural Revolution in Great Britain, France, Italy, and the United States.* Oxford: Oxford University Press, 1998.

Matusow, Allen J. *The Unraveling of America: A History of Liberalism in the 1960s.* Athens: University of Georgia Press, 2009.

Newfield, Jack. *A Prophetic Minority.* New York: New American Library, 1966.

Patterson, James T. "The Rise of Rights and Rights Consciousness, 1930s–1970s." In *Contesting Democracy: Substance and Structure in American Political History, 1775–2000,* edited by Byron E. Shaefer and Anthony J. Badgers, 201–23. Lawrence: University of Kansas Press. 1996.

Perlstein, Rick. *Before the Storm: Barry Goldwater and the Unmaking of the American Consensus.* New York: Nation Books, 2009.

Rosen, Ruth. *The World Split Open: How the Modern Women's Movement Changed America.* New York: Penguin, 2006.

Rossinow, Doug. *The Politics of Authenticity: Liberalism, Christianity, and the New Left in America.* New York: Columbia University Press, 1998.

Sale, Kirkpatrick. *SDS.* New York: Random House, 1973.

.

Index

16th Street Baptist Church bombing (Birmingham, AL), 10